D0072670

THE EVER-EVOLVING ENTERPRISE

THE EVER-EVOLVING ENTERPRISE

Guidelines for Creating Your Company's Future

Stephen C. Harper

Foreword by Brett Martin
Founder and CEO of Castle Branch, Inc.

 PRAEGER

AN IMPRINT OF ABC-CLIO, LLC
Santa Barbara, California • Denver, Colorado • Oxford, England

Library of Congress Cataloging-in-Publication Data

Harper, Stephen C.
    The ever-evolving enterprise : guidelines for creating your company's future / Stephen C. Harper; foreword by Brett Martin.
        p. cm.
    Includes bibliographical references and index.
    ISBN 978–0–313–39183–5 (cloth : alk. paper) — ISBN 978–0–313–39184–2 (ebook)
    1. Business enterprises. 2. Leadership. 3. Organizational learning. 4. Technological innovations—Management. I. Title.
HD2351.H37   2011
658.4—dc22   2010031675

ISBN: 978–0–313–39183–5
EISBN: 978–0–313–39184–2

15 14 13 12 11   1 2 3 4 5

This book is also available on the World Wide Web as an eBook.
Visit www.abc-clio.com for details.

Praeger
An Imprint of ABC-CLIO, LLC

ABC-CLIO, LLC
130 Cremona Drive, P.O. Box 1911
Santa Barbara, California 93116-1911

This book is printed on acid-free paper ∞

Manufactured in the United States of America

Dedicated to Randy Pausch (1960–2008)
His "Last Lecture" and life remind us that we need to seize and
savor the moment.

———⬦⬦⬦———

Firms that can sense sooner, analyze quicker, learn quicker, decide quicker, innovate quicker, implement quicker, and make adjustments to plans as they are being implemented quicker will evolve quicker and get favorable results quicker. As we venture into the future there will only be two types of firms; the quick and the dead.

—Stephen C. Harper

Contents

Foreword

As you read this foreword I trust that the economic storm of 2008 through 2010 has long since passed you by and today you are enjoying an economy that is both robust and kind. A robust economy provides all members of the global community with opportunities and prosperity.

When reading a book, it is important to consider when it was written and how the times might have influenced its author. Dr. Harper wrote this book during a remarkable time in our country's history; the "Great Recession," as it will forever be remembered, left an indelible mark on our society. In less than 24 months our economy shed millions of jobs, stock markets plummeted by over 50 percent, retirement accounts went from 401Ks to 201Ks, house values spiraled to historic lows and, most significantly, many Main Street American men and women, for the first time in their lives wondered and worried what was going to happen next.

While the economic skies have started to clear, I remind you that as one storm passes, another looms over the horizon. Ultimately, the only difference between the storms of the past and the storms of the future is whether you have learned to better navigate through them. Dr. Harper is a rare author. He is always looking to the future in an effort to never repeat the mistakes of the past. While many look to the past as a guide, Dr. Harper understands that the strategies we used before the great economic storm will no longer deliver success in today's economy. He makes a most compelling argument that today is a most appropriate time to learn and practice corporate entrepreneurship.

Corporate entrepreneurship can be the difference between survival and death for many American companies. The "Great Recession" quickly separated those who had failed to innovate from those who would become the great corporate entrepreneurs of our time. The economic storm left businesses with very few options when it came to survival: Option One: cut to the bone and wait out the storm; Option Two: cut into the bone and bury your head in the sand; Option Three:

(selected by millions and millions of businesses around the country) close the door and turn off the lights.

There was a fourth group: a number of businesses that did not die, and that did not merely survive. They were a group of businesses that thrived. They were the entrepreneurial ones, the ones who saw and evolved to a rapidly changing economy. They were the companies that had, over the years, invested in their entrepreneurial employees and their business development divisions. They were the ones who had spent years innovating, and now with a well-honed entrepreneurial framework in place, the leaders of these companies turned to their entrepreneurial employees as well as their innovators and said, "Find us a path through the storm."

In the last 20 years we have seen an incredible surge of entrepreneurial spirit that is like a giant wave lifting this country up and into the new economy. Entrepreneurs were creating new companies at a frenzied pace, often out of thin air and from the ground up. Some were good, some were great, and some were destined for failure. The one common denominator they all shared was "new": new ideas, new technology, new products, new services, new methods, new models, new money! "New," the ever-changing environment that an entrepreneur thrives in.

Dr. Harper deeply appreciates and, in this book, explores the new veracity with which our economy changes. Our economy has experienced change in every decade but never before have we witnessed the speed and magnitude of change that we experience today. Never before have we been required to embrace change as the very fuel, the oxygen that feeds our entrepreneurial and innovative spirit which results in our success.

Many of the start-up companies that defined the dotcom boom, after making it through their formative years failed to embrace change. They failed to focus on the fundamentals that brought them success in the first place. They stopped innovating and started focusing on driving profit. Blinded by profits alone, they stopped looking forward and turned inward. They forgot that what was new today would soon change. The change came with tremendous force and speed. In what felt like overnight, the global economy went from red hot to ice cold. For many, the change was overwhelming, devastating.

Everything is clear in hindsight, but when your company is growing by double digits it is easy to get comfortable with what you have. It is easy to not force yourself and your company to innovate. In the early days of the twenty-first century, companies simply unlocked the front door, turned on the lights, and by the sheer strength of the economy their company would grow by 20 percent. It was a world where survival was easy. It was a world where the status quo became an easy trap for companies to fall into. Unfortunately, for many firms the failure to evolve was fatal.

Today that 20 percent cushion is gone. If you want growth, you have to go and get it. You have to fight for it, tooth and nail. You cannot count on your core clients to get you through a storm. You can only count on your ability to attract new business. You can only count on the entrepreneurial employees and innovators that make up the foundation of your organization.

Companies that are tooled to adapt to change have a tremendous competitive advantage. Companies with vibrant entrepreneurial spirits will find and exploit new and profitable opportunities. Companies with established business development teams will give their leaders the ability to not only get through a storm, but also to grow through a storm. Ultimately, corporate entrepreneurship offers the company's leaders not just the tools to merely survive, but the power to thrive.

Brett Martin
Founder and CEO of Castle Branch, Inc.

Acknowledgments

I want to thank Brian Romer, Senior Acquisitions Editor for Praeger, for recognizing the value of this book and working with me to make it a reality. I also want to thank Stan Wakefield who submitted my proposal to Brian. Stan has been instrumental in getting my last three books published.

I want to thank three of my colleagues—Thom Porter, Dave Glew, and Jonathan Rowe at The University of North Carolina Wilmington—who have been coauthors of some of my recent articles, including some that served as the springboard for this book. They recognized that writing for practitioners is different from the usual scholarly writings of academicians. Each one of them provided valuable insights and suggestions. They also made me a better writer.

I want to thank Larry Clark—Dean of the Cameron School of Business at the University of North Carolina Wilmington. Dean Clark has been supportive of everything I have done. His unlimited energy, combined with his leadership by example, has been a source of inspiration as I enter my fifth decade as an educator.

I want to thank the Institute of Industrial Engineers for allowing me to use portions of some of the articles it published in *Industrial Management* and *Industrial Engineer* in this book. These two magazines served as a good launch pad for some of my thoughts.

I want to thank three other groups for making my professional journey so rewarding. First, I want to thanks the students I have worked with at The University of North Carolina Wilmington, Duke University, and Arizona State University. They have made teaching a pleasure, and I learned from them as well. I want to recognize two students in particular. Tiago Sommacal—a student from Brazil—demonstrated an insatiable curiosity for learning. Nathan Snell "educated" me on the power of information technology by providing me with a continuing stream of ideas. Second, I want to thank the business thinkers who have put pen to paper and provided ideas that have been incorporated into my philosophy and mental framework. Third, I want to thank the executives—particularly the ones who I have known personally—who have provided me with insights into today's challenges. They have taught me a lot about various industries, markets, and firms. They also have helped me see the world through various perspectives.

As always, I want to thank my family for bringing joy to my life.

Introduction

Evolve or Die: The Nature of the Ever-Evolving Enterprise

If we are to achieve results never before accomplished we must employ methods never before attempted.

—Sir Francis Bacon

If you want take your firm to the next level and beyond, then your firm must be an ever-evolving enterprise. It cannot continue doing what it has been doing or merely trying to keep up with its competitors. Future success will be contingent on the extent to which it is innovative and a learning organization. To excel, it must be able to create and maintain significant competitive advantages. It must be able to offer products and services that give it a competitive edge. It will also have to develop processes that enable it to be faster, provide higher quality products or services, be more efficient, and/or be more convenient to its target market.

This book is based on six premises: First, what worked well yesterday will be less effective today, ineffective tomorrow, and obsolete the day after tomorrow. Second, change is no longer an exceptional occurrence. Change is the rule. Change can be evolutionary, or it can be revolutionary, depending on how executives approach the future. Third, executives need to focus more of their attention on creating the company's future than on improving its present. Fourth, breakthrough leadership will be required if the company is to thrive in the ever-evolving marketplace. Traditional leadership techniques that served their companies well in times of continuous improvement will not be enough for the company to break away from the pack.

Fifth, breakthrough leadership should not be the chief executive officer's exclusive domain. To excel, companies need to have breakthrough leaders at all levels and in every unit. Every person has the potential to make a difference, and every person should play an integral role in moving the company forward and creating its future.

The sixth premise may be the most important one. It is the essence of the ever-evolving enterprise. It is the idea that change does not guarantee success or even survival. For a firm to thrive in the years ahead, it must initiate the right changes, at the right time, and in the right way. Change should never be just for the sake of change. Changes that are not in sync with prevailing realities will fail. Changes that are not timed and implemented well will fail.

This book provides insights, ideas, and examples about how your business can be smarter, quicker, more adaptive, and more innovative. Being an ever-evolving enterprise involves looking for things others do not look for (scanning internally and externally), seeing things others do not see (kaleidoscopic perspective), seeing things before others see them (strategic learning), thinking thoughts others do not think (mental dexterity), doing things others do not do (innovation), and recognizing the need to modify what you are doing (adaptability and operational learning) when others do not see the need to change. Being an ever-evolving enterprise also calls for having the courage to do what you and possibly no one else has done.

Ever-evolving enterprises approach change in a similar manner to how savvy investors manage their investments. Change should be managed like a portfolio that balances risk and return as well the short-, medium-, and long-term horizons. Some of the changes will be the product of comprehensive planning. Other changes will be more adaptive. Some of the changes will be revolutionary, while other changes will be more evolutionary. Some of the changes will be designed to foster game-changing breakthroughs. Other changes will be more incremental. Some of the changes will be organic, while others may be the result of acquiring ideas and practices from other firms.

Creating the company's future requires more than just keeping pace with the changes that are happening outside the company. The ever-accelerating rate of change places a premium on the company's ability to evolve in a revolutionary manner. Companies that learn more quickly and innovate better than other companies will thrive. Companies that are slow to learn and merely imitate other companies will be relegated to a very precarious existence.

Becoming an Ever-Evolving Enterprise Requires the Right Type of Corporate Culture

Becoming an ever-evolving enterprise takes more than occasionally developing a new product, service, or process. It takes more than developing a "platform" for launching a group of new products or services. To truly be ever-evolving, your firm must have a culture that fosters substantive, multifaceted, and proactive change.

Every company has a distinct culture, just as every person has a unique personality. A company's culture is the result of numerous factors and forces. It affects the type of people the company hires as well as how it motivates and rewards people. Corporate culture determines the type of ideas the company will embrace as well as the extent to which people are encouraged to experiment, explore, innovate, and take risks.

Corporate culture plays a crucial role in times of ever-accelerating change. It serves as an invisible guidebook for employees. It indicates what the company values, what it encourages, and what it rewards. If the company's strategy calls for the development of innovative products, the company will need a culture that welcomes experimentation and exploration. If the prevailing culture abhors risk taking and punishes mistakes, then the company's strategy is destined to fail.

The company's culture will have a lot to do with whether people create the company's future or the company languishes in the present. All products, services, processes, and profits come from people. The company's future is directly related to the quality of ideas that are developed and the extent to which they are executed well by people at all levels in the company.

Create Your Company's Future

Executives with a long-term horizon and mental dexterity are able to develop different perceptions of the future. If you identify an emerging opportunity early enough, you have a head start over everyone else. You have the time to study potential foreign markets and to learn the "ropes" about selling products in those markets. With lead time, you will not be rushed into anything. This reduces uncertainty and takes a lot of the anxiety out of doing something you have never done before. Additional lead time also gives you a chance to get the bugs out and develop a high level of proficiency before competition enters the scene.

The future will offer an almost unlimited number of opportunities. The companies that thrive in the years ahead will be the ones that identify emerging markets early and develop the ability to meet the market segment's needs to the point that no other company will even consider entering that market. Executives need to develop a list of possible *strategic* positions for the company. Unfortunately, too many executives use an "incremental" approach to positioning their companies. Even if they are able to identify where they want their companies to be in three years, their targets tend to be an extension of the last few years' growth. At the end of this year, they will simply add another year to their plan. Too many corporate strategies are nothing more than minor modifications of existing product lines, efforts to expand sales territories, and attempts to fine-tune operations to improve efficiency.

Strategic learning has offensive and defensive dimensions. From an offensive perspective, it may enable your company to be a path maker and to set the rules for how the game will be played. Success will be partly contingent on the extent you anticipate potential opportunities and position your company to capitalize on them. From a defensive perspective, strategic learning helps you anticipate potential threats and position your company to minimize their corresponding detrimental effects.

It will be impossible for you or your company to foresee every factor or force. Our ever-accelerating, ever-changing, multidimensional world will challenge the brightest executives and the most extensive data bases. No one will be able to anticipate every key event. No scenario or simulation will be able to capture every possibility, every probability, and every potential state of nature. Your company will thrive in the years ahead to the extent that it sees the future first and the extent that it evolves by learning new ways to do things and new things to do.

The book contains numerous "reality checks" that either encourage you to reflect on your practices or are particularly candid in making a point. Here are a few reality checks to see if your firm is positioned to be an ever-evolving enterprise.

Reality Check: How frequently do you do a systematic analysis of what your competitors are doing and contemplate what they may be considering in their effort to take your customers?

Reality Check: How much time do you spend each week contemplating what your market (competition. customers, technology, etc.) will be like three years from now?

Reality Check: Have you truly considered the consequences of losing your top two customers, one or more of your best people, what would happen if you lost your major supplier, and what would happen if your information system was corrupted or destroyed?

Reality Check: If you are not monitoring key trends, exploring possible events that can help or hinder your firm, and developing contingency plans to address various situations that have certain risks and consequences, then you are not doing your job in creating your company's future.

Reality-Based Learning Enhances Performance

The marketplace is changing too rapidly for companies to operate from a reactive stance by responding only to today's needs and relying on today's technology. The ever-evolving marketplace will require continuous scanning, continuous learning, continuous improvement, continuous adaptation, and continuous innovation.

Your firm must recognize that what worked well yesterday will not work as well today, will be ineffective tomorrow, and will be obsolete the day after tomorrow. How you spend your time and how you approach situations will determine whether your firm will be able to evolve to the next level or if it will slide into mediocrity. The Levels of Managerial Proactivity profiled in Table I.1 highlight the differences between good managers, better managers, and exceptional managers.

TABLE I.1.   Levels of Managerial Proactivity

Types of Managers	Approach to Situations
Good Managers	They spend their time solving problems and trying to come up with the answers to existing questions. Their perpetual fire fighting drains their firms of critical time, energy, and resources.
Better Managers	They move their firms forward by spending some of their time identifying the problems that will need to be solved and coming up with better answers to current and future questions.
Exceptional Managers	The best managers create their firm's future by preventing problems from happening so they have time to identify and capitalize on future opportunities. They also come up with the answers before anyone else—including their customers and competitors—even know the questions. They combine learning, change, and innovation to take their firms to the next level and beyond. They create their firm's future by changing the possibilities, probabilities, and payoffs in their world.

Reality Check: How do you spend your time? If you frequently say, "Someday I need to take the time to seriously think about the future and find significant ways to enhance my firm's competitiveness," then you are leading your firm to extinction. Creating your firm's future cannot be on a time-available basis. Do not procrastinate—start now.

Reality Check: If your firm is not changing as much as the world outside it, then you are leading your firm to extinction.

Reality Check: If you and your staff are not developing the skills you will need to outthink your competitors, then you are leading your firm to extinction.

Reality Check: If your firm's technology, processes, and information system are not keeping up with competition and customer expectations, then you are leading your firm to extinction.

Learning is defined as an awareness that changes behavior. It involves finding new ways to do things and new things to do. If you are serious about learning, then you need to step back and look at your firm and your industry through *irreverent* glasses. You and your staff must look at current and future realities. This involves looking at every situation, every practice, and every assumption, and asking, "Is there a better way?" Then you develop the better way.

Ever-evolving enterprises incorporate processes that resemble "tough love." You must create an environment that fosters introspection, multi-directional communication, and constructive criticism throughout the company. When the company is confronted with a problem, or performance falls below expectations, people must be free to challenge the key assumptions, prevailing perceptions, and the way things are done. For substantive learning to take place, there can be no sacred topics, no sacred practices, and no sacred cows.

Ever-evolving enterprises recognize that to improve their current performance and to prepare for the future they need to divide their activities into five areas: (1) things that need to be deleted, (2) things that need to be reduced, (3) things that need to be continued, (4) things that need to be improved, and (5) things that need to be initiated.

Reality Check: Timing plays a critical role in change efforts. Change is not the issue. The right change at the right time is the issue. There are times when you need to embark on a new initiative and times when you should stick with what you have been doing. If you are too far out in front in your efforts to be first to market (first mover), then you may be there when there is no market. There is a difference in being at the leading edge and being at the bleeding edge. If your timing and approach are not in sync, then being first to market may mean you are also first to fail. There are advantages to being a fast follower. It gives you a chance to learn from the first mover's errors. Someone once noted that being the first mover is not as important as being the first one to cross the finish line (first finisher). Conversely, if you are too late because you were late in recognizing the opportunity or because you were trying to reduce your risk by doing extensive analysis, then you may miss the opportunity altogether.

Many Firms Are "Change Impaired"

The saying "You cannot teach an old dog new tricks" is often applied to established firms. Emerging firms can also get set in their ways. The young dog must keep learning new tricks as it matures. It is ironic that a firm's success can contribute to its decline. Firms that experience success—especially overnight success—often fall prey to the "paradox of success." The key to evolving is to keep the firm from becoming arrogant and complacent. Arrogance and complacency lead to mediocrity, and mediocrity causes the firm to be irrelevant in the marketplace. Firms that adopt the "If it isn't broken, don't fix it" mentality must recognize that if they do not break it, some other firm will. Firms that fall into the "We should not launch the new model until the current model's demand wanes" mentality need to keep launching new models even if they cannibalize the current models in the short term. The moral to the story is if it isn't broken, then break it anyway.

Firms that state "You cannot argue with success" develop the Midas Touch syndrome where they believe everything they do will turn into gold. Successful firms need to develop a healthy case of paranoia. When Jeff Bezos was asked about how he deals with Amazon's success, he said he tells his people that they should wake up scared each morning.[1] Andy Grove, who was the CEO of Intel, recognized the value of paranoia in his book, *Only the Paranoid Survive*.

Reality Check: If you and the people in your firm feel you do not need to change, that you know more than anyone else, and you know what is best for your customers, employees, and suppliers, then your arrogance is about to be blindsided by new realities. Psychologist Morris Massey noted that some people will not take a hard look at their basic attitudes and behavior until they have a "significant emotional event." Do not let the loss of one or more of your major accounts or key people create a crisis that becomes your wake-up call.

Reality Check: When your firm starts being overrun with "challenges" you need to ask, "Am I the one who should be leading this venture?" There is a point when you or key staff members just may not have what it takes.

Some firms and managers actually experience the opposite of the paradox of success. They become very conservative and cautious. Even the savviest executives make mistakes. That is part of learning. You or your people will speed your company's slide into mediocrity if you adopt the attitude, "If I don't try anything new, then I won't make any mistakes." The greatest mistake a company can make is to not experiment with new products, new services, and new processes.

Reality Check: There is a time to think, a time to analyze, a time to decide, and a time to act. Leadership involves making judgment calls and having the guts to take action when it needs to be taken. Do not fall prey to paralysis by analysis.

The saying, "Show me a water skier or a snow skier who never falls, and I'll show you a skier who never gets better" also applies to enterprises. If you want to take your firm to the next level, then you must put your company in a situation where it is consistently experimenting and learning from its successes and mistakes.

Someone once told me he must not be a very good manager because he has so many problems to solve. I noted there are two types of problems. The first type involves the problems associated with clinging to the past—the unwillingness to change. These problems are a reflection of reactive management. Then I noted that there is a second type of problems. They are the "problems of progress" that come from trying new things that will move the firm to the next level.

I also shared a tip about using the word "problems." I suggest to almost every manager I meet that they drop the word "problem" from their vocabulary. I suggest that they substitute the words "situation" or "challenge" whenever they would use the word "problem." Using situation or challenge is far more positive. If you start every meeting with, "What problems do we have?" that conveys a sense of negativity. If you start your meeting with, "What situations or challenges are we facing or may be on the horizon?" people tend to approach the challenges with a more positive frame of mind. By the way, when the White House faces a major military or political challenge, the top brass meets in the "situation room," not the problem room. The essence of management is to transform potential problems into lucrative opportunities.

I then shared another tip that I have found very useful. I suggested that he no longer use the term "someday" when he refers to something he or his firm *should* do. Most people postpone doing things they know they should do to "some day." I noted that *someday* does not appear on any calendar. It is not the 25th hour of the day, the eighth day of the week, and so forth. I suggested that whenever he is about to use the term *someday* that he set a specific date instead of someday. Nike captured the need to be proactive and to have a sense of urgency with its "Just do it" slogan. How compelling would Nike's slogan have been if it was "Just do it someday" or "Just do it when you get around to doing it"?

Reality Check: If your firm is blindsided by numerous surprises, is not attracting new customers, and misses key deadlines, it has learning disabilities. If it has inconsistent product or service quality and is not gaining efficiencies, it has learning disabilities. If sales are coming in way below forecasts and your firm has to make major concessions to keep its customers, it has learning disabilities. And your firm has learning disabilities if you and your staff exclaim, "Why didn't we think of that?"

Techniques and Suggestions for Learning How to Evolve

Whole books have been written about how people learn and how to help them learn. The following sections highlight a few techniques and offer a few suggestions for how to foster learning in your venture so it can be an ever-evolving enterprise.

Being Future-Oriented Fosters Proactive Learning

Learning helps people improve what they are doing by making better decisions and executing them. There are an almost unlimited number of ways to enhance learning in organizations. Learning involves generating knowledge and insights through analysis, developing "lessons learned" from various experiences, learning from collecting knowledge including best practices of firms in and outside your industry, sensing potential problems and opportunities through anticipatory management, solving existing problems, sharing knowledge with others in your firm, and breaking down barriers that impede learning. Learning can also reduce the chance people will be blind-sided.

Reality Check: Are you accessible and approachable, or are you removed and handle things in only a very formal manner? If you want your people to suggest ideas, then you need to do more than just have an open door and provide a suggestion box. You need to solicit their ideas, provide timely feedback on their ideas, and quickly act on the ones that have merit.

Reality Check: Are your people free or even encouraged to challenge your ideas? Are they free to speak out and state, "The emperor has no clothes"? Do you openly admit when you have made a mistake? If you will not, then others will not, and then how will you know what needs to be fixed?

Reality Check: How often do you and your people call a time out after doing something to analyze deliberately and candidly what went well and what went wrong? How often do you just move on to the next activity without trying to identify the "lessons learned" that will help you and others in the future? How often do you just do things as they have been done before? How often do you and your staff make a deliberate effort to tap a knowledge network (best practices and internal lessons learned database) *before* doing something you have done before or for the first time?

Learning organizations are characterized by the probing nature of the questions that are asked and their open and quick flow of information. They are also characterized by how they are able to step back and analyze what is going on and then to reposition themselves. They know:

- You need to have a system where bad news (which tends to be covered up) travels quicker to decision-makers quicker than good news.
- If you want to hear the bad news you cannot shoot the messenger.
- There are no "dumb" questions.
- "Conventional wisdom" may be an oxymoron.
- You should look for causes and not the culprits.
- You need to look beyond the symptoms and find the underlying causes.
- In some situations you should "solve the solution" rather than focus on the causes.
- Learning follows from candid analysis of disparities between predictions and outcomes.

- Denial and rationalization need to be addressed head on.
- Cross-functional teams are more likely to develop insights and innovative approaches

Developing a learning organization also involves reducing and eliminating barriers to learning. The barriers include the destructive political games that are played as well as senseless paperwork, reports, committees, and meetings. Robert Townsend suggested that firms create the position "Vice-President of Killing Things" when he was CEO of Avis.[2] He noted in his book, *Up the Organization*, that when firms are embarking in many directions, they also need to counterbalance the initiatives by deliberately killing things that no longer contribute to the firm. He also noted that "sacred cows"—activities that have been considered out-of-bounds for various illogical reasons—should be killed.

Asking the tough questions, challenging assumptions, and making every effort to gain perceptive insights into the unique nature of the situation are essential components for learning organizations. Psychologists Chris Argyris and David Schon recommend that organizations incorporate "double-loop learning."[3] Most companies use single-loop learning. With single-loop learning, an adverse variation from expected interim results initiates actions until the variation is corrected. With double-loop learning, however, management deliberately steps back and analyzes the whole situation ... including the objectives, strategies, plans, tactics, and timelines. Instead of the typical knee-jerk of "see a variance, fix the variance," that assumes the overall strategy is still the right path to take, management goes all the way back to ground zero and challenges the assumptions and objectives that served as the basis for the development of the strategy being implemented.

Double-loop learning is similar to zero-based budgeting. Instead of deciding how much to allocate to various on-going projects, zero-based budgeting first asks if the project should be continued at all. With zero-based budgeting, nothing is given—everything has to be justified in terms of the extent it is mission-critical.

Double-loop learning encourages managers to re-examine their mental models and the corresponding cause-and-effect relationships. For example, if monthly sales for a product is falling below expectations, management should go beyond the usual single-loop learning response of increasing advertising or lowering its price. With double-loop learning, management steps back and re-examines the product's position in its life cycle and whether the resources invested in that product could be deployed more favorably in the development of a new product to serve an emerging market.

With double-loop learning, departures are seen as opportunities to learn, not just things to be fixed. If management really embraces the concept of double-loop learning, then it will not wait for variances to raise fundamental questions about whether the company is doing what it really should be doing. If the company is truly a learning organization, then serious questioning of basic issues will take place on a regular basis. It is easy to get caught up in just what is happening at the moment. You need to step back periodically and look for trends, what could be just over the horizon, and see the big picture. Learning organizations deal with strategic issues on a regular basis, they don't save them for annual planning retreats or major crises.

In the Following Chapters . . .

This book shows you how to blend transformational change concepts, anticipatory management, breakthrough leadership, strategic positioning, speed and perceptiveness, corporate entrepreneurship, learning organization principles, developing a culture that fosters innovation, and smart execution to achieve exceptional results. It helps you develop a mental framework for creating your company's future and to become an ever-evolving enterprise.

This book demonstrates how visionary thinking and planning "two markets ahead" will help you spot emerging opportunities. It shows how breakthrough leadership and "corpreneurial" strategies can help you catch the waves of change so your company can continue moving forward . . . as other companies fall by the wayside. It helps you frame a compelling vision and monitor performance so there will be fewer surprises.

This book offers hundreds of ideas, insights, and examples. It is not intended to be just for people who are already at the helms of their companies. It is intended for people at all levels in the company. It will help those who want to get to helm as well as those who want to make a difference in their current positions. It is based on the premise that if you look at the world differently, then you will see things others do not see, think thoughts others do not think, make decisions others will not make, and take actions others will not take. This will set you apart from others in your firm. It will also help you set your firm apart in the marketplace.

Conclusion: Good Bye and Good Riddance to the Comfort Zone

If you want to take your firm to the next level and beyond, then you will create an environment that encourages your people to embrace change rather than resist it. People are far more likely to embrace change if they are the initiators and beneficiaries of the change rather than the recipients or casualties of change.

Your firm's future success will be tied to its ability to sense what your customers will want and your ability to develop products, services, competencies, and processes that will delight them. These factors will enable your firm to determine how the game will be played and to gain the industry high ground. Firms that are smart, proactive, and innovative will be far more successful than firms that are slow to learn and sloth-like. The U.S. West ad, "You either make dust or eat dust," captures the need for and benefits to be gained from being an ever-evolving enterprise.

All products, processes, patents, and profits come from people. If you create an environment that encourages and rewards learning, change, and innovation, then your people will direct their resourcefulness to efforts that will create your company's future. If you create an environment that does not tap their resourcefulness, then they may jump ship and share their innovative talents with a competitor or even create their own companies to compete against you. When it comes to innovative talent and ideas, you either use them or lose them!

Being proactive means not waiting for a crisis to change what your firm is doing. Take the following Ever-Evolving Enterprise Quiz in Table I.2 to see where you and your firm stand in your ability to create an exceptional future.

We have to release this death grip on the past and deal with the future.[4]

—John Naisbitt, author of *Megatrends*

TABLE I.2. Ever-Evolving Enterprise Quiz

How does your firm rate on the following dimensions? *Scoring Level: 1 = not at all, 2 = rarely, 3 = occasionally, 4 = frequently, 5 = ongoing/extensive	Level*
1. To what extent does your firm have a specific and challenging vision for its future that fosters a high level of energy and commitment in people at all levels to be engaged and stretch to their potential?	1-2-3-4-5
2. How frequently does your firm do a systematic analysis of what your competitors are doing and contemplate what they may be considering in their effort to take your customers?	1-2-3-4-5
3. How often does your firm contemplate what your market (competition, customers, technology, etc.) will be like three years from now?	1-2-3-4-5
4. How often does your firm truly consider the consequences of losing your top two customers or one or more of your best people?	1-2-3-4-5
5. To what extent does the firm have a succession plan for key leadership positions in place so the talent will be there to meet future challenges?	1-2-3-4-5
6. To what extent do the firm's leaders invest time and money in developing the firm's human resources for future challenges?	1-2-3-4-5
7. Has your firm truly considered what would happen if your information system was corrupted or destroyed? 1 = no, 3 = somewhat, 5 = seriously.	1-2-3-4-5
8. How often does your firm monitor key metrics to identify even the smallest change or trend?	1-2-3-4-5
9. How often does your firm actively solicit employee, supplier, and customer ideas for new ways to do things and new things to do?	1-2-3-4-5
10. To what extent does your firm encourage constructive criticism, for people to challenge the way things are being done, and questioning the assumptions that are the basis for plans and decisions?	1-2-3-4-5
11. To what extent does your firm make a deliberate effort to learn from other firms?	1-2-3-4-5
12. To what extent does your firm have formal processes in place to learn from its experiences and share what it has learned to improve future performance?	1-2-3-4-5

(continued)

TABLE I.2. (Continued)

How does your firm rate on the following dimensions? *Scoring Level: 1 = not at all, 2 = rarely, 3 = occasionally, 4 = frequently, 5 = ongoing/extensive	Level*
13. To what extent does your firm hire people with diverse perspectives and experiences?	1-2-3-4-5
14. To what extent is your firm working on break-through innovations?	1-2-3-4-5
15. To what extent does your firm have mechanisms searching for emerging opportunities in and outside its current markets?	1-2-3-4-5
16. To what extent does your firm have processes in place to reduce bureaucracy, kill sacred cows, discontinue out-of-date practices and eliminate legacy mindsets?	1-2-3-4-5
17. To what extent does your firm have processes in place for people from various departments to share their thoughts, to cross-pollinate ideas, encourage skunkworks, etc.?	1-2-3-4-5
18. To what extent are people at all levels of the firm encouraged, reviewed, and rewarded for being innovative?	1-2-3-4-5
19. To what extent does your firm have formal processes in place to continuously improve operations?	1-2-3-4-5
20. To what extent does your firm have formal processes in place to identify and correct deviations from planned performance?	1-2-3-4-5
Total points	

Scoring Key

90–100	Congratulations, your firm demonstrates most of the qualities of an ever-evolving enterprise.
80–89	Your firm has many qualities of an ever-evolving enterprise, but still has areas that can be improved.
70–79	Your firm has some strengths, but there is a lot of room for improvement.
60–69	Your firm has some significant impairments that impede its ability to learn and change.
20–59	Your firm may be beyond hope. It will take a radical change in management, corporate culture, systems, and processes to have any chance of being competitive in the future.

Notes

Portions of the material in this chapter originally appeared in the article, "The Ever-Evolving Enterprise" by the author and David J. Glew in *Industrial Management*, March/April, 2008. Reprinted with the permission of the Institute of Industrial Engineers, 3577 Parkway Lane, Suite 200, Norcross, GA 30092, www.iienet.org. Copyright 2009 by Institute of Industrial Engineers.

1. "Nerd of the Amazon," *60 Minutes*, February 3, 1999 (CBS Video).

2. Robert Townsend, *Up the Organization* (New York: Alfred A. Knopf, 1970), 93.

3. Chris Argyris and David A. Schon, *Organizational Learning* (Westminster: Addison-Wesley, 1978), 2, 3.

4. John Naisbitt, *Megatrends* (New York: Warner Books, 1984), 13.

Chapter 1

Guidelines for Transformational Change

Leadership will always play a key role during those times when a group faces a new problem and must develop new responses to the situation. One of the functions of leadership is to provide guidance at precisely those times when habitual ways of doing things no longer work, or when dramatic change in the work environment requires new responses.

—Edgar H. Schein, M.I.T. Professor

The new economy is like the opening line, "It was the best of times, it was the worst of times," in Charles Dickens's *A Tale of Two Cities*. For firms that are ever-evolving, it can be the best of times. They will be the ones that sense and seize opportunities. For firms that are not in sync with new realities, it will be the worst of times. They will be the casualties of change.

The last few decades have seen incredible change. Things that people thought could not happen did happen. Things that were supposed to take decades to happen took just a few years. Things that were supposed to take years took place in a few months. We live in a world where products and services that did not exist ten years ago are common in most households, offices, or automobiles. We also live in a world where things that once were common are now artifacts of the past.

The new economy is a place where the rules have changed so much that you wonder if there are any rules. It is an economy where power has been equalized between buyers and sellers. It is an economy where a startup's revolutionary product can make the market's leading product obsolete. It is an economy where there are no time-outs and no commercial breaks. It is an economy where change is changing, ever-accelerating, and increasingly complex. It is an economy where change comes at a company from all sides. It is an economy where change comes at a company like a relentless and merciless series of waves. It is an economy where change makes it difficult to catch your breath and stay on your feet. It is an economy where change can be so unanticipated, so radical, so comprehensive that it sucks the air right out of your lungs!

The new economy presents new challenges. So many changes have occurred on so many fronts in such a short time that many companies have been caught off guard. Their executives appear to be frozen in time like deer caught in the headlights of an oncoming truck. The new economy is catching large and small companies in its headlights. Even successful companies have been stunned by the speed that revolutionary technology has been developed, new products have been introduced, and existing markets have been reconfigured.

The new economy operates 24/7 at "net speed." In the new economy, companies need to develop products that will cannibalize their own products before other firms cannibalize them. Instead of focusing on beating their competitors' products, companies need to move forward and create new products that make their own existing products obsolete.

The rules of business have not only changed; they are being rewritten each day. The premise "If it isn't broke, don't fix it" has been replaced with "Break it before your competitors do." The premise that your company will succeed if it incorporates continuous improvement processes has been replaced by the premise that only the innovative will survive. Incremental and linear change used to be enough for a company to be competitive. Today, the market beckons for breakthrough innovations and bold initiatives.

The new economy is an idea economy. It is an economy that rewards firms that find new ways to do things and new things to do. An economy of ideas is also an economy of insights and revelations. Executives who are savvy to market dynamics will be in a position to prevent potential problems and capitalize on emerging opportunities. When Jeff Bezos learned about the projected increase in the use of the Internet, he quit his job in New York City and headed west in search of the best opportunity to pursue. Bezos's perceptiveness was an epiphany. It was a sudden realization that electronic commerce would be like a tsunami hitting the business world. He dropped everything he was doing so he could ride the wave of change. His perceptiveness made him one of the richest people in the world as the founder of Amazon.com. The lack of perceptiveness and flexibility by established book, music, and video retailers caused them to be blindsided by the electronic commerce wave. It is an economy where startups like Amazon, eBay, Google, YouTube, Facebook, Skype, and firms that have yet to be launched can garner millions of customers and an extraordinary valuation within just a couple of years.

Creating Your Company's Future by Developing an Ever-Evolving Enterprise

Change can be dramatic or it can be traumatic. Executives who want to move their company forward and create its future must embrace the prelude to Star Trek. They must be willing to "Boldly go where no company has gone before." They must be able to take their companies forward to the next level and beyond. Their people must be able to think thoughts they have never thought, to do things they have never done—or no one has ever done! They must be able to develop new technology and to harness it to create significant competitive advantages. They must know their customers better than their customers know themselves. Companies that can anticipate where the market is going will be in a position to create their future.

The ever-evolving enterprise is like a magnet. It attracts customers, employees, investors, and allies who want to be partners in its journey into tomorrow. Developing an ever-evolving enterprise involves doing everything that is possible to be the employer of choice, the provider of choice, the investment of choice, and the customer of choice. It is about creating a company where highly talented people will stand in the rain for the opportunity to be considered for a position. It is about having a corporate culture that unleashes people and enables them to surprise themselves with what they can think and do. It is about creating an environment where people are committed to making possible what the marketplace considers impossible. It is about having the answers before anyone else even knows the questions. It is about developing products, services, and processes that make the competition irrelevant.

Developing an ever-evolving enterprise is not about maintaining your competitive position; it is about launching preemptive strikes. Creating the company's future goes well beyond preserving market share and keeping existing customers; it involves searching for emerging markets and attracting new customers. Creating the company's future goes well beyond satisfying customers; it involves delighting customers.

Developing an ever-evolving enterprise requires irreverence for almost everything that exists. Creating your company's future takes vision and the guts to do what needs to be done today to create a better tomorrow. Creating your company's future involves developing an environment where change is the way of life, where repetition is abhorred, and where maintaining the status quo is sinful. Creating your company's future involves slaughtering sacred cows and encouraging everyone to blow a whistle when they run across any form of "b.s."

The Model for Creating Your Company's Future

Executives who want to create their company's future must become venture "catalysts." They must be committed to building a great company rather than acting like venture capitalists who are preoccupied with cashing out for considerable personal gain in a relatively short period of time. Unlike venture capitalists who are almost solely concerned about generating wealth for investors, venture catalysts take pride in what their companies offer, care about their company's employees, and foster mutually beneficial relationships with all the company's other stakeholders.

The competitive bar continues to be raised. The ever-changing marketplace will reward companies that have their acts together and trample companies that are out of sync. Companies that are able to develop and sustain competitive advantages on multiple fronts will have a higher probability of success than those that stand out in only one area. Excellence in just one competitive facet may not be enough to win in the marketplace.

A few years ago, companies that provided excellent quality stood out in the crowd. Today, anything less than excellence and the company is out of the game. Yet, in a world where excellence is becoming the standard, companies must be more than excellent. They must be *exceptional* if they want to win in the marketplace. The Creating Your Company's Future Model profiled in Figure 1.1 reflects various dimensions executives need to keep in mind if they want to transform their companies into exceptional enterprises.

The model, which serves as part of the foundation for this book, reflects a causal flow from left to right. Certain prerequisite conditions must exist before the company can gain these competitive advantages. These prerequisites need to be in place before the drivers of change can emerge which, in turn, facilitate the emergent factors that foster the development of the company's competitive advantages.

These advantages include the company's ability to: (1) keep pace, if not stay ahead of, changing conditions, (2) be either first-to-market or

FIGURE 1.1.   Creating Your Company's Future Model

	Creating Your Company's Future		
Prerequisite Conditions →	Drivers of Change →	Emergent Factors →	Competitive Advantages
Breakthrough Leadership	Talent	Leaders at All Levels	Ever-evolving Enterprise
Anticipatory Management	Insights	Lucrative Opportunities	Temporary Legal Monopolies
Innovative Systems	Ideas	Innovative Products/Services	Delighted Customers/ Addicts
Revolutionary Culture	Commitment	Inspired Employees	Champions/Fanatics

to have such superiority as a fast follower that it blows its competitors out of the market, (3) meet its target market's needs so well that its customers do not even consider other companies, and (4) create an environment where employees identify with the company to the point that they cannot imagine working for any other enterprise.

Creating Temporary Legal Monopolies

Companies must seek opportunities where they can "own the market." Executives should make every effort for their company to be so superior that other companies think twice before they consider competing against it. Executives should also make every effort to anticipate emerging markets so they have the lead time necessary to develop products and services to meet their needs when the "window of opportunity" opens. Being first-to-market provides the company with a *temporary legal monopoly!*

Ever-evolving enterprises rely on "corpreneurial" strategies to gain temporary legal monopolies. Corpreneurial strategies which are profiled in chapter six involve focusing on emerging market opportunities and developing innovative products and services rather than making minor modifications to existing products in established markets. Ever-evolving enterprises, through their corpreneurial strategies, resemble the efforts by entrepreneurs to change the way the game is played. The spirit of corpreneurship is emphasized throughout this book.

Creating Delighted Customers and Addicts

Marketing has been defined as the process whereby the company tries to "create and maintain customers for a profit." When the "marketing concept" was developed, it was asserted that corporate success was contingent on the company's ability to "serve" the market. Serving the market at that time meant providing products and services that were in tune with market expectations. With the passage of time, however, customer expectations and the availability of competitive alternatives have increased.

Today's marketplace is experiencing the emergence of a whole new level of consumer expectations. Every minute of every day is a "moment of truth" for companies. The days of "let the buyer beware" and mass marketing are over. Serving and satisfying customers will not cut it. Customers expect customized solutions. Customers expect to be "wowed and delighted."

If companies want to create and maintain customers and to gain temporary legal monopolies, then they must be designed to wow and delight their customers to the level that they are almost addicted to their products and services. Business schools may tout the value of developing barriers to entry to keep competitors out. When you wow and delight your customers you are creating a *barrier to exit* where they cannot imagine buying from any other firm.

Creating Champions and Fanatics

Executives need to pay as much attention to the people within the company as they do to targeted customers. All products, processes, patents, and profits come from people. Your company's future is tied directly to the quality of its human resources and the extent they are committed to creating your company's future. No company will ever have the best people. Companies will succeed only to the extent that they are able to *bring out the best* in their people. Ordinary people can do truly extraordinary things under the right conditions.

Change Needs to be Approached with the Proper Mental Framework

Change efforts are rarely simple. Executives who want to initiate change need to recognize that change must be seen in a contextual manner. They will succeed only to the extent they take into consideration the uniqueness of their corresponding situations. The greater the

FIGURE 1.2.   Contextual Change Model

Step One: Identify specifically the "desired results."

Step Two: Develop an "awareness" of the unique factors and forces at play in the situation.

Step Three: Develop an "understanding" of how the factors and forces are interelated. Model the situation as a system.

Step Four: Formulate your change strategy and plan its implementation.

Step Five: Implement the change strategy and monitor its degree of success. Change if necessary.

Step Six: Determine if the change produced the "desired results." Debrief on what you learned and how what you learned can benefit future action.

complexity, the greater the likelihood that factors and relationships will be missed that could affect which change effort is selected as well as the effectiveness of the change effort.

The Contextual Change Model profiled in Figure 1.2 identifies the six steps associated with initiating effective change. It begins with identifying the desired results. Organizations are created to achieve certain results. This notion is captured in Steven Covey's principle that executives need to "begin with the end in mind." Management must have a results-orientation in everything it does. Change should never be for the sake of change. Change should be initiated so the company can achieve specific results.

Executives will serve their companies well if they identify the company's key result areas and set specific objectives for each area. Once the desired results are identified, attention needs to be directed to the awareness stage. Management has to take the company's unique situation into consideration to achieve the desired results. Stage two encourages management to identify all the factors and forces that are relevant to the company's situation that may have some bearing on the change effort. Every relevant factor and force is listed in stage two. These factors include (among other things) the nature of competition, economic conditions, the rate of technological change, government regulations, and the company's available resources.

Stage three encourages management to analyze how the factors and forces may be interrelated. We live in a world of cause and effect relationships. Few things exist in isolation. The understanding stage can be seen as an attempt to build a model that reflects the whole situation, its parts, and the relationships among the parts. The model is then used to capture the expected sensitivities among various factors and forces. Scenarios and simulations are helpful in identifying possible relationships and their relative sensitivities.

The first three stages are critical in the management of change. Too often, managers enter the decision-making process prematurely. They either go in with too little understanding of the situation they are facing, or they approach today's decisions with yesterday's information. A decision can only be as good as the information that goes into making it. Managers need to recognize that in times of change every situation is unique.

Stage four represents the decision-making side of change management. When management is satisfied that it has a true understanding of the unique situation, it can direct its attention to generating and evaluating possible change strategies. Alternatives need to be generated for how to achieve the desired results given the unique situation at hand. The alternatives then need to be evaluated in terms of their ability to achieve the desired results effectively and efficiently. The availability of resources and the degree of risk will also affect which alternative is selected.

When the change strategies under consideration are ranked, management can select the change effort that best fits the company's unique situation. Management then makes all the corresponding decisions for implementing the decision. The decisions include: what is to be done, how it is to be done, who will do it, what resources will be needed, and when it will need to be done. Contingency plans may also be developed during this stage.

Stage Five represents the initiation of change to achieve the desired results. Stage Five recognizes that decisions do not implement themselves. Management needs to recognize that every plan is based on a set of assumptions about reality. If the assumptions do not hold up, then the plans may need to be modified. Implementation includes monitoring the change effort's success on a periodic or ongoing basis.

Monitoring frequency will be contingent on the volatility of the situation, the consequences of an unfavorable variation, as well as the length of time and amount of resources it takes to address the variation. The greater the sensitivity, the greater the need for more frequent monitoring. Life is full of surprises and few things go as planned, so this stage may involve adjusting the change effort or launching a contingency plan to get the company back on track.

Stage Six is a reality check. It involves making sure the change effort fulfilled the original performance expectations. If the company was unsuccessful in its efforts, then management needs to recognize that its decisions for the change effort were probably built on a weak foundation.

Change Must Be Approached in a Holistic Manner

Creating your company's future will require that your firm's vision, strategy, culture, systems, and structure be aligned. The Holistic Change Model profiled in Figure 1.3 profiles how these dimensions are interrelated.

The Vision: Your firm needs to have a clear and compelling vision. Your vision should indicate where you want it to be at a specific date in the future. This is the bull's-eye for your target.

Strategy: Your strategy reflects how you plan to create and maintain customers for a profit. It identifies your competitive advantage(s).

Values: Your firm's values may affect decisions and actions by identifying what is appropriate.

Culture: Your culture reflects your firm's key values. A corporation's culture is like a person's personality. It affects how people see the world and their propensity to behave in certain ways.

Systems and Structure: These affect how things are done. They reflect the processes, policies, and practices that affect behavior and performance.

Leadership: Leadership ties all the other factors together. It is the force that fosters the development of an exceptional enterprise.

The External Environment: Nothing happens in a vacuum. The firm succeeds only to the extent that it is in sync with current and future realities and the extent that it provides value to its target market(s).

FIGURE 1.3.   The Holistic Change Model

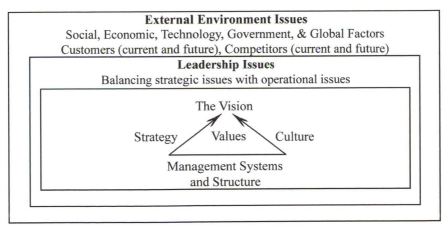

New Realities Call for New Approaches to Leadership

The ever-accelerating nature and ever-increasing magnitude of change call for a whole new perspective in viewing the change process. Transformational change begins by noting the following realities:

Principles of Change Management

- Change is not just a set of tools and techniques; it is a state of mind.
- Change is not about fixing yesterday's mistakes; it is about preparing for a new tomorrow.
- Change is not about surviving; it is about thriving.
- Change is not just about the bottom line; it is about focusing on the "top line."
- Change is not just about putting out fires; it is about blazing new trails.
- Change is not the enemy; it is about making change an ally.
- Change is not about creating a fuzzy mission statement; it is about creating a compelling vision.
- Change is not about developing detailed and inflexible plans; it is about "futuring."
- Change is not about competing in the future; it is about creating the future.
- Change is not about incrementalism; it is about breakthrough innovation.
- Change is not about isolated tweaks; it is about multifaceted change efforts.
- Change is not about coping; it is about making change a way of life.

Change Is Not Just a Set of Tools and Techniques; It Is a State of Mind

Transformational change is an attitude. It is the way you approach situations and challenges. It is about how you see the future, technology, risk, innovation, and people. Executives who understand the complexities of transformational change will be able to break away from the pack. Executives who continue approaching the world around them with the same mental models and approaches will be left behind.

Change Is Not about Fixing Yesterday's Mistakes; It Is about Preparing for a New Tomorrow

There is a story about two managers supervising teams of workers who are cutting their way through a forest. While one manager is busy measuring the group's progress, the other manager climbs a tree and yells down, "We're in the wrong forest!" New realities call for a new breed of leaders. Albert Einstein noted, "The significant problems we face cannot be solved at the same level of thinking we were at when we created them." Hopefully the days that were devoted to "stopping the bleeding" can be replaced with a commitment to building strength and creating the firm's future.

Change Is Not about Surviving; It Is about Thriving

Transformational change involves gaining temporary legal monopolies in target markets by outthinking and outdoing your competition. It is about sensing change before others so you have a "mental head start" over your competitors. It is about being the first to see opportunities so you can develop competencies that will help your company thrive . . . as other companies desperately try to survive.

Change Is Not Just about the Bottom Line; It Is about Focusing on the "Top Line"

Top-line management encourages companies to seek new revenue opportunities. It encourages executives to scan the horizon for emerging opportunities and to be more entrepreneurial. It also encourages the company to do exploratory marketing to find new markets to serve and new ways to serve existing markets. Top-line management embraces being first-to-market and making preemptive strikes. Top-line management recognizes that companies that are first-to-market may have the opportunity to establish brand identity and to set the rules for how the competitive game will be played.

Change Is Not Just about Putting Out Fires; It Is about Blazing New Trails

Few things capture people's excitement more than being part of a vibrant entity and exploring new possibilities. Capitalizing on growth opportunities and developing innovative approaches capture the human spirit far more than efforts geared to downsizing and outsourcing. Executives will serve their companies well if they direct their attention to looking at the world through new eyes. If they view their companies as if they are a fresh sheet of paper, then they will find opportunities for their companies to excel.

Change Need Not Be the Enemy; It Is about Making Change an Ally

Transformational change means being the initiator and beneficiary of change rather than the recipient and victim of change. Rosabeth Moss Kanter, author of *The Change Masters*, noted, "Change can either be friend or foe, depending on the resources available to cope with it and master it by innovating. It is disturbing when it is done to us, exhilarating when it is done by us."[1] She also noted, "Change can be exhilarating, refreshing—a chance to meet new challenges, a chance to clean house. . . . Change brings opportunities when people have been planning for it, are ready for it, and have just the thing in mind to do when a new state comes into being."[2]

Change Is Not about Fuzzy Mission Statements; It Is about Creating a Compelling Vision

Executives need to have a strong future orientation. They also need to develop a vision for where their companies should be in that future. In a sense, the vision is the "call to arms" that empowers people at all levels to make exciting things happen.

Change Is Not about Developing Detailed Plans; It Is about "Futuring"

A vision statement cannot be developed unless executives scan the horizon for what may be ahead. Leadership must make sure the company keeps its eyes on the horizon. Karl Albrecht, author of *The Northbound Train*, emphasizes the need for executives to do "futuring." He defines futuring as a "constantly active mental process that generates action strategies for capitalizing on the unfolding environment."[3] Plans that are inflexible and too formal are like quicksand. They may elicit a degree of organizational rigidity that will impede the company's ability to adjust to the ever-changing world. Executives who recognize future discontinuities will keep tomorrow from being a linear extension of the past.

Change Is Not about Competing in the Future; It Is about Creating the Future

Transformational change is not about preparing for the future; it is about creating your company's future. Transformational change is about breaking the rules, making new rules, and then changing the rules again. It goes beyond managing in a world of change; it means leading the change. Transformational change is about being proactive and entrepreneurial. It involves having the ability to change the probabilities, the payoffs, and the states of nature. Transformational change involves pondering what opportunities may exist and then positioning your company to create its future by capitalizing on the opportunities. Transformational change embraces Alan Kay's philosophy, "The best way to predict the future is to invent it!"[4]

Change Is Not about Incrementalism; It Is about Breakthrough Innovation

Creating a world-class company calls for more than making minor changes in existing products. Philip Aines noted, when he was Vice President of Research and Development at Pillsbury, "It's much more difficult to come up with a synthetic meat product than a lemon-lime cake mix because you know exactly what the return is going to be. A synthetic steak is going to take a lot longer, require a much larger investment, and the risk of failure will be much greater."[5] The irony is that Aines made that statement over forty years ago. Unfortunately, too many firms today do not have the courage to develop breakthrough products and services.

Change Is Not about Isolated Tweaks; It Is about Multifaceted Change Efforts

Organizational contexts are as multifaceted as a diamond. Executives need to approach change from a holistic or systems perspective. Executives need to recognize that a company is part of a much larger ecosystem. Change efforts need to recognize that a company is actually a web of relationships. Executives need to be able to differentiate between causes of problems and symptoms of problems. Changing one component of the system will affect other components. Some effects will be obvious; others will be subtle. Some effects will be immediate; others may not appear for quite some time. Executives need to view change as if they were throwing a stone into a pond. They need to anticipate the ripple effect and make sure the overall effect is what they desire before they throw the stone.

Change Is Not about Coping; It Is about Making Change a Way of Life

Coping has become a way of life for most companies. Too many executives focus on just making it through the day. They spend too much time and energy trying to make sure things do not fall through the cracks. They also spend too much time bracing themselves for the next wave of change. An organization has only so much energy. The energy can be spent defending and maintaining its current position or it can be directed to initiating change and moving forward to the high ground. Karl Wallenda, the great high-wire performer captured the inherent energizing force of change when he stated, "Being on the wire is living; everything else is waiting."[6] Transformational change creates opportunities for everyone in the company to feel alive by providing them opportunities to make a difference.

Lead or Get Blown Out of the Way!

The business world is not a forgiving place. It is a world where competitors do not take prisoners. It is a world where being a day late means going out of business. There used to be room in the marketplace for good companies and good managers. As long as companies offered something within reason, at an acceptable price, they could make a reasonable profit. It is clear now that the classic twentieth century saying, "Lead, follow, or get out of the way." is being replaced with the reality that you either lead or get blown out of the way. In times of rapid change, there is little room for companies that follow. If you are not markedly better; you are dead.

Leading Change Is as Multifaceted as a Diamond

Transformational change is not a simple process. Numerous factors need to be considered. The more the factors are incorporated into the change process, the more likely it will produce beneficial results. Transformational change is more of an art than a science. It cannot be engineered and managed with the same precision that an assembly line can be designed and managed. It takes perceptiveness and finesse. The following sample of insights may prove beneficial before embarking on a change effort:

Corporate Change "Facts of Life"

- Change is a fact of corporate life. Most people resist change, especially if they are not prepared for it. Create an environment where people embrace it rather than brace themselves to resist it.
- Change is occurring at an ever-accelerating pace. Improve your company's ability to sense it while it is on the horizon when people can see it coming and prepare for it.
- Change is more acceptable when people see it as beneficial to them rather than a threat. Show them that it is relevant and worth the effort.
- Change will be implemented better if the people who must make it happen are coarchitects of the change.
- Change is more acceptable when it is prompted by a sense of reality than if it is imposed from above as a "Just do it!" edict.
- Change is more likely to be accepted if it follows a successful change effort. Capitalize on the momentum.
- Change is more likely to be accepted if is initiated after a previous change has been assimilated rather than if it is initiated while a major change is underway. Let your people catch their breath for a brief moment before moving on.
- Change is more likely to be accepted if it is the result of deliberate analysis rather than a knee-jerk response to an unanticipated event or crisis.
- Change is more likely to be accepted by people who have limited experience than by people who are accustomed to doing things in a particular way.
- Change is more likely to be accepted if the people in the company are familiar with change models and change processes.
- Change is more likely to happen if executives set the right example for others to follow.

Leading Change Requires Commitment from All Involved

Transformational change calls for more than going through the motions. Leading change is not for those looking for quick fixes. Change calls for total commitment, not just participation. Transformational change recognizes the difference between commitment and participation. When they are asked to describe the difference they say, "It's the difference between eggs and bacon. While the chicken participated in making the breakfast possible, the pig was truly committed!"

Transformational change succeeds only to the extent that leaders are able to create an environment where people want to get on board. Change efforts may encounter varying levels of commitment. Some change efforts are expedited because they start with a high level of commitment. Other change efforts are almost destined to fail because they face stiff resistance. The following levels of commitment may be encountered in a change effort:

The Seven Levels of Commitment

Champions: Those who are the architects or initiators of the change.

Committed: Those who embrace the change at face value.

Participants: Those who accept the change and will voluntarily implement it.

Observers: Those who watch from the sidelines and withhold judgment of the need for and merit of the change.

Skeptics: Those who need to be convinced of the need for and merit of the change.

Overt Resistors: Those who openly resist change.

Covert Resistors: Those who resist the change behind the scenes.

People can be in one category for one change effort and a different category for another. If people believe the company is in a "change or die" situation and have a chance to be coarchitects of the change effort, then they may welcome the opportunity to play a leading role in it. Conversely, people who have been left in the dark and have been burned by change efforts in the past may resist it with the utmost vigor.

People leading change efforts should be realists. Resistance is a natural part of most change processes. Few people embrace change that will affect them when someone else proposes it. The only person who welcomes change is a baby with a soiled diaper. People leading change efforts should recognize that people's resistance may have merit. They should try to learn why people are reluctant to accept and implement the proposed change. When people do not understand the need for change or what is involved in the change effort, their resistance may actually be confusion. Their questions should not be seen as resistance. People who propose change should remember that other people have not been thinking about the change as much or for as long. They also need to recognize that other people do not have extrasensory perception. They should look at change through the other people's eyes.

Resisters need to see the benefits of making the change and the consequences for the company and for them if the company does not make the change. There will be times, however, when resistors must face a "moment of truth." They should given the opportunity to "get on the

Reality Check: You may be able to learn something from the resistors. Most people do not wake up in the morning saying, "Let's see how I can keep the company from moving ahead today." People who resist change believe they have a good reason for resisting the change. They may see something you do not see. Resisters can serve as a timely "reality check." They keep us from having blind faith and being overly infatuated with our own ideas.

bus." But the invitation to get on board should make it clear that once the decision is made to go ahead, they need to be mentally and physically committed or find a job with a company that shares their perceptions.

Change leaders need to keep an eye on the covert resistors. John Kotter, author of *Leading Change*, stresses the need for change leaders to not drop their guards once the change effort is initiated. These people look for the first sign of problems to show the change effort was ill conceived. They may even look for the first sign of success to indicate the problem has been resolved and that the company can return to its old ways.[7]

Transformational change recognizes three other aspects associated with people's commitment to change efforts. First, the absence of resistance should not be mistaken for commitment. Going back to the chicken and pig story, there are a lot of chickens out there. Effort needs to be directed to gaining their commitment. Second, while people may resist change, few people resist improvement. Change efforts need to indicate how the change will lead to a better tomorrow. Emphasis should be placed on how things will be better instead of just different. Third, change efforts need to be led by people at all levels of the company. Top management may foster change by providing air cover, but change efforts should not rely on charismatic style to gain commitment. Charisma has two drawbacks. It is a rare commodity, and most people would rather decide for themselves if they are to join the change effort rather than rely on someone else's personality to sway them.

Mid-level managers, first-line supervisors, and hourly employees should also have the opportunity to play a leadership role. Top management needs to be sure mid-level managers support the change. Mid-level managers can make change happen or kill it in its tracks. They can expedite change by endorsing it or they can derail it by dragging their feet.

Mid-level managers also play a crucial role in making sure two-way communication flows unimpeded.

Top management also needs to be in tune with what is happening on the front lines of change. Front-line personnel will be more committed to the change effort if they have a sense for the overall context of change. First-line supervisors live where the rubber meets the road. Employees usually support change only to the extent their supervisors support them and the change effort. In many ways, their commitment to the company is tied directly to their commitment to their supervisor. Change has the best chance for success when the whole organization operates as a web of formal and informal change champions.

Leading Change Means Sloughing Off Yesterday and Today

Transformational change involves learning. Most change efforts fail because managers do not understand the nature of learning. For people to learn new ways to do things and new things to do, they first need to discontinue what they are currently doing. The Lewin Three-Step Change Model profiled in Figure 1.4 provides a framework for managing change. Years ago, psychologist Kurt Lewin noted that change needs to be viewed as a three-step process.[8]

Most managers think that initiating change is a one-step process. Kurt Lewin noted that change efforts are destined to be exercises in futility if people are unwilling to discontinue what they have been doing. Most people are unwilling to change if they are in their comfort zone. More and more people are clinging to the way they have done things. Many people may prefer their comfort zone even with its drawbacks to the potential benefits associated with an uncertain future. Lewin noted that

FIGURE 1.4.   Lewin's Three-Step Model for Initiating Change

Step One: Unfreezing >>> Step Two: Initiating the Change >>> Step Three: Refreezing

Step One: Unfreezing
> Breaking away from the way things have been done.

Step Two: Initiating the Change
> Identifying and trying new ways to do things or new things to do.

Step Three: Refreezing
> Reinforcing the new ways or new things to do.

before people can change the way they see the world or how they behave it in, they must discontinue, forget, or what Lewin calls "unfreeze" their current mindset and/or behavior.

Executives need to create an environment where people realize they cannot prepare for tomorrow unless they are first willing to let go of the past and present. The first step involves unfreezing the prevailing approach to getting things done. Before executives try to introduce change they need to create a situation where the people involved in the change recognize the shortcomings and risks associated with continuing the present into the future. Some people refer to this situation as having people recognize they are on a burning platform where they cannot stay where they are.

Transformational change efforts have the best chance for success when those involved in the change recognize the need to let go and welcome the prospect of doing something new. Unfortunately, some people are not willing to let go of past and current practices, approaches, and mental models.

Executives need to be prepared to deal constructively with people who are unwilling to let go. Unfreezing involves having people realize new realities require adopting new approaches. In step one, management needs to communicate the risks associated with continuing what they had been doing. There are two basic strategies for fostering the unfreezing process. The first strategy is called "burn the village." This strategy is based on the premise that if you want people to move to a new territory, then burn their village so they have to move on.

Reality Check: It is said that the Spanish explorer Hernando Cortes burned his ships when he arrived in the New World. Cortes recognized that as long as the ships were anchored off shore, his men could think about returning to their homes. By scuttling the ships, Cortes's men had to deal with the new world. If you want your people to journey into the future, then you may have to provide the spark that burns their comfort zones so they cannot cling to the present. The most effective spark may be information that shows that we either change or die!

The second strategy for getting people to realize they cannot continue what they are doing involves more finesse. If you give people the opportunity to analyze a situation and to see where it is going, then *they* may realize that there is no future in maintaining the status quo. You will not have to burn the village; *they* will burn it.

People are far more likely to embrace change if they see the need for it and how it is relevant and beneficial to their future. When people recognize that the path they are on will not take them where they want to go, they are far more likely to look for, consider, or even create a new path. This is why it is important for your firm to have an information system that monitors current performance and compares it with expected performance. Learning often occurs when people see disconfirming information—when information indicates things are not working, they are not on the right path, or that they are not in the right forest. Running scenarios may also reveal the need to change.

Reality Check: What will it take for your people to want to leave their comfort zones to make the changes that will be necessary to take your firm to the next level? Will it take stretch goals, more lucrative incentives, or pride? Or will it take startling information, some event, or a crisis?

Reality Check: There will be some situations when you will have to let people go who are not willing to let go.

Peter Drucker's "strategic planning gap" model, profiled in chapter four helps the unfreezing process. Executives need to ask, "Where is the company at this point in time?" "Where should the company be at a future point in time?" and "Where will the company be at that future point in time if it does not change what it is presently doing?" The strategic planning gap is the difference between where the company wants to be and where it will be if it does not change. The larger the gap, the greater the need for change and the greater the magnitude for the change effort.

Leaders must transform the anxiety and risks associated with uncertainty into constructive efforts rather than debilitating behavior. Chris Argyris captured the nature of anxiety associated with change and the propensity for people to not want to leave their comfort zones. He noted people may experience two different types of anxieties. Anxiety 1 is associated with the risks of doing something the person has never done before. The person's perception of the risks may keep him or her from changing. It includes the risks associated with making a mistake, of looking stupid, and of being punished. Anxiety 1 is quite natural and should be expected.[9]

Argyris noted that whenever people are put in a situation where they try to do something new, they are temporarily incompetent—they are not in control. This explains why so many people are hesitant to leave their comfort zones. Anxiety 2 occurs when the person realizes that the risks and consequences of *not changing* are greater than the risks and consequences of changing.[10] Anxiety 2 frequently involves the fear of missing an opportunity or even recognizing the potential for regret or feeling guilty for not doing something.

For change to occur, Anxiety 2 must be greater than Anxiety 1. Jeff Bezos noted that he quit his job in New York when he saw statistics about how Internet commerce was expected to grow exponentially. When he quit his job he did not know what types of products he would sell, but he knew he had to catch the Internet wave. When Bezos was asked about what drives him, he stated that his decisions and behavior are based on his "regret minimization framework."

The second strategy involves giving the people who are expected to change the opportunity to play an integral role in determining the change effort. People are far more likely to embrace and implement a change effort is they have a chance to be co-architects of the change efforts. This is often the difference between whether things are done well or just done. Jim Collins noted in his book *Good to Great* that if you have the right people (capable and engaged employees) on the bus, they will determine where the bus should go.

Management needs to recognize that transformational change can be a time-consuming process that involves learning, experimentation and anxiety. It can also be a time when performance drops. People rarely excel at first when the try new approaches. Management needs to make sure that the proper conditions exist for people to learn in a risk-free environment. Management needs to make sure the proper training, equipment, encouragement, and resources are provided so people's confidence and competence support the new approach.

Bob Knowling, a master change agent while at U.S. West, captured the nature of Anxiety 1. He stated, "Once people have figured out something very different is happening, fear permeates the organization. You can cut it with a knife. I've come to the conclusion that you can unfear an organization. You have to tell people that if they allow fear to paralyze them, it will become a self-fulfilling prophecy; it will be their undoing because they're immobilized; they can't make decisions."[11] A scene from the film *12 O'Clock High* provides an extreme example of how to get people to let go of what they are doing. When the commanding general recognizes the bomber crews are reluctant to fly, he tells them, "Consider yourselves already dead. Once you accept that idea it won't be so tough."

Emphasizing the benefits of sloughing off current practices may be more fruitful than utilizing scare tactics to get people to let go. You can reduce the anxiety associated with trying new things if you provide the people who are involved in the change process with a safety net. People are far more willing to experiment if they have the freedom to fail; that is part of learning.

People will be more willing to embark on a new journey if they see they will have the opportunity to make a difference. Steve Jobs had been unsuccessful in his attempts to recruit John Sculley away from his heir apparent position at Pepsi to run Apple Computer in Apple's early years. Jobs's stock offer and generous perquisites were not enough to get Sculley to change his career. Sculley tendered his resignation, however, when Jobs challenged him with the question, "Do you want to spend the rest of your life selling sugared water, or do you want a chance to change the world?"[12]

Henry David Thoreau captured the essence of Anxiety 2 when he observed, "The mass of men live lives of quiet desperation."[13] People like Bezos who embark on the entrepreneurial journey or jump at the opportunity like John Sculley to be part of a major change initiative either have low levels of Anxiety 1 or high levels of Anxiety 2. People who relish the challenges of doing something new are less likely to be constrained by Anxiety 2. These people welcome the opportunity to the do things they—and possibly no one else—have ever done before.

Organizations that are future oriented and opportunity driven will be less likely to encounter Anxiety 1. Leaders can expedite change by creating an environment where the opportunity cost of Anxiety 2 exceeds the risks associated with Anxiety 1. People will jump on the bus when they see the benefits of getting on the bus headed to a new and exciting destination far outweigh the benefits of staying at the station by continuing the status quo. The same also applies when the consequences of continuing the status quo (staying on a burning platform) outweigh the consequences (including the fear of the unknown, etc.) of the proposed change effort.

Once the unfreezing process has taken effect, step two in Lewin's three-step change process—the introduction of change—can begin. This step has multiple dimensions. New ideas can now be developed to address new challenges. Yet, executives need to be selective, recognize the importance that timing plays, and demonstrate finesse. The process for identifying and developing the change initiative incorporates decision theory and creative problem-solving techniques.

The second step often involves introducing a new perspective and priorities as well as a new way to do things. Again, there are two strategies that may be used to introduce the change. The first approach is similar to Cortes's approach. The manager simply announces that effective immediately people are to use a different approach. This rarely produces the level of commitment needed for the change to be effective.

Reality Check: If you are the type of person who prefers to tell people what to do rather than giving them the opportunity to be coarchitects in taking your firm to the next level, then at least take the time to communicate why the proposed behavior is important and how to do it well. But recognize that telling is not the same as leading. Telling only gets compliance. Leading brings out people's best.

Step two works best when the people involved in implementing the change as well as those who will ultimately be affected by it are given the opportunity to share their thoughts. The more the people who are going to be involved in implementing the change are given the opportunity to be the coarchitects of it, the greater the probability they will be committed to making it a success. The more the people to be affected by the change understand its need and benefits, the less likely they will be to resist it.

The third and final step in the process is called "refreezing." Even though the new perspectives, priorities, and behavior may appear to management to be far superior to current practices, the people who are expected to adopt the new behavior need to have the opportunity to try the new approach without the fear of being punished if they do not perform well at first. Learning involves experimentation which may result in mistakes or a drop in performance. Management needs to create an environment where people learn from their mistakes and are not punished as they learn new approaches.

Refreezing is crucial because many people will revert to the "old ways" when things get tough. People need to believe the new behavior is the right behavior. If they believe they will be better off with the old way, then they may revert back to it rather than demonstrate the new behavior. The rewards for the new behavior must be better than the rewards for continuing the status quo.

The need to create an environment that encourages and rewards change efforts is particularly important. Step three increases the likelihood that the new way of doing things becomes the way of life. One of the guiding principles of psychology is the concept of "behavioral modification." Behavioral modification stresses the need to reward desired behavior whenever it is demonstrated. Positive reinforcement does two things. First it indicates that the new behavior is valued. Second, it reduces the likelihood that people will continue the former behavior. Behaviors that are rewarded tend to be repeated. Behaviors that are no longer rewarded tend to be discontinued. Step three will also have a greater chance for success if the people involved in the change effort see they are making progress. Their efforts will be strengthened if they are rewarded, even symbolically, for their efforts.

Reality Check: Learning can be defined as replacing an old habit with a new habit. Be careful when you refreeze the new behavior. If you make a big deal out of how the new way is the best way—even the only way—to do things, when the time comes that you have to replace it with a new behavior it may be very difficult to get them to discontinue what they now feel comfortable doing. The moral to the story is to make it clear that to be an ever-evolving organization, change is written in pencil that can be erased, rather than in permanent ink.

Change Needs to be Deliberate and Systematic

Very few firms approach change in a deliberate and systematic manner. All too often change is postponed until the time is available. And when management initiates change, it is done in a haphazard, reactive manner. All too often it is done when the firm is faced with a crisis. Most firms operate in such a fire-fighting, day-to-day mode that when they are faced with a deadline for doing something, they tend to do what they have done before rather than look for ways to do it better. The following insights and tips foster more effective change efforts. They are not provided in any particular rank or order.

Insights and Tips for Fostering Transformational Change

- You need to create a sense of urgency—have people recognize they are on a burning platform.
- You have to create an environment where people recognize they need to leave their comfort zone.
- Your people should to not get too comfortable with their new approach because they will need to leave it in the near future.
- Your people need to be comfortable doing what they have not done before (and possibly no one else has either).
- Your people need to recognize that just because something has not been done before does not mean that it cannot be done.
- Your people need to recognize that just because they have not done something before does not mean they are not able to do it.
- Your people need to recognize that when you are at the innovative edge or trying to take your firm to the next level you are going from the known to the unknown. They will not have perfect information, road maps, and other forms of guidance. They will have to make informed estimates or judgment calls.
- You and your people will need to make a deliberate effort to identify the "critical unknowns" and to transform them into key insights. Foresight can give your firm a mental head start over your competitors.
- Your people need to recognize learning is like the practice of triage in an emergency room.
- Your people need to differentiate between what can and should be changed from the things that should not or cannot be changed. You may benefit from serenity prayer, "God, grant me the serenity to accept the things I cannot change, the courage to change the things I can, and the wisdom to know the difference."
- Your people need to recognize that to learn quickly they have to be able to forget or unfreeze quickly.

Lewin's "Force Field" Model Helps Foster Change

Kurt Lewin's second change model provides a useful framework for expediting the acceptance of change. His "force-field model" indicates that most situations exist in a state of dynamic equilibrium.[14] Lewin noted that equilibrium exists when the forces supporting change are

FIGURE 1.5.   Lewin's Force-Field Change Model

Driving Forces >>> Present Balance Point <<< Restraining Forces

counterbalanced by the forces restraining change. The force-field model profiled in Figure 1.5 serves as a reality check. Restraining forces will exist in almost every change effort. If they are not identified and addressed, then the change effort will be jeopardized.

The force-field model notes that change will occur when at least one of the following three conditions occurs. First, management can increase the forces supporting the change. This can be done by increasing training opportunities and by providing rewards for adopting the desired behavior. Second, management can try to reduce the restraining forces. Knocking down the barriers that hold people back will foster change. Creating an environment where people have a punishment-free opportunity to try the new behavior represents one of the best ways to reduce the risks associated with change. Third, management can try both approaches.

The two-stage "red-light green-light" approach to transformational change builds on Lewin's ideas. Certain facets of the proposed change may represent stoplights that stop change efforts in their tracks. If the goal of the change effort is to have employees go from point "A" level of performance to point "B" level of performance, then managers need to create an environment that makes the improvement in performance possible. Change efforts should begin by asking employees to identify the *red lights* that slow them down and/or impede their journey. The red lights may include poor equipment, lack of training, insufficient information, and so forth. These factors impede performance and sap motivation. If these factors exist, then employees quickly conclude that management is not committed to them and/or the change effort. Management needs to address the red light factors before initiating the change effort.

Management should then direct its attention to providing *green light* factors. Green lights enhance commitment. They give people a reason to get out of bed in the morning and improve their performance. Green lights are important because the elimination of red lights—even though it may be appreciated by the employees—rarely generates high levels of performance. If management wants high levels of commitment and high levels of performance, then it will have to provide support, empowerment, and high levels of rewards. Management also needs to make sure the rewards are relevant to the people involved, that they are large enough to make the effort worthwhile, and that they are tied directly to and proportional to the level of performance.

The two-stage red-light green-light approach provides a good explanation for why employees may not jump at the chance to be part of a change effort. If they do not join the change procession to point "B," it is because management has not eliminated the red lights and provided enough green lights to make the journey worthwhile. If employees do not jump on the bus, then management is at fault, not the employees.

Concluding Comments: Leading Change Is about Changing Oneself

Organizational transformation requires personal transformation. You must be prepared to lead by example. You must be prepared to change yourself before you attempt to influence other people. To expect others to be flexible while not being willing to make similar changes yourself is hypocrisy. You must undergo an honest self-appraisal by looking at your own behavior when you are seeking an explanation for why people do not jump on the change bus.

Chris Turner—Xerox Business Services's Learning Person—noted, "You have a choice. You can be the last of the old generation of managers, or you can be the first of a new generation."[15] Alan Webber, as editor of *Fast Company* noted, "The revolution is going to happen. It's just a matter of whether you're with it or you're behind it."[16]

As a leader, you cast a shadow in everything you do. Every action and every word either reinforces or undermines the change effort. You must be willing to apply the "rule of finger" which suggests you look at your hand when you point the finger of blame at others. If you look at your hand, you will see *three* fingers pointing back at you. You must be the stimulus that fosters the desired response from everyone involved in the change effort. If the results are not there, then it is because you did not create an environment conducive to the results.

Caveat emptor! Most books on instituting change focus on how leaders can get the other people in the company to change. This book focuses on how leaders need to change themselves first. It encourages you to not wait for someone else to save the day. It encourages you to seize the challenge right now and take the initiative to create your company's future.

This book is like a mirror and a coach. It encourages you to identify your strengths, shortcomings, and blind spots. It encourages you to say goodbye and good riddance to what you have done and how you have done it. It means you will have to leave your comfort zone—and never have a comfort zone—unless the process of initiating change and embarking on new journeys is what you consider to be your *new* comfort zone. Transformational change will occur only when the anxiety associated with doing the same things the same way is far greater than the anxiety associated with doing things you have never done before!

Take the Transformational Change Quiz in Table 1.1 to see where you and your firm stand in your ability to foster change.

TABLE 1.1.   Transformational Change Quiz

How does your firm rate on the following dimensions? *Scoring Level: 1 = not at all, 2 = rarely, 3 = occasionally, 4 = frequently, 5 = on-going/extensive	Level*
1. To what extent is your firm involved in trying to introduce game changing products and to make your competitors' products obsolete?	1-2-3-4-5
2. To what extent is your firm customer-centric?	1-2-3-4-5
3. To what extent does your firm have a deliberate set of processes for reviewing its product/service portfolio to determine current and future worthiness?	1-2-3-4-5
4. How often do you contemplate what your market (competition, customers, technology, etc.) will be like three years from now?	1-2-3-4-5
5. To what extent does your firm have contempt for the status quo? To what extent are current practices, processes, policies, and assumptions challenged?	1-2-3-4-5
6. To what extent does your firm have a culture that fosters high levels of commitment in your people?	1-2-3-4-5
7. To what extent does your firm have leaders at all levels?	1-2-3-4-5
8. To what extent does top management make a deliberate effort to identify the uniqueness of the situation—rather than approaching the decision the same way it has in the past—when making decisions?	1-2-3-4-5
9. To what extent does top management make a deliberate effort to monitor and anticipate changing conditions in its external environment?	1-2-3-4-5
10. To what extent does top management welcome the changes and opportunities the future will bring?	1-2-3-4-5
11. To what extent does top management recognize that before your firm can embark on a new path it must make a deliberate effort to discontinue current practices?	1-2-3-4-5

TABLE 1.1.   (Continued)

How does your firm rate on the following dimensions? *Scoring Level: 1 = not at all, 2 = rarely, 3 = occasionally, 4 = frequently, 5 = on-going/extensive	Level*
12. To what extent does your firm have formal processes in place to learn from its experiences and share what it has learned to improve future performance?	1-2-3-4-5
13. To what extent does top management approach change in a systematic and integrated manner rather than on a piecemeal basis?	1-2-3-4-5
14. To what extent does your firm have a crisp and compelling vision for its future for guiding decisions rather than a nebulous mission statement?	1-2-3-4-5
15. To what extent is does management try to sense who may resist a specific initiative and make a deliberate effort to learn about why they do not support the change effort?	1-2-3-4-5
16. To what extent is does management deal constructively yet firmly with people who are not committed to change efforts?	1-2-3-4-5
17. To what extent do your firm's executives recognize that in order for the firm to change, they must change and set the example for others to follow for the change?	1-2-3-4-5
18. To what extent do your firm's executives practice the "rule of finger" concept by acknowledging that when things do not go as planned that they are the ones who are responsible for the shortcomings?	1-2-3-4-5
19. To what extent are people at all levels of the firm encouraged, reviewed, and rewarded for being innovative?	1-2-3-4-5
20. To what extent does your firm have formal processes in place to continuously improve operations?	1-2-3-4-5
Total points	

Scoring Key

90–100	Congratulations, your firm demonstrates most of the qualities associated with effective organizational transformation.
80–89	Your firm has many qualities associated with organizational transformation, but it still has areas that can be improved.
70–79	Your firm has some strengths, but there is a lot of room for improvement.
60–69	Your firm has some significant impairments that impede its ability to be transformed into an exceptional enterprise.
20–59	Your firm may be beyond hope. It will take a radical change in management, corporate culture, systems, and processes to have any chance of being competitive in the future.

It is easy to find fault with a new idea. It is easier to say it can't be done, than to try. Thus, it is through the fear of failure that some men create their own hell.

—E. Jacob Taylor

Notes

Some of the material in this chapter originally appeared in the article, "Leading Organizational Change" by the author in *Industrial Management*, May–June 1998. Reprinted with the permission of the Institute of Industrial Engineers, 3577 Parkway Lane, Suite 200, Norcross, GA 30092, www.iienet.org. Copyright 2009 by Institute of Industrial Engineers.

1. Rosabeth Moss Kanter, *The Change Masters* (New York: Simon & Schuster, 1984), 64.

2. Ibid.

3. Karl Albrecht, *The Northbound Train* (New York: Amacom, 1994), 62.

4. Alan C. Kay, "Predicting the Future," *Stanford Engineering* 1, no. 1 (1989): 1.

5. "The Breakdown of U.S. Innovation," *Business Week*, no. 2419 (1976): 57.

6. Warren Bennis and Burt Nanus, *Leaders* (New York: Harper & Row, 1985), 69.

7. John P. Kotter, *Leading Change* (Boston: Harvard Business School Press, 1996), 133.

8. Kurt Lewin, "Frontiers in Group Dynamics: Concepts, Method, and Reality in Social Science," *Human Relations*, no. 1 (1947): 5–41.

9. Edgar Schein, "How Can Organizations Learn Faster? The Challenge of Entering the Green Room," *Sloan Management Review* 34, no. 2 (1993): 87.

10. Ibid.

11. Noel M. Tichy, "Bob Knowling's Change Manual," *Fast Company*, no. 8 (1997): 80.

12. John Sculley, *Odyssey* (New York: Perennial Library, 1987), 90.

13. Henry David Thoreau, *Walden* (New York: Branhall House, 1951), 22.

14. Kurt Lewin, *Field Theory in Social Science: Selected Theoretical Papers* (New York: Harper & Brothers, 1951), 259.

15. Alan Weber, "XBS Learns to Grow," *Fast Company*, no. 5 (1999): 51.

16. Ibid.

Chapter 2

The Breakthrough Leader's Role in Creating the Company's Future

There is nothing more difficult to take in hand, more perilous to conduct, or more uncertain in its success, than to take the lead in the introduction of a new order of things.

—Niccolo Machiavelli

The ability to lead change will be more important in the years ahead than at any time in the past. The accelerating rate of change coupled with the breadth of change will challenge even the most talented breakthrough leaders. While the future may be uncertain, one thing is clear: without breakthrough leaders to guide them into the future, companies will have no future.

Creating your company's future involves more than taking the road less traveled; it involves creating the road yet to be traveled. It is not about taking the company to the next rung on the ladder; it is about creating a whole new ladder to climb where there are no other climbers.

Breakthrough leaders recognize that two prerequisites must exist before executives can create their company's future. First, they must be willing to discontinue everything that impedes forward progress. Embarking on a new journey is a lot less difficult when executives are not loaded down with anchors of the past and present. Second, they must look reality straight in the eyes and not blink. Creating your company's future is about changing reality. Changing reality requires a no-holds-barred environment where people are free to challenge everything, think new thoughts, and launch game-changing initiatives.

Reality Check: Breakthrough leadership is not about creating a better tomorrow; it is about creating an entirely different tomorrow. Breakthrough leaders know that evolutionary change may be too slow. They also know that radical change may backfire if the company is not ready for it. Breakthrough leaders recognize that creating their company's future will require revolutionary evolution!

Creating your company's future will require bold thinking and bold action. Breakthrough leaders do not sit around talking about their dreams; they lead revolutions. They do not spend their time pushing data; they recognize that revolutions start with ideas. They do not expect ideas to implement themselves; they know ideas will succeed only to the extent they are executed well. They do not wait for their turn; they stick their neck out. They do not dwell on finding fault or rationalizing; they develop solutions. They do not wait for someone else in the company to take the lead; they take the initiative. They do not wait to be asked; they volunteer. They do not wait for the opportunity to knock; they find the door and kick it open. General George Patton noted, "You will never know what is going on unless you can hear the whistle of the bullets."

Breakthrough leaders do not seize *the* moment; they seize *every* moment. They do not wait until the time is right—when they have all the resources, the time, the information, the authority, the talent, and support from above. They make things happen in spite of the odds. They know leadership is not given to you. They know you have to seize the opportunity to lead.

Breakthrough leaders have the guts to approach things in a real-time manner, to commit resources, to take a stand, and to say "We can make it happen!" They have the guts to eliminate the word *someday* and to squash anything that resembles procrastination. They have the guts to start what should have already been started. They also have the guts to drop what should have been dropped years ago.

Breakthrough leaders know they must have a sense of urgency, a tolerance for turbulence, the ability to deal with ambiguity, and a bias for action. They know creating the company's future is more like exploring than navigating. They know that when they go where no one has gone before there are no maps or signs to guide them. They recognize you have to make judgment calls and that you cannot be right 100 percent of the time. They know that if you want to be at the leading edge, you do not have the luxury of spare time and complete information. They know that for the company to be more entrepreneurial you cannot succumb to paralysis by analysis. They also know that for companies to go the distance, they must avoid quick fix management fads and being seduced by short-lived opportunities.

Breakthrough leaders see reality and attempt to create a whole new reality. They have the courage to ask the questions that need to be asked, to challenge the ways things have been done, and to take the company where other companies fear to tread. They have the ability to create an environment where people can make a difference. They recognize that for the company to thrive in the years ahead, people at all levels of the company must come up the answers to tomorrow's questions today.

Breakthrough leadership means that where the company has been and where it is now may have little bearing with where it needs to go. Breakthrough leadership rarely involves incrementalism. The automatic linearity associated with continuous improvement rarely provides the ability to blow competitors out of the water. Breakthrough leadership is far more likely to occur when you operate with a clean slate. You cannot create your company's future by merely adding one more dot each year to a series of older dots. Breakthrough leadership usually involves starting a whole new vector! While the company may bring some of its core competencies along on the journey, that does not mean that the company should automatically bring its existing products, processes, and services. Breakthrough leadership involves developing new competencies, new products, and new processes to capitalize on new opportunities.

Breakthrough leadership incorporates a number of the qualities found in new ventures. Entrepreneurs start ventures because they see an emerging opportunity or a gap in the marketplace. In short, they see a reality and attempt to change it, or they see a new reality emerging and they attempt to capitalize on it. New venture success is usually contingent on the size of the gap and the extent to which the venture introduces innovative products/services/processes.

Ventures that merely offer continuous improvements may survive, but they will not thrive. Ventures that produce discontinuous change—where nothing on the market even comes close—will thrive. The entrepreneur's ability to see what *is* and what *can be* provides the basis for creating a company. The breakthrough leader's ability to see what *is* and what *can be* provides the basis for creating the company's future.

The Strategic Deployment of Self

Leading change is a way of life for breakthrough leaders. They recognize the risks associated with doing the same things the same way. Decades ago, Thomas Watson, Jr., as CEO of IBM noted, "There never has been any future in the status quo. In business, the status quo means inevitable failure."[1] While most people recognize that change is a fact of life, a number of people share "if it isn't broke, don't fix it." philosophy.

Breakthrough leaders have contempt for the status quo. They constantly look around for "gaps." They constantly ask, "Are we doing what we should be doing?" and "Should we still be doing this?" Breakthrough leaders know good enough is not good enough anymore. They also know that if you are merely trying to be competitive, you will always be eating someone else's dust. Breakthrough leaders are committed to creating an exceptional enterprise.

Change must go well beyond rhetoric; it must be internalized and operationalized. Change cannot be done on a "virtual organization" basis. It cannot be outsourced. Change takes time and hard work. Change requires commitment to go the distance. Change should not be expected to produce overnight successes. Transforming a company into an exceptional enterprise could take years. Change must be seen as a never-ending journey. Change takes commitment from everyone in the company. Change must be encouraged, enabled, reviewed, and rewarded at every level in the company.

Breakthrough leaders recognize change is not an occasional proposition. There are no short cuts, no time-outs, and no commercial breaks. They recognize that no facet of the organization is immune, nothing can go untouched, and nothing is sacred. Change is not something that is done when it is convenient. It cannot be ignored, and it cannot be postponed. Change must be substantive and continuous. It must involve bold initiatives as well as continuous fine-tuning.

The process of creating the company's future is light years away from becoming an exact science. Change is so multifaceted that it is nearly impossible to be aware of all the factors and forces at play. It is even more difficult to determine the dynamic relationships among the factors and forces. Breakthrough leadership requires perceptiveness, flexibility, and finesse. There will be times when the company will need go ahead at full speed and times when it may be wiser to pull back on the throttle and reassess the appropriateness of company's course of action. There will be times when the breakthrough leader will need to be out front leading the charge, and there will be times when working behind the scenes will be more effective in making the right things happen.

Breakthrough leaders need to use their talents in a strategic manner. They need to deploy their talents with the same skill as they deploy their company's resources. Leaders need to allocate their time and attention in such a manner that they get the greatest return per unit of time, just as they allocate the company's capital to get the highest return per dollar invested.

Breakthrough leaders recognize two important points about how they spend their time. First, it is impossible to lead every change effort. There are not enough hours in the day for them to be involved in every facet of change. Second, it will not be in the company's best interest to be directly involved in every change effort. Breakthrough leadership involves creating an environment where people at all levels of the company are playing a leading role in the change process. Breakthrough leaders should champion the company's *overall* change rather than be *the* champion for individual change efforts.

Breakthrough leaders recognize the need to be selective in their involvement. If they are too removed from change efforts, then the troops may wonder whether anybody at the top really cares about the challenges and risks they are facing. If they are ever-present, then they will have lost the opportunity to appear at just the right time to break down a barrier or to give the troops a psychological boost. Being ever-present may also indicate a lack of faith in the employees' judgment and ability to make things happen.

Self-awareness plays an integral role in the strategic deployment of the leader's time and talents. Every person has shortcomings. Leaders who are aware of their shortcomings should surround themselves with people who have talents they lack. They should also surround themselves with people who will tell them like it is when the situation calls for objectivity and candor. Leaders need to recognize that as situations change, so must their talents. Paul Wieland, former President of Independence Bancorp and founder of The Center for Advanced Emotional intelligence, noted that at some point your strengths become liabilities. According to Wieland, "Most of us have become successful by developing a set of strengths and working around our weaknesses, but inevitably we push these strengths too far, and they become weaknesses."[2]

Breakthrough leaders recognize that every word they speak and every action they take can send ripple effects throughout the company.

A leader's comments are never off-the-record. At no time is the leader offstage. Times of change are times when even the slightest action or lack of action can make a major difference in whether a change effort moves forward or stalls.

Every person in the company casts a shadow. Breakthrough leaders make every effort to cast the type of shadow that fosters positive change. They recognize that to lead, you must lead by example. They know that asking or expecting others to do what they are not willing or able to do themselves is hypocrisy. They will have to take risks before they can expect anyone else to take risks. They know they will need to understand the dynamics of technological change before they can expect others to embrace new technology. When you lead by example you gain the respect of those around you. When you expect others take a journey you are not willing to take, then you are sowing the seeds of distrust, contempt, and resistance.

Guidelines for Breakthrough Leaders

New challenges call for new approaches to leading change. The following qualities characterize breakthrough leaders. It is unlikely that any person will demonstrate high levels of all the qualities. The key for people who aspire to be breakthrough leaders is to incorporate these qualities into their personal repertoire. These qualities should help you lead your company through the minefield of new realities.

Guidelines for Breakthrough Leaders

- Breakthrough Leaders craft a compelling vision of a better tomorrow.
- Breakthrough Leaders avoid the "boiled frog" syndrome.
- Breakthrough Leaders demonstrate courage and resilience.
- Breakthrough Leaders demonstrate "impatient patience."
- Breakthrough Leaders are decisive; they do not fail the "match test."
- Breakthrough Leaders provide the spark that ignites commitment.
- Breakthrough Leaders create early victories.
- Breakthrough Leaders need to beware of covert resistance and yes people.
- Breakthrough Leaders get the right people on the bus.
- Breakthrough Leaders establish relevance.
- Breakthrough Leaders demonstrate integrity and build trust.
- Breakthrough Leaders get others involved.
- Breakthrough Leaders build coalitions.

- Breakthrough Leaders develop leaders.
- Breakthrough Leaders ask the right questions.
- Breakthrough Leaders are learners.
- Breakthrough Leaders create a learning organization.
- Breakthrough Leaders prevent the "paradox of success."
- Breakthrough Leaders recognize the need for the firm to compete against itself.

Breakthrough Leaders Craft a Compelling Vision of a Better Tomorrow

Crafting the company's vision may be the most important role breakthrough leaders can play in creating their company's future. Breakthrough leadership involves developing a shared and compelling vision for what can be, what should be, and what must be. The ability to develop such a vision is contingent on having the ability to envision and embrace what the future may hold.

Breakthrough leadership will only be possible if the company has a clearly articulated vision. The vision serves three purposes. First, it serves as the company's North Star. All decisions, plans, and activities should be directed to fulfilling the company's vision. Second, the vision must be compelling. It should give each person in the company a reason to jump out of bed each morning. Third, the vision can serve as the glue which holds all of the company's components together.

Breakthrough leaders use the process of crafting the company's vision to explore possible futures for the company. Steven Rebello noted, "Truly successful people have the ability to see new paths and the power to persuade others to follow. . . . Vision is the ability to fill in the blanks, to see beyond the blind spots and to move forward while the others are still standing around rubbing their eyes. . . . Visionaries make their mark by breaking rules, taking risks, forging connections. And they alter the landscape with innovations we were hardly aware we couldn't live without. Visionaries share the capacity to see what others can't (or won't) and the courage to bring their vision to life."[3]

Breakthrough leaders recognize that the visioning process is not for dreamers. They know that creating the company's future calls for a combination of imagination and realism. Their job is to explore the possibilities and then create the company's future realities. Breakthrough leaders recognize that revolutions begin with ideas. They also know that imagination is the source of great ideas.

Breakthrough Leaders Avoid the "Boiled Frog" Syndrome

There is a story that if you put a frog in a frying pan and slowly turn up the heat, the frog will boil to death rather than jump out. If you drop a frog into boiling water, however, it will jump out immediately. Breakthrough leaders can reduce the likelihood the company will fall prey to the boiled frog syndrome if the people sense a significant "gap" between where they are and where they need to be. When people see the gap or feel they are on a burning platform, they will get out of their comfort zone and change what they are doing.

Edgar Shein noted that managers must make disconforming data highly visible to all members of the organization, and the data must be convincing. Just saying that the organization is in trouble because profit levels are down, market share is being lost, customers are complaining, costs are too high or good people are leaving is not good enough. He observed, "Employees often simply do not understand or do not believe it when management says, 'We are in trouble.' "[4]

John Kotter, author of *A Sense of Urgency*, considers creating a *sense of urgency* to be the first step in leading change. He noted, "Sometimes executives underestimate how hard it can be to drive people out of their comfort zones. . . . When the urgency rate is not pumped up enough, the transformation process cannot succeed and the long-term future of the business is put in jeopardy. . . . The urgency rate is high enough when 75 percent of a company's management is honestly convinced that business as usual is totally unacceptable. Anything less can produce very serious problems later in the change process."[5] Over 50 percent of the companies Kotter studied failed to create the sense of urgency needed to enact change.[6] Kotter, in his book, *A Sense of Urgency* differentiates constructive *true urgency* and destructive *false urgency*. True urgency creates a commitment to moving ahead and winning. False urgency is evident in stress-filled, frantic efforts that consume energy and time, but do not move the firm ahead.[7]

While breakthrough leaders may see the need for the company to change what it is doing, executives should recognize that it may take an extra effort to jump start other people's perceptions of the need to discontinue what they are doing. Ignorance, arrogance, and complacency abound in many organizations. Companies on the brink of disaster frequently operate from a state of denial.

If the company is not facing a crisis, then management may need to *create* a sense of urgency. Jan Timmer, as CEO of Phillips Electronics, may get the prize for attempting to get his people's attention. He handed out a hypothetical press release stating that Phillips was bankrupt to the company's top one hundred executives at a retreat.[8] When managers look for reasons why the company got itself in such a bind via the loss of accounts, missed deadlines, and the like, they should remember the immortal words of Pogo, "We have met the enemy and he is us!"

Breakthrough Leaders Demonstrate Courage and Resilience

The process for crafting and implementing the company's vision also calls for guts and resilience. If the company wants to be at the leading edge, then creating the company's future will call for bold initiatives rather than fine-tuning the present. The bolder the vision, the greater the risks and the need to let go of what the company is doing. Breakthrough leadership involves having the courage to go boldly where no company has gone. It also takes the courage to deal with the challenges that will come from those who have a vested interest in maintaining the present or some other course of action that meets their needs.

Breakthrough leaders recognize that taking the company in a new direction or trying to achieve even higher levels of performance involves risks. They know that you cannot steal second base if you keep one foot on first base. They also realize that performance and morale may drop at the beginning of the journey. It takes time for people to learn. When people try new things, they also make mistakes. Change takes people out of their comfort zones. People may feel incompetent when they try to do things they have not done before. Breakthrough leaders build the learning period into the change plan and let people know in advance that mistakes are part of the learning process. While they may not encourage mistakes, they do expect them to occur.

Breakthrough leaders also recognize they need to be the keepers of the faith. They must have the courage to protect the company's basic values when others are tempted to compromise the integrity of the company. There will be moments of truth when management can either demonstrate its commitment to doing what the company says it values or take the easy way out. In those instances, leaders step forward and do the right thing without hesitation.

Breakthrough leaders create an environment where people at all levels know what the company values. They recognize that a strong set of values can provide far better guidance than a one-thousand page company policy manual. Nordstrom demonstrated its commitment to doing the right thing when it developed its "rules" for decision making, "Rule #1: Use good judgment in all situations. There will be no additional rules."[9]

Breakthrough Leaders Demonstrate "Impatient Patience"

Most people consider the concept of impatient patience to be an oxymoron. Breakthrough leaders know the difference between forcing the issue and giving it time to germinate. Carlo Brumat noted, "Leaders need to transmit a sense of urgency, a feeling life is short and that there's a lot to be accomplished. But if a leader is unreasonable—if he or she expects results overnight—the effect on morale can be devastating. The best leaders balance a sense of urgency with persistence."[10]

Being decisive has its merits, but if the people who have to play a role in the change effort do not recognize the need for change, then decisiveness will have little effect. The purpose of decision-making is not to make decisions. The purpose of decision-making is to make decisions that will be implemented. Without implementation, the change effort dies on the vine.

Breakthrough leaders recognize that decisions are rarely embraced when they are forced down people's throats with a "Just do it" tone. Decisions that require input and the support of others may need some time to germinate. People who develop ideas should not expect their ideas to be embraced immediately by others in the company. They should also recognize that when others ask questions about the idea it does not necessarily mean they are opposed to the idea. Questioning should be encouraged so they have the opportunity to "see the light" for themselves.

Mark Maletz, a principal with McKinsey & Company, provides the following observations to effecting real change:

> First, realize that you probably did not stumble over your brilliant insight or ingenious project idea in one glorious moment. Undoubtedly, you arrived at your idea over time. It was a process. Second, when others (including your boss) don't understand your ideas immediately, don't label them as ignorant bureaucrats—a force to be reckoned with. That attitude will back others against a wall and make it difficult for you to get your point across. Instead, recognize that others may have to go through a similar journey of understanding that you traveled to "get there." Third, self-discovery is much more powerful than any preaching from on high—or from below. Help others discover what you're

proposing, and you'll find that you won't have to waste time maneuvering or dodging.[11]

Breakthrough Leaders Are Decisive: They Do Not Fail the "Match Test"

Breakthrough leaders recognize change calls for decisiveness. The words *someday* and *maybe* have no place in the process of creating the company's future. Breakthrough leaders create a sense of urgency so people will resist the temptation to procrastinate or to fall prey to paralysis by analysis. They create a situation where people do not sit on their hands waiting for additional information that may not be available or worth the additional time.

Decisiveness appears to increase with experience. People who have been on the firing line in various situations are more willing to make decisions. Breakthrough leaders are also more willing to trust their intuitive skills when data is limited. The accelerating rate of change and the consequences of being a day late place a premium on having leaders who do not freeze up when they are confronted with a major decision.

Too many people in today's companies would fail the "match test." The match test forces people who have been reluctant to take the risks associated with making a decision to make a decision with minimal delay. When they are presented with a decision, they must hold a lighted match in their hand. They have to make a decision while holding a lit match. They learn that you either decide or get burned.

Breakthrough Leaders Provide the Spark That Ignites Commitment

In a perfect world, every person in the company would embrace the company's vision and be self-motivated to make it a reality. Breakthrough leaders recognize that people rarely have blind faith in the company's leaders. They also recognize that people will be committed to the company's vision and creating the company's future only to the extent that the journey will contribute to their own future. Breakthrough leaders make every effort to show how fulfillment of the vision will enhance each person's well-being.

Breakthrough leaders create an environment where people who are motivated to fulfill the vision will be empowered and rewarded for their efforts. They create an environment where people who are moderately motivated see the merit in contributing at a higher level. They also create an environment where people who are dragging their feet get with the program or get out. If leaders are in tune with what turns each person on, then they may be able to create an environment where good people are transformed into fanatics. The level of fanaticism is evident in whether people jump out of bed on Monday morning with greater zeal than they look forward to quitting time on Friday afternoon.

Breakthrough Leaders Create Early Victories

Breakthrough leaders recognize that they do not have carte blanche, nor do they have an unlimited amount of time to introduce the change. Executives need to identify those actions that optimize importance and urgency. If they get wrapped up in initiating change efforts that will take years before they provide any return, people may throw in the towel before embarking on the journey. Conversely, if they spend all their time on urgent but relatively insignificant efforts, people may not believe tomorrow will be better than today.

While people may be receptive to new ways to do things and new things to do, finesse should be demonstrated when introducing change. Each change effort needs to represent an essential part of an overall game plan for transforming the company. Management needs to make sure the change effort is not seen as another "flavor of the month." Bob Knowling noted, "If you come in and announce, 'Here's the next change program,' you're dead. You just painted a target on your chest."[12]

People need to see that the new way of doing things produces results. Executives need to identify opportunities for "early victories" when they develop their change efforts. While management may have total faith in the change effort's eventual success, the sooner the rest of the people see they are making progress the better.

The untapped potential for ideas is particularly evident at the lowest levels of the company. The average Japanese worker submits over a hundred ideas each year. Toyota has averaged over two million ideas per year from its workers ... and implemented nearly 80 percent of them.[13] American workers rarely submit more than a handful of ideas each year. John Gardner noted, "There is usually no shortage of new ideas; the problem is to get a hearing for them."[14] He also observed, "The still untapped source of human vitality, the unmined lode of talent, is in those people already recruited and thereafter neglected."[15]

Veteran breakthrough leaders know the importance of being able to pick "low-hanging fruit." Low-hanging fruit represent events or milestones that are easy to accomplish and produce beneficial results in a short period of time.[16] They are tangible indicators of progress. Low-hanging fruit have three benefits. First, as people see the merit in their efforts, they begin to believe the new way is the better way. Second, low-hanging fruit also keep the naysayers at bay who have been skeptical about the change. Third, capturing low-hanging fruit provides the impetus to reach for higher-hanging fruit. The higher-hanging fruit may include tackling major challenges or seeking breakthrough innovation. Chapter six differentiates jewels and low-hanging fruit. Jewels also require a low-level commitment of time and resources, but they have a higher yield. Early victories can be accomplished with a combination of these two efforts.

The pursuit of early victories should not to be confused with the pursuit of quick fixes. Quick fixes are superficial efforts that tend to give the false impression the battle has been won. Early victories represent situations where there is tangible evidence the company is making progress in its transformation. They also help maintain the momentum and energy needed to win the war.

Breakthrough Leaders Need to Beware of Covert Resistance and Yes People

Breakthrough leaders recognize that change efforts may be resisted in many ways. Some resistance may be direct. Some resistance may occur in a more covert manner. Change creates a state of disequilibrium. It takes people out of their comfort zones. It also alters people's positions of power and influence.

Mark Maletz offers four observations about resistance. First, "If change has not been very successful in the past, then you need to prepare for the inevitable opposition." Second, "Beware of people who say they are supportive of the change effort, but who are not. They will either fail to support/sign off on it or sabotage it." Third, "Change agents should not automatically resist resistance—they should learn from it." Fourth, "From the very first day, make the change process transparent. If you are going to make the process transparent, you've got to be willing to admit when you're wrong, or when someone else has a better idea."[17]

Breakthrough leaders create an environment where people who initially have reservations about the proposed change are free to voice their concerns and to challenge the assumptions that were part of the decision process. Breakthrough leaders are also prepared to provide information to support the course of action. The best way to reduce resistance is to give people, especially those who may be skeptical about the need for change, the opportunity to: (1) participate in analyzing the company's current situation, (2) craft the vision, and (3) develop the change effort to make the vision a reality. When it comes time to implement the decision, breakthrough leaders do what is necessary to gain overt commitment from everyone involved in the change effort. They know the company will not be able to break away from the pack if people just go along to get along or just go through the motions.

Breakthrough leaders make it clear that there is a time to discuss, a time to decide, and a time to act. They make it clear that if you are not willing to be committed to the change effort, then you should find an employer that shares your perceptions of the future and what it will take to get there. Jim Collins, coauthor of *Built to Last* provides one view of how to deal with resistance. He stated, "How do you get people to share your values? You don't. You find people who share them and eject those who don't."[18] Wayne Calloway as CEO of Pepsi indicated there may be times when drastic action needs to be taken to deal with people who may jeopardize the change effort. He stated, "Occasionally, it's very important to have a public hanging."[19]

Breakthrough leaders recognize the best way to reduce ongoing resistance to change is to show that it is producing results. The sooner the change effort shows it is making tangible progress toward its goal, the sooner the resistance will be reduced. Particular attention should be directed to breaking the change effort into periodic milestones. Meeting the milestone targets can be seen as mini-victories for the change effort. A change effort's momentum and early victories can help bulldoze lingering resistance.

Breakthrough Leaders Get the Right People on the Bus

Breakthrough leaders recognize the points made by Jim Collins in his book, *Good to Great*, when he stressed the need to have the right people involved in the change effort. Collins noted: (1) that you need to have the right people on the bus—if you have the right people you will not need to motivate them, (2) that they need to be in the right seats—in the positions that will use their talents, and (3) that you need to get the wrong people off the bus. He also noted that if you have the right people, they will determine where the firm should go and how it should get there.[20]

Breakthrough Leaders Establish Relevance

Management's effort to create a sense of urgency will not gain a high level of commitment unless they also establish a sense of relevancy for all involved. Paul Strebel noted, "Managers must put themselves in their employees' shoes to understand how change looks from that perspective and to examine the terms of the personal compact between the employees and the company."[21] Gerry McQuaid found the ability to create a sense of relevance was critical to gaining a high level of commitment from employees. When he was Site Manager for Corning's optic fiber plant, he recognized management's earlier efforts to gain a high level of commitment to quality were unsuccessful. Management had emphasized the need to increase Corning's profitability, stock price, and dividends. Workers did not jump on the quality bus because they did not consider themselves to be directly in Corning's financial loop.

The workers jumped on the quality bus only when McQuaid created an environment where they realized foreign competition was trying to put each of them in the unemployment line. They embraced quality not because it would improve Corning's financials: they embraced the quality initiative when they realized it was essential for *their* financial security.

Breakthrough Leaders Demonstrate Integrity and Build Trust

People are far more willing to embark on a journey if they have faith in their leader's judgment and trust that person to act in their best interests. Trust does not come with one's position. Trust, like respect, arises from an ongoing relationship. Trust is more likely to occur when people are involved in the change process from the earliest possible stage. They are more likely to support and implement ideas and plans they helped develop than ideas and plans that are dropped on them from above.

Breakthrough leaders recognize that listening and asking may be more effective than telling people what to do. Kotter noted, "The key is not having all the answers . . . but asking probing questions. If you come in and announce what should be done, then they are less likely to trust you. If you ask for their views, then they tend to believe you value their views. This is important for building trust."[22]

Breakthrough Leaders Get Others Involved

People at the top of the company often believe they can initiate change by edict. They may get *reluctant* compliance, but they will rarely get the level of commitment needed to leapfrog the competition. Change works best when it is a collaborative effort by people who are allied to one another.

The ability to form an alliance is particularly valuable if the person who wants to initiate the change is not at the top of the company. Resistance may come from all sides rather than just from below. This is why it is so important to establish a network of relationships based on trust and respect throughout the company. Barbara Reinhold noted, "You have to understand the metabolism rate—the tolerance for change—of your boss or of your organization might be dramatically different from your own. Then look around. Find other people who are willing to take the change journey with you. Never go it alone. Undoubtedly others in your company feel as you do. Your task is to find them."[23]

Warren Bennis noted, "If you're a leader, you've got to give up your omniscient and omnipotent fantasies—that you know and must do everything. Learn to abandon your ego to the talents of others."[24] Bill Breen and Cheryl Dahle noted, "Change starts with finding a backer—someone who can sell your plan to the senior team. Change dies without a fighter—someone smart enough and skilled enough to win over the opposition."[25]

Breakthrough Leaders Build Coalitions

Change efforts need to be broad-based rather than the effort of just one or two individuals. While the effort may initially be led by a handful of people, for it to gain momentum, more people need to be brought in to drive the change effort. Breakthrough leaders bring people together and help them develop a shared strategy for moving the company forward into the future.

Change efforts are more likely to succeed when they are coalitions of individuals and/or groups that have common interests. Coalitions are particularly beneficial in two areas. First, they provide a broader base of ideas. This reduces the likelihood the change effort will be based on a myopic perspective. Second, coalitions also provide a broader base of support for the change. John Kotter noted that a lone executive can be an easy target for those who want to derail a change effort. A change effort that represents a broad-based coalition is much harder to derail.[26]

Breakthrough leaders recognize the political side of organizations. While a few companies may offer the freedom to challenge the status quo, breakthrough leaders need to recognize their vulnerability. Bob Knowling stresses the need for change agents to be savvy to organizational politics and organizational turf. He noted, "As a change agent you have to pick which battle you really mean to fight, and never sacrifice the war over a little skirmish . . . a dead change agent doesn't do anybody any good."[27]

Breakthrough leaders need to remember that new ideas usually replace existing ideas. The person who came up with the idea for the way things are currently being done probably will not welcome any effort that will modify, reduce, or discontinue her idea. When you suggest a new way of doing things you are in a sense *firing* the current idea. You are declaring the way things are currently being done to be obsolete. You may see the *constructive* side to constructive criticism, but the originator of the current strategy will see the *criticism* part of constructive criticism. The originator of the current strategy will be less likely to be a resistor if given the opportunity to be a coarchitect of the change effort.

Breakthrough Leaders Develop Leaders

Breakthrough leadership involves more than just getting people to follow or even be allies. Leaders do much more than develop followers; they develop leaders. They know the company cannot rely on one or two leaders to create the company's future. A company will need leaders at all levels if it is to excel in the marketplace.

Creating the company's future involves a deliberate and continuous effort to create the company's future leaders. Breakthrough leaders create an environment where people are given the opportunity to lead themselves. As people gain experience and confidence, they are given the opportunity to lead others. Every manager's performance review should identify whether the manager is developing people to their potential and developing leadership skills within the group. A Midwestern manufacturer was so serious about the need for leaders to develop other leaders that it established the policy, "Any manager who does not have a ready replacement will be terminated!"

Companies that are committed to developing leaders at all levels do not leave the process to chance. They commit considerable time and resources to the development of leaders. Stratford Sherman indicated, "Perhaps the simplest, hardest, and most telling measure of any company's leadership development program is the allocation of the CEO's time."[28] Senior executives—particularly the CEO—must be prepared to commit at least one-third of their time to developing leaders throughout the organization either through direct involvement or through leadership development seminars.

There is an interesting story about how one CEO approached developing leaders. According to the story, a young engineer was summoned to the CEO's office one day. When the CEO asked the engineer why he thought he was summoned, the young engineer replied, "I was in charge of a $10,000,000 project that failed. I am here to be fired." The CEO responded, "Fired, no way! We are going to keep you around to see what you learned." The CEO noted that the company needed people who can manage $100,000,000 initiatives and that he considered the $10,000,000 to be an "investment" in the engineer.

Breakthrough Leaders Ask the Right Questions

Breakthrough leaders recognize that you can only come up with the right answers if you ask the right questions. The next chapter on anticipatory management profiles how making inquiries can lead to insights which may serve as the basis for launching key initiatives. By challenging assumptions and pondering what the future may hold, people are encouraged to do reality checks and mentally break away from the present.

Assumption analysis, benchmarking and the analysis of best practices can also stimulate recognition that something can be done better or something better should be done. John Grant and Devi Gnyawali believe assumption analysis provides the opportunity to raise some interesting questions about the likelihood that the present is prologue to the future. Assumption analysis also helps executives determine which drivers of current performance are apt to remain predictable in the near future and which may be jolted by foreign competition, technological advances, and regulatory changes.[29]

Breakthrough Leaders Create a Learning Organization

Competitive advantages used to be based on the extent to which a company had more capital than its competitors. Today, knowledge and ideas may be a company's greatest competitive advantages. Success is now contingent on being able to out-think and out-innovate rather than out-spend one's competitors. To do different things, however, you need to think different thoughts. To think different thoughts, you need to see things differently. That is what learning is all about.

Being the market leader does not come from maintaining the status quo nor does it come from imitating other companies. Market leadership will not go to incrementalists. Market leadership will go to companies that: (1) are able to generate breakthrough ideas, (2) have the courage to boldly go where no company has gone before, and (3) have the managerial acumen to operationalize the ideas so they become a reality.

Market leadership comes from busting through the ceiling of commonality. Competitive advantages reflect an organization's ability to do certain things better than other companies. Competitive advantages are the result of experimentation, of learning what works and what does not work. It comes when people find new things to do and new ways to do things.

Companies that want to be at the leading edge will need to learn from their various stakeholders. Stakeholders need to be asked, and asked often, what they want and what they expect from the company. Customers, employees, suppliers and distributors' ideas need to be solicited, and they must be given the opportunity to be coarchitects in the company's change efforts.

Revolutions begin with insights and ideas. To get revolutionary ideas, you need a revolution in thought patterns, not just knowledge.[30] Ideas are the product of one's thought patterns (mental models) and one's perceptions of how the world works (paradigms). One's mental models and paradigms should not be inhibited by conventional thinking and a myopic perspective.

Reality Check: Organizations, like individuals, can have learning disabilities and blind spots. Managers and management teams may have selective perception that keeps them from processing information that is inconsistent with their present managerial mindsets. When this happens, they will either fail to see the new realities or they may not be able to modify their current behavioral repertoire to meet new challenges.

Continuous learning is essential for your company to be an ever-evolving enterprise. Learning in its most fundamental form is about asking, listening, reflecting, challenging, experimenting, unlearning, and discontinuing. Learning provides the insights that serve as the cornerstone for the strategies, products, services, and processes that will enhance the company's competitiveness, performance, and vitality.

Learning occurs best in environments where there is contempt for the status quo, where the past and present are not revered, and where there are no sacred cows. Leading change means creating an environment where everyone is free to challenge every assumption and every practice. It also means creating an environment where there are no dumb questions and no dumb ideas. In such an environment, making mistakes is considered part of the learning process. Mistakes are acceptable as long as people learn from them and do not make the same mistake twice. It also means that complaints from internal and external stakeholders are considered to be learning opportunities rather than an assault on the company. They should be solicited, welcomed, and rewarded.

Leading change is as much an attitude as it is an overall process. Learning organizations do not refer to negative situations as "problems." They consider problem situations to be "challenges" that need to be addressed. People tend to avoid problem situations because they have a negative air about them. People tend to be far more motivated when they are faced with the challenge and opportunity to make things better.

Running scenarios can provide interesting insights into what the future may hold. When people realize that certain changes are possible and, in some cases, inevitable, then they are far more likely to commit themselves to dealing with the new realities. The same is true with best practices and benchmarking. The analysis of companies in and outside one's industry may be an eye-opening experience for people at all levels of the company. Benchmarking analysis and the study of best practices may be particularly beneficial for people who have adopted the state of Missouri "show me" attitude.

Benchmarking helps remove mental blinders that keep people from seeing what is possible. It also represents a way for managers to deal constructively with people who say, "There's no way we can do that!" When people claim it is not possible to reduce the packaging error rate to less than 1 percent, they see things differently when they learn L. L. Bean ships well over 100,000 packages a day at Christmastime with an error rate of less than one-tenth of one percent.

Breakthrough Leaders Are Learners

Breakthrough leaders recognize they too have to be willing to learn, to experiment, *and* to make mistakes. They also recognize that how they handle their mistakes as well as the mistakes of others can have a dramatic effect on people's willingness to experiment. Carlo Brumat noted, "No one knows what the future will bring, how a market will respond, whether a new technology will work. Yet so often, whenever a desired outcome fails to materialize, leaders look for scapegoats. That reaction freezes people's mindsets and destroys imagination. In the sciences, researchers don't look upon a failed experiment as a mistake to be blamed on somebody. Instead, they see it as an opportunity to change their view of how things work. Business leaders need to adopt the same attitude."[31]

Breakthrough Leaders Prevent the "Paradox of Success"

Executives should exercise caution when they refreeze the new behavior and celebrate success in making progress. Leading change is a never-ending process. While Frederick Taylor and his movement toward scientific management may have stressed the need to find the "best way," it is clear that there may not be *one* best way and what may appear to be the best today may be obsolete tomorrow.

The moment you believe you have found the best way, you are dead. Executives need to recognize that today's change, which may appear to be the best way, is tomorrow's status quo. What is refrozen today in step three in Kurt Lewin's three-step change process—profiled in chapter one—may need to be unfrozen tomorrow. Today's great ideas may be obsolete in the near future.

While it is important to have quick victories, celebrations should be put in perspective. John Gardner noted, "Self-congratulation should be taken in small doses. It is habit forming, and most organizations are far gone in addiction."[32]

John Kotter noted premature victory celebrations kill momentum. He stressed the need for continued movement forward. Kotter believes that without momentum, the powerful forces associated with tradition take over. After the celebration is over, the resistors may point to the victory as a sign the war has been won and the troops should be sent home.[33]

Executives need to stress that all change is subject to change and that no one should get too comfortable with the way things are done.

Rosabeth Moss Kanter observed, "Organizations with a formula that works well are doomed to replicate it, handing over their operations to people who control things so that there are no deviations from the formula."[34] Noel Tichy and Stratford Sherman noted in their book, *Control Your Destiny or Someone Else Will*, "In an environment of unceasing change, few business ideas remain useful for long; after a while, even successful concepts must be abandoned."[35]

Breakthrough Leaders Recognize the Need for the Firm to Compete Against Itself

Market leadership comes from competing against oneself rather than one's competitors. When companies focus their energy on what competitors are doing, they take their eyes off their customers. They get caught up in market share and competitive response. A "competitor-orientation" leads to the tendency to react to other companies, rather than to focus on what the market values and where the market is headed.

When you compete against yourself in your ability to delight your customers, there is never an end to learning, experimenting, and evolving. When you compete against other companies, there is a tendency to celebrate when you are out in front. This elicits corporate arrogance. Arrogance quickly degenerates into complacency. Rapidly changing markets and escalating customer expectations show little mercy or patience for companies that are complacent and out of sync.

Chunka Mui, coauthor of *Unleashing the Killer App: Digital Strategies for Market Dominance*, noted the need for companies to commit themselves to creative destruction. She observed, "Cannibalize your markets, treat your assets as liabilities, ensure continuity for the customer, not yourself. Smart companies are preemptively destroying their own value chains. Recognizing that change is coming that will (render) obsolete their infrastructure, force them into a commodity role, or remove them from the process altogether, many are choosing to hasten the end of the old model."[36]

Concluding Comments: Keep Moving Forward

The ever-accelerating, never-ending nature of change resembles a relentless set of waves crashing into the shore. Breakthrough leadership is a relentless process. It involves meeting the challenges of change head on and by ensuring your company is an ever-evolving enterprise.

Your company must avoid being caught in the paradox of success. Your company cannot afford to celebrate its successes for more than a moment. You need to be directing your attention to tomorrow and tomorrow's tomorrow. Roger Enrico, as CEO of Pepsi noted, "As soon as everyone is on the bandwagon with one growth idea, a leader should be working on the next one."[37] Creating your company's future is a never-ending process. You can never let up. The moment you ease up is the moment when the world starts to pass your company by. Take The Breakthrough Leader's Role in Creating the Company's Future Quiz in Table 2.1 to learn the extent you and your firm are positioned to foster significant change.

All problems become smaller when you don't dodge them but confront them. Touch a thistle timidly and it pricks you; grasp it boldly, and its spines crumble.

—Admiral William S. Halsey

TABLE 2.1. The Breakthrough Leader's Role in Creating the Company's Future Quiz

How does your firm rate on the following dimensions? *Scoring Level: 1 = not at all, 2 = rarely, 3 = occasionally, 4 = frequently, 5 = ongoing/extensive	Level*
1. To what extent is your firm willing to take the road less travelled or to even create its own roads rather than traveling down established roads?	1-2-3-4-5
2. To what extent do people at all levels in your firm have the "We can make it happen" attitude?	1-2-3-4-5
3. To what extent is your firm committed to creating breakthroughs and changing the competitive landscape rather than focusing on linear and incremental change?	1-2-3-4-5
4. To what extent is your firm committed to evolving on a continuous—almost relentless—basis rather than an on-and-off reactive and occasional change basis?	1-2-3-4-5
5. To what extent do the leaders in your firm understand and exhibit the concept of the strategic deployment of self? Do they recognize the situations when they should selectively get involved and exhibit the qualities they seek in others?	1-2-3-4-5
6. To what extent does your firm have a vision that is a "call to arms" and fosters a level of commitment that excites its people to do extraordinary things?	1-2-3-4-5

(continued)

TABLE 2.1. (Continued)

How does your firm rate on the following dimensions? *Scoring Level: 1 = not at all, 2 = rarely, 3 = occasionally, 4 = frequently, 5 = ongoing/extensive	Level*
7. To what extent do the leaders in your firm have the courage to do what needs to be done and the resilience to hang in there when it would be easier to go with the flow and do what other firms are doing?	1-2-3-4-5
8. To what extent does management ask probing questions and encourage others to challenge conventional wisdom, current practices, and the validity of key management assumptions?	1-2-3-4-5
9. To what extent does top management create a sense of urgency so people "want to get on the bus" and make things happen *now* rather than falling prey to paralysis by analysis?	1-2-3-4-5
10. To what extent does top management create early victories to generate commitment for substantive initiatives and to silence naysayers?	1-2-3-4-5
11. To what extent do your firm's leaders demonstrate their commitment to learn what needs to be learned to enhance the firm's competiveness?	1-2-3-4-5
12. To what extent do your firm's leaders create an environment that fosters learning new ways to do things and new things to do at all levels?	1-2-3-4-5
13. To what extent does your firm compete against itself so that it does not fall prey to the paradox of success and become complacent?	1-2-3-4-5
14. To what extent does management consider establishing coalitions and/or alliances with other organizations to create synergies that will give the firm an edge?	1-2-3-4-5
Total points	

Scoring Key

62–70	Congratulations, your firm's leaders demonstrate most of the qualities of breakthrough leadership.
54–61	Your firm has many of the qualities of breakthrough leadership.
46–53	Your firm has some strengths, but there is a lot of room for improvement.
38–45	Your firm's leaders have significant impairments that impede the firm's ability to make the changes it needs to make if it wants to excel.
14–37	Your firm may be beyond hope. It will take a radical change in management, corporate culture, systems, and processes to have any chance of being competitive in the future.

Notes

Some of the material in this chapter originally appeared in the article, "Leading Organizational Change" by the author in *Industrial Management*, May-June 1998. Reprinted with the permission of the Institute of Industrial Engineers, 3577 Parkway Lane, Suite 200, Norcross, GA 30092, www.iienet.org. Copyright 2009 by Institute of Industrial Engineers.

1. Thomas J. Watson, Jr., *A Business and Its Beliefs* (New York: McGraw Hill, 1963), 79.

2. Pamela Kruger, "A Leader's Journey," *Fast Company*, no. 25 (1999): 124.

3. Stephen Rebello, "Visionaries," *Success* 45, no. 2 (1998): 39.

4. Edgar Schein, "How Can Organizations Learn Faster? The Challenge of Entering the Green Room," *Sloan Management Review* 34, no. 2 (1993): 87.

5. John Kotter, "Leading Change: Why Transformation Efforts Fail," *Harvard Business Review* 73, no. 2 (1995): 60, 62.

6. Ibid., 60.

7. John P. Kotter, *A Sense of Urgency* (Boston: Harvard Business Press, 2008), 5–9.

8. Paul Strebel, "Why Do Employees Resist Change?" *Harvard Business Review* 74, no. 3 (1996): 89.

9. Nordstrom orientation packet.

10. Eric Randsell, "School for Leaders," *Fast Company*, no. 23 (1999): 50.

11. Anna Mudio, "Boss Management," *Fast Company*, no. 23 (1999): 102.

12. Noel Tichy, "Bob Knowling's Change Manual," *Fast Company*, no. 8 (1997): 80.

13. Daniel Gross, "Power of Suggestion," *Attaché* October (2000): 16.

14. John Gardner, *No Easy Victories* (New York: Harper Colophon, 1968), 41.

15. Ibid., 40.

16. Robert Slater, *The GE Way Fieldbook* (New York: McGraw-Hill, 1999), 61.

17. Anna Mudio, "Mint Condition: His People Are As Good As Gold," *Fast Company*, no. 30 (1999): 396.

18. Stratford Sherman, "How Tomorrow's Best Leaders Are Learning Their Stuff," *Fortune* 132, no. 11 (1995): 92.

19. Ibid., 93.

20. Jim Collins, *Built to Last* (New York: Harper Business, 2001), 41.

21. Ibid., 87.

22. Thomas A. Stewart, "Why Leadership Matters," *Fortune* 137, no. 4 (1998): 82.

23. Mudio, "Boss Management," 94.

24. Ibid., 92.

25. Bill Breen and Cheryl Dahle, "Field Guide for Change," *Fast Company*, no. 30 (1999): 384.

26. Kotter, *Leading Change: Why Transformation Efforts Fail*, 62.

27. Tichy, ibid., 82.

28. Noel Tichy and Christopher DeRose, "Roger Enrico's Master Class," *Fortune*, 132, no. 11 (1995): 102.

29. John Grant and Devi Gnyawali, "Strategic Process Improvement Through Organizational Learning," *Strategy and Leadership Journal* 23, no. 3 (1995): 30.

30. Arian Ward, "Lessons Learned on the Knowledge Highways and Byways," *Strategy and Leadership Journal* 23, no. 3 (1996): 19.

31. Randsell, ibid., 50.

32. John W. Gardner, *No Easy Victories* (New York: Harper Colophon Books, 1968), 42.

33. Kotter, *Leading Change: Why Transformation Efforts Fail*, 66.

34. Rosabeth Moss Kanter, *The Change Masters* (New York: Simon & Schuster, 1983), 70.

35. Noel M. Tichy and Stratford Sherman, *Control Your Destiny or Someone Else Will* (New York: Harper Business, 1994), 37.

36. Leigh Buchanan, "Killer Apps," *Inc.* 20, no. 6 (1998): 94.

37. Noel Tichy and Christopher DeRose, 106.

Chapter 3

Anticipatory Management: Carpé Futurum!

These days, unless you devote an enormous amount of time to anticipating the future, you won't have any future.

—Ron Chernow, American biographer

"If only I had known, then I could have done something about it" is being heard with increasing frequency in firms of all sizes and in all industries. Managers at all levels are exclaiming, "How could this have happened?" and "How could we have seen this coming?" These questions reflect the shattering stress and disorientation that occurs when people are subjected to too much change in too short a time. Alvin Toffler profiled this phenomenon in his book *Future Shock*. He noted that future shock is a process in which the future *invades* the present and catches people unprepared for new realities.

Toffler noted that "future shock" is similar to the culture shock people experience when they travel to a markedly different country. People who are unprepared for the new realities fail to get the most from the experience. They are also more likely to behave inappropriately. If the culture shock is extreme, then the traveler may freeze up or return to the comfort zone of his/her home land. When future shock occurs, however, there is no option to return to the past.

Executives need to be more than planners, they need to be deeply involved in *thinking* about what the future may hold and what the company can do to create its future. This chapter emphasizes the need for executives to adopt the principles of anticipatory management.

Anticipatory management encourages executives to extend their mental time horizons and to scan the horizon for emerging opportunities and potential threats. It also stresses the need to run scenarios so the firm will have a head start over its competitors and not be blindsided by new realities. Anticipatory management enables firms to launch strategic initiatives that will give them the ability to seize the future.

Reality Check: Coping will not cut it. While technological breakthroughs have created new opportunities and changed the way we live and work, quite a few organizations are like deer frozen in the headlights of an oncoming truck. Too many managers merely try to "cope" with the relentless waves of change. In a world of ever-accelerating change, coping will not be enough.

This chapter is not about coping. It is about contemplating what may be over the horizon or around the bend. It is about sensing and seizing opportunities to give your firm significant competitive advantages. It is about anticipating and preventing problems—or at least minimizing their impact by positioning your firm to handle the challenges—rather than being overrun by change. The message here goes beyond the Latin "carpé diem" or "seize the day." To succeed in today's environment, managers and firms must seize the future: Carpé futurum!

Top Management Is Asleep at the "Future" Wheel

Although executives may say they think about the future, the evidence indicates otherwise. Gary Hamel and C. K. Prahalad noted in their book, *Competing for the Future*, that on the average, senior management is devoting less than 2.4 percent of its time to building a collective view of their firm as a whole for what markets the firm should serve, what technologies it should master, which customers to tailor its products and services to, and how to get the most from its employees.[1] This "corporate perspective on the future" is the result of a deliberate and time consuming process of asking tough questions and challenging key assumptions.

Hamel and Prahalad's "2.4 percent" observation raises the question, "If the top executives of some of the top companies are not focusing on their company's future, then who is?" Their research provides good news as well as bad news. The bad news is that most top executives are managing more than leading. Without a strategic perspective, executives are destined to live a perpetual "fire-fighting" existence. The good news is that any company with executives at the helm who commit serious time to preparing for the future will have a significant advantage.

> Reality Check: Someone once said that because the world is changing so much on so many dimensions that firms should direct their attention to reacting to change rather than planning. Managers should direct some of their time to responding to changes, but the advice to not plan for the future is foolhardy.

Planning is more crucial today for at least two reasons. First, it helps you avoid what is called "tyranny of the urgent." Too many managers focus just on what is needed right now. Second, developing plans that indicate expected milestones and results as well as your assumptions puts you in a better position to know when things are not going as planned and to make timely changes.

Leadership involves identifying and dealing proactively with current and future realities. It involves making decisions today that make for a better tomorrow. It involves more than just adding another dot to a linear series of dots. It involves differentiating the issues that have extended long-term significance from urgent issues that have limited long-term significance. It involves taking the mental journey from the known into the unknown. It also involves having the courage to discontinue what the firm has done so it can do what it has not done.

Some Thoughts about Sensing and Seizing the Future

Change is the law of life. And those who look only to the past or present are certain to miss the future.

—John F. Kennedy

At every crossway on the road that leads to the future each progressive spirit is opposed by a thousand men appointed to guard the past.

—Maurice Maeterlinck, Nobel Laureate

For knowing afar the evils that are brewing they are easily cured. But, when for want of such knowledge, they are allowed to grow until everyone can recognize them, there is no longer any remedy to be found."

—Machiavelli, *The Prince*

Anticipating the future belongs to those who see possibilities before they become obvious.

—Theodore Levitt,
former Editor of the *Harvard Business Review*

A danger foreseen is half avoided.

—Thomas Fuller, M.D.

Having a "Legacy" Mindset: Out of Touch, Out of Sync, and Then Out of Business

Our mindsets affect how we see the world, how we process information, the decisions we make, and how we behave. Too many firms have legacy mindsets. These mindsets may have worked well in the past, but they prevent firms from seeing and accepting new possibilities. The terms being "Delled," "Amazoned," or "Southwested" apply to many firms. Dell changed the way computers were made, marketed, and distributed. Amazon challenged the very foundation of bricks and mortar retail businesses. Southwest Airlines offered air fares that no one in the industry thought were sustainable. These and other firms like Netflix, Skype, and NetJets changed the way business is conducted by changing the game itself rather than just tweaking the existing rules. Meanwhile, established firms either ignored them or ridiculed them as entrepreneurial follies. As we now know, their legacy mindsets were the equivalent of saying, "The world is flat."

Companies that are out of touch or rely on outdated mental models are not able to align their strategies with new realities. History provides numerous examples of people and companies that were blindsided by new realities or that underestimated the speed at which the future would invade the present. Here are a few noteworthy examples from *The Experts Speak* by Christopher Cerf and Victor Navasky, and *Bad Predictions* by Laura Lee.

Man will not fly for 50 years.[2]

—Wilbur Wright to his brother Orville in 1901.
Two years later their plane flew.

A severe depression like that of 1920–21 is outside the range of probability.[3]

—The Harvard Economic Society,
November 16, 1929

I think there is a world market for maybe five computers.[4]

—Thomas Watson, Chairman of IBM in 1958

With over fifty foreign cars already on sale here, the Japanese auto industry isn't likely to carve out a big slice of the U.S. market for itself.[5]

—Business Week, August 2, 1968

640K ought to be enough for anybody.[6]

—Bill Gates, speaking of computer memory requirements in 1995

I predict the Internet . . . will soon go spectacularly supernova and in 1996 catastrophically collapse.[7]

—Bob Metcalfe, coinventor of the Ethernet and founder of 3Comm in 1995

Each statement reflects how even people who should have a grasp for the future can be totally off base. Samsung encourages its people to ponder what the future could bring. Samsung was so concerned about being blindsided about possible events that it put a picture of a jet exploding into the side of the World Trade Center in New York over the urinals in one of its facilities to encourage its people to think the unthinkable.[8] The 9-11 Commission's report concluded that the Bush administration and its associated intelligence agencies lacked the imagination to consider the hijacking of commercial airliners to use them as flying bombs to be a threat. The investigation also revealed that the towers were built to have a reasonable chance of withstanding the collision of an airliner. Unfortunately, the scenarios did not include the consequences when the fuel created an inferno.

Anticipatory Management Incorporates "Futuring"

Karl Albrecht, author of *The Northbound Train*, cautions against the tendency for companies to get too wrapped up in the planning process. He notes that many organizations are so engrossed in planning that it impairs their ability to respond to changes, threats, and opportunities. Albrecht states that in some instances developing a plan is "such an exhausting process that thereafter nobody wants to change it, even if some major environmental event occurs."[9] He recommends that executives do "futuring" rather than traditional, comprehensive long-range "planning."

Whether it is referred to as long-range or strategic planning, one thing is clear: most people approach it in a too mechanistic and deterministic manner. If the marketplace was stable and the future fairly predictable, then the development of detailed long-range plans might be relatively simple. The marketplace, however, is anything but stable. The accelerating rate of change, technological breakthroughs, new competitors, and the emergence of all new markets have produced discontinuities.

Reality Check: Most planning efforts are doomed before they even begin. They are too rigid and too incremental. Conventional planning techniques that were developed in a linear and incremental world do not have the flexibility needed to address multifaceted and rapid-paced change. Conventional planning techniques also fail to incorporate entrepreneurial forces that often change what it takes for businesses to succeed.

While plans still need to be developed, targets identified, and deadlines set, the overall planning process needs to become more flexible. When planning incorporates future possibilities and the impact of innovation, it resembles "futuring" more than planning.

Futuring Is Not Forecasting Nor Is It Incremental

Futuring is different from long-range planning in at least three distinct areas. First, it recognizes that the future will not be an extension of the past. Futuring expects events to occur that cause "discontinuities." Second, there may be numerous possible futures. The future will be a function of various factors as well as various possible relationships among those factors. Third, innovation will play an even greater role in the future. Innovation has the potential to accelerate the rate of change. It also can cause fundamental shifts in the nature of business and life.

Reality Check: Traditional forecasting techniques have drawbacks because they tend to be extrapolations from the past. Unexpected events, however, cause discontinuation from the past and present. A forecast is like a mental model that does not change with changing times. Executives are frequently blindsided because forecasts miss early indicators of discontinuities. These discontinuities can be the result of environmental factors like the truly unusual weather patterns caused by El Niño, the emergence of all new markets or industries caused by a technological breakthrough, or the shock waves that have been taking place in the near collapse of the U.S. economy.

Few companies foresaw the exponential growth of the Internet. Most retailers believed it would be retail "business as usual" where established companies would be competing against each other for market share. Few companies foresaw how quickly wireless communication would be developed or the breadth of impact it would have on our lives. Few companies foresaw the near collapse of U.S. financial institutions, the auto industry, the housing market, and so forth.

Discontinuities destroy linearity and predictability. Discontinuities cause turbulence for those who expect stability. Yet discontinuities are what creating the company's future is all about. Creation is defined as the act of bringing something new into the world. Creation involves starting a new vector rather than adding another dot to a linear series of dots. Creation involves exploring, experimenting, and testing the limits. Creation involves doing what others say cannot be done that way, for that little cost, that well, that fast, or at all. Creating the firm's future involves creating discontinuities that give the company a competitive edge or make competition irrelevant.

Success: The Confluence of Preparation and Opportunity

The Roman philosopher Seneca defined luck as "what happens when preparation meets opportunity." While luck may contribute to a firm's success, anticipatory management does not rely on luck. Instead, it relies on perceptiveness and resourcefulness. It relies on systematically scanning the horizon for trends and events that could help or hurt the firm. It relies on running scenarios that identify possibilities and probabilities. It relies on having the ability to change what the firm is doing so it has a head start over its competitors. It helps firms create game-changing products, services, and processes.

The introduction of this book noted that executives can be divided into three groups. The first group is comprised of *reactive* managers who spend all their time solving problems. Their perpetual fire-fighting existence is not only extremely tiring, but it also keeps them from preparing for the future and finding ways to improve what they are doing. When executives operate from a reactive stance, they have less time to think things through or to explore the possibilities. When time is of the essence, most executives tend to approach situations as they did in the past or by trial and error. This can be costly for two reasons. First, what worked well yesterday may be totally inappropriate tomorrow. It takes time to develop innovative approaches. Second, even when the trial and error process associated with "winging it" produces an occasional success, it places considerable stress on the company's human resources.

The second group is comprised of *preventive* managers who spend less time and resources solving problems because they have taken measures to avert problems. It is amazing how many problems can be prevented with a little foresight and resourcefulness. Preventive managers outperform reactive managers, but their focus is on preventing problems rather than sensing and seizing opportunities.

The third group is comprised of *anticipatory* managers. Anticipatory managers take a *mental journey* to the future to create their company's future. They elevate themselves above problem solving and even problem prevention to the point where they can direct their attention and the company's resources to creating, cultivating, and capitalizing on emerging opportunities. They also direct their attention to improving existing products and processes. While they may not have heard Peter Drucker say that within every problem is at least one disguised opportunity, they recognize that their firm's success is tied to its ability to sense and seize the future.

Anticipatory management is captured in Wayne Gretzky's approach to playing hockey. The story goes that when Gretzky was asked how he had scored so many goals, he responded that most people play the puck *where it is*. He stated that he anticipated *where the puck would be* and skated to that point. While he may not have earned an MBA, Gretzky's approach illustrates how being the first-mover can be advantageous when a window of opportunity is about to open.

Anticipatory Management Opens the Company to Unlimited Opportunities

Executives should direct their attention to exploring future possibilities and identifying the position the company should occupy in the years ahead. Instead of trying to develop detailed formal plans, executives need to adopt the proactive philosophy of "anticipate, if not create change." Proactivity is based on two premises. First, your job is to influence the world around you as much as possible. Second, if you are to be subject to change, then be the initiator of the change.

> Reality Check: There is an interesting irony associated with managing in today's marketplace. The question has been raised, "Does there have to be a crisis for a leader to emerge?" Executives who are particularly good at preventing problems, via foresight and resourcefulness, do not get a lot of fanfare. By preventing fires rather than fighting fires, they do not make the news. By preventing fires, they do not need to be involved in high profile actions or speeches. Their foresight and resourcefulness put their company on a path that allows them to evolve without radical reorganizations, crash programs, or a desperate search for a charismatic leader.

In times of rapid change, it is easy for companies, especially growing companies, to "drive beyond their headlights." The ever-accelerating rate of change puts companies in a situation where they may not be able to see what is in front of them until it is too late to do anything constructive about it. Anticipatory management encourages executives to do three things. First, executives need to consider various possibilities for what may be ahead of them. By asking, "What if . . . " questions, executives may be able to identify potential threats in time to either prevent them or minimize their consequences. Second, executives are encouraged to extend their "mental headlights." By extending their time horizons, executives will not only see things earlier, they will have the lead time needed to deal with them in a constructive and evolutionary manner. Anticipatory management reduces the need for the company to swerve or hit the brakes. Third, it encourages executives to broaden their radar to have a 360 degree sweep. This will reduce the likelihood they will be surprised or blindsided by factors and forces that are not in their line of sight.

Anticipatory Management Begins with Asking the Right Questions

Anticipatory management recognizes that the process of asking questions and coming up with answers has a vital role in fostering organizational success. A key difference among reactive, preventive, and anticipatory managers is how they approach this process. Reactive managers spend most of their time trying to come up with answers to today's questions. Unfortunately, they may not be asking the right questions. Preventive managers have a better grasp of today's questions and spend most of their time developing and implementing better answers. In contrast, anticipatory managers ask the questions that need to be answered and then develop the answers *before* others (particularly their customers and competitors) even know the questions. They recognize that sensing opportunities is not enough; they also need to be prepared to seize them.

Anticipatory managers recognize that you will only come up with the right answers if you ask the right questions. If you ask the right questions early enough and often enough and you give people considerable latitude to be innovative, then they will usually deliver game-changing answers. A sample of questions anticipatory managers ask is given in Table 3.1.

TABLE 3.1.   Questions Anticipatory Managers Ask

1.	What business should we be in?
2.	What will it take to make our vision a reality?
3.	What competencies, resources, assets, skills, processes, technology, facilities, etc. will it take for our business to succeed in the next five years?
4.	How can we preempt our current and potential competitors' actions?
5.	How can we anticipate our current and future customers' needs?
6.	Do our assumptions about the future reflect emerging realities?
7.	Are our predictions and assumptions based on objective analysis or just intuition?
8.	How often do we need to update our predictions?
9.	Are we monitoring the right trends and events? What events—especially discontinuities—could change everything?
10.	Are we looking at the right indicators for what the future may hold?
11.	Do we have an effective early warning system (similar to radar, sonar, CT scan, seismographs, listening posts) in place to detect variances from expectations early?
12.	Do we have contingency plans in place to address mission-critical opportunities and threats?
13.	What can we do that will change the way the game is played so that we make our competition irrelevant?
14.	What can we do to create barriers to entry for other firms that are considering entering our markets?
15.	What can we do to create barriers to exit for our current customers?

One of the qualities of truly effective executives is their courage to ask the first question. While they may spend some of their time focusing on whether the firm is operating efficiently, they continuously ask whether the firm is doing what it should be doing in the first place. Stated another way, they frequently ask, "Are we in the right forest?"

Anticipatory Management Uses the Three "I's" of Strategic Learning

Strategic learning will help you create your company's future. Strategic learning incorporates the "Three I's" of strategic learning that are depicted in Figure 3.1. It encourages managers to do strategic "inquiries" that lead to strategic "insights" that serve as the basis for launching strategic "initiatives."

Strategic learning encourages managers to extend their mental time horizons. Two things happen when you extend your time horizon. First, you approach change and innovation with a more open mind. In the short term you cannot change much, so you have to do the best with what you have. In the medium term, you can make moderate changes in your products, services, and processes. In the long term, however, almost everything can be changed; almost anything is possible. You can consider developing all new products, entering all new markets, and even creating new industries.

Second, with an extended time horizon your perceptions of probabilities change. Things that you thought were impossible may be considered possible. Things that you thought were unlikely may be viewed as inevitable. These insights can be like an epiphany. They alter the way you see the world to the point that they are like a call to action to change what you are doing. However, strategic learning is far from automatic. Table 3.2 lists eleven important concepts that will help you turn inquiries into insights and insights into initiatives.

FIGURE 3.1.   The Three "I's" of Strategic Learning

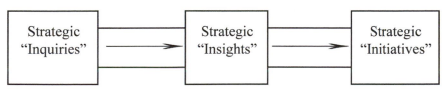

TABLE 3.2.   What Anticipatory Managers Know

1.	Bad news tends to get covered up. Bad news needs to travel to decision-makers more quickly than good news.
2.	If you want to hear the bad news, then you cannot shoot the messenger.
3.	There are no "dumb" questions.
4.	"Conventional wisdom" may be an oxymoron.
5.	It is not just what you know that matters. It is how soon you know it, what you plan to do about it, and how quickly you deal with it that matters.
6.	When time is of the essence, "solve the solution" rather than focusing on the cause.
7.	Learning flows from a candid analysis of disparities between predictions and outcomes.
8.	Denial and rationalization need to be addressed head on.
9.	Openness and brutal honesty are essential. People need to be free to say, "The emperor has no clothes!"
10.	Cross-functional teams are more likely to develop insights and innovative approaches than an individual working alone.
11.	A specific person or group must be designated and held responsible for scanning the horizon and reporting to decision makers what the future may hold.

Strategic learning ties directly to Gary Hamel and C. K. Prahalad's concept of industry foresight. Strategic insights into what the future may hold may serve as the basis for gaining industry foresight. When you have an idea for what might be, you can begin contemplating the corresponding set of factors and forces that will accompany the corresponding changes. Hamel and Prahalad observed that there is more to industry foresight than just gaining one or two insights. They noted, "Industry foresight is based on deep insights into trends in technology, demographics, regulations, and lifestyles, which can be harnessed to rewrite industry rules and create new competitive space."[10]

Scenarios Play an Integral Role in Anticipatory Management

It is easy to contemplate obvious events. The development of scenarios is a much more in-depth activity that fosters serious discussions about what the future may hold. Time should be made available for people to explore numerous possibilities, their corresponding probabilities, and resulting consequences because there are an unlimited number of possible futures. The saying, "Hope for the best, but prepare for the worst" captures the value of running scenarios.

Most forecasts tend to be linear extrapolations of the present. Scenarios should not just focus on trends; they should also consider discontinuities. Discontinuities are events that are not part of a trend but can change the world. A breakthrough innovation can make everything in the market obsolete. A new government regulation can stop a company in its tracks. A fire in a major supplier's facility can bring an assembly line to a standstill. The loss of a key staff member can leave a company without the knowledge to secure or complete a project.

Reality Check: Scenarios should not, however, be restricted to events that could jeopardize the company. Factors, forces, and events that can have a beneficial effect on the company should also be identified.

Scenarios can foster a "kaleidoscopic perspective" of multiple possible futures. They encourage managers to ask, "What's missing in this picture?" and also to ask, "What should not be in the picture?" In a world of innovation, creative destruction, and cannibalization, the products, services, processes, skills, and facilities that seem commonplace today may be obsolete tomorrow. In addition, what is unheard of today may be the norm in the not-too-distant future. Table 3.3 lists twelve tips for anticipatory managers to more effectively develop scenarios for their organizations.

You need to recognize that even though you would like to be able to call a time-out periodically to plan and analyze things and to improve what you are doing, your competitors and customers are not standing still. You need to adopt anticipatory management so you can be in sync with various future realities and not just in sync with today's realities. This is why it is important for your firm to do a "future" SWOT analysis with your "current" SWOT analysis. Current SWOT analysis focuses on current strengths, weaknesses, opportunities and threats. Future SWOT analysis projects strengths, weaknesses, opportunities and threats two to five years into the future. Future SWOT analysis looks for future competitors, competitive advantages you may be able to develop, where you may be vulnerable, opportunities that may be emerging in other markets and industries, and threats that may arise from competitors and market forces that do not appear on your radar screen.

TABLE 3.3.   What Anticipatory Managers Do

1.	Look for things others do not look for.
2.	Expect the unexpected.
3.	See things before others see them.
4.	Look at critical situations from various vantage points and perspectives.
5.	Contemplate what are the things that if changed would change almost everything.
6.	Develop the ability to change quickly when others do not see the need to change.
7.	Think thoughts others do not think.
8.	Have a keen sense of current and future organizational realities.
9.	Have the courage to do what they and possibly no one has done before.
10.	Think long-term backward rather than short-term forward.
11.	Explore and exploit new business opportunities.
12.	Try to make possible what others consider impossible.

Warren Bennis and Burt Nanus in their book, *Leaders,* offer a particularly useful technique for using scenarios to foster strategic inquiries, insights, and initiatives. Their Quick Environmental Scanning Technique (QUEST) is based on the logic used in brainstorming.[11] With QUEST, managers and staff specialists and/or a select group of industry experts identify various possible situations ranging from changes in government regulations, to major technological breakthroughs, dramatic shifts in consumer demand, a return to double-digit inflation, the loss of a key raw material, and so forth. Once the list of key factors, events, and/or trends is generated, then scenarios can be constructed to reflect a string or cluster of events that could unfold over a period of time. Bennis and Nanus profile how an airline ran scenarios to gain insights into what the future may hold. The factors included: a surge in airline terrorism, a merger between two major airlines, and a declaration that a major type of aircraft is unsafe.[12] It is ironic that the scenarios were run decades ago; since then, almost every possible situation—as well as some that were not projected—has happened.

QUEST's major strength lies in the development of a "cross-impact matrix." The cross impact matrix provides a vehicle for looking at the interrelatedness of possible events and situations. This technique encourages executives to look at each possible event or situation from various angles and in the context of other events and situations. Executives usually gain new insights when they try to place a probability on the likelihood of occurrence for each possible event and attempt to determine the interrelatedness of the events. When the matrix is completed, it indicates situations which could have a favorable impact as well as those which could have a detrimental or even devastating effect on the company.

Contingency Plans Can Provide for Quick and Constructive Responses

Scenarios can provide a reality check or "wake-up call" for firms. The sooner a firm realizes or accepts that something is inevitable or more likely than expected, the sooner it can prepare itself to deal constructively with it. Anticipatory managers do not put off to tomorrow what should be addressed today. They recognize that "never" may indeed happen and that "someday" could be tomorrow.

Anticipatory management will not provide executives with a crystal clear picture of the future. It should, however, provide insights into possible futures. By asking perceptive "What if?" questions and running "If, then . . ." scenarios, executives may be able to develop strategies that will position their companies to capitalize on emerging opportunities. The process of asking questions and running scenarios may also provide insights into factors and forces that could derail their companies.

The insights uncovered by vigilant firms can be extremely valuable. Only with foresight of new realities can innovative approaches be developed to deal with them. Insights into a range of possible futures also give management the incentive to create alternative plans to address various possible situations. By posing "What if?" questions, managers can consider preparing "If, then" contingency plans.

Executives also need to realize they cannot build fail-safe systems. The lack of certainty about what tomorrow will bring makes the development of contingency plans a necessity. For every area of opportunity or vulnerability, executives should develop at least one contingency plan. By developing contingency plans in advance, the company may be able to respond quickly when it becomes apparent that the company's original plan will not produce the desired results.

All strategies, tactics, and budgets are based on assumptions about what the economy, customers, competition, technology, and so forth will do as the company's plan is being implemented. As situations unfold, executives need to monitor performance and conditions to determine if the plans need to be modified or replaced by another plan. The appropriateness of the contingency plan and how quickly it is implemented will determine whether the company will be able to maintain its forward progress.

No company has the luxury of having the time needed to develop contingency plans for every possible threat or vulnerability. Contingency plans should be developed, however, when: (1) the probability of error is high, (2) the consequences of error are too high, or (3) when both conditions exist.

Concluding Comments: Carpé Futurum!

Foresight and commitment go hand in hand. If you want to create your company's future, you must be committed to looking to the horizon, to championing breakthrough innovation, and to positioning your firm to sense and seize opportunities as well as minimizing and/or preventing threats. You must also make a commitment to not be seduced into jumping on the bandwagon of short-term opportunities or succumbing to quick fixes.

You may not be able to predict the future, but you do have the ability to gain insights into future possibilities. Anticipatory management will not enable you to foresee every possible event. There will still be surprises, Murphy's Law will still show itself, and the best laid plans are still destined to have some flaws. Nevertheless, efforts to sense trends, clues, and cues for what the future may hold will give your company an edge over companies that focus on the present.

Your company will be more likely to thrive in the years ahead if you: (1) have the foresight to start the company's journeys early, (2) build buffers into plans, (3) monitor ongoing performance, (4) sense exceptional deviations early, (5) have contingency plans ready to implement at the first sign of variance, and (6) have resources in reserve to make the changes possible.

The future is out there. The only question is, "What role will you play in creating your firm's future?" Will you seize it or let external forces determine your firm's destiny? Maya Angelou noted, "The horizon leans forward, offering you space to place new steps of change."[13] Anticipatory management involves changing the possibilities and changing the probabilities. It is about making great things happen and keeping bad things from happening.

Anticipatory management enables you to create your firm's future—carpé futurum! Take the Anticipatory Management Quiz to get a better sense of where you are now and what steps you need to take to more fully embrace anticipatory management. Take the anticipatory management quiz in Table 3.4 to learn the extent you and your firm are positioned to sense and seize the future.

To every man there comes in his lifetime that special moment when he is figuratively tapped on the shoulder and offered that chance to do a very special thing, unique to him and fitted to his talent; what a tragedy if that moment finds him unprepared or unqualified for what could have been his finest hour.

—Winston Churchill

TABLE 3.4.   Anticipatory Management Quiz

How does your firm rate on the following dimensions? *Scoring Level: 1 = not at all, 2 = rarely/barely, 3 = occasionally/ somewhat, 4 = frequently/sufficient, 5 = ongoing/extensive	Level*
1. To what extent does your firm have a specific and challenging vision for its future that fosters a high level of energy and commitment in people at all levels to be engaged and stretch to their potential?	1-2-3-4-5
2. To what extent is your firm searching for emerging opportunities in and outside its current markets?	1-2-3-4-5
3. To what extent is your firm spending time looking at the horizon for emerging opportunities?	1-2-3-4-5
4. To what extent is your firm spending time looking at the horizon for potential threats?	1-2-3-4-5
5. How frequently does your firm do a systematic analysis of who your competitors will be in the next three years and contemplate what their competitive advantages will be in their effort to take your customers?	1-2-3-4-5
6. How often does your firm probe what your current customers will want in three years? To what extent are you probing to identify their unarticulated needs as well as their unmet needs?	1-2-3-4-5
7. To what extent does your firm encourage constructive criticism, for people to challenge the way things are being done, and question the assumptions that are the basis for plans and decisions?	1-2-3-4-5
8. To what extent does your firm try to identify who your customers should be in three years—especially those who are not your current customers?	1-2-3-4-5
9. To what extent does your firm have an early-warning system for monitoring changes in its external environment?	1-2-3-4-5

(continued)

TABLE 3.4. (Continued)

How does your firm rate on the following dimensions? *Scoring Level: 1 = not at all, 2 = rarely/barely, 3 = occasionally/ somewhat, 4 = frequently/sufficient, 5 = ongoing/extensive	Level*
10. To what extent does your firm have a real-time system in place for informing management of variances or deviations from the assumptions that were the basis for forecasts and resulting plans?	1-2-3-4-5
11. How often does your firm monitor key metrics to identify even the smallest change or trend?	1-2-3-4-5
12. To what extent does your firm monitor changes in technology that can have a significant impact on how it does business and its ability to compete?	1-2-3-4-5
13. How often does your firm truly consider the consequences of losing its top two customers?	1-2-3-4-5
14. How often does your firm truly consider the consequences of losing one or more of your best people?	1-2-3-4-5
15. To what extent does the firm have a succession plan for key leadership positions in place so the talent will be there to meet future challenges?	1-2-3-4-5
16. To what extent do your firm's leaders invest time and money in developing the firm's human resources for future challenges?	1-2-3-4-5
17. Have you truly considered what would happen if your information system was corrupted or destroyed? 1= no 3 = somewhat, 5 = seriously.	1-2-3-4-5
18. To what extent does your firm have formal processes in place to identify and correct deviations—including contingency plans—from planned performance?	1-2-3-4-5
Total points	

Scoring Key

80–90	Congratulations, your firm demonstrates most of the qualities of anticipatory management.
70–79	Your firm has many qualities of anticipatory management, but still has areas that can be improved.
60–69	Your firm has some of the qualities of anticipatory management, but there is a lot of room for improvement.
50–59	Your firm has some significant shortcomings that will impede its ability to stay in sync with the ever-changing marketplace.
18–49	Your firm is very reactive and may be beyond hope. It will take a radical change in management, systems, and processes to have any chance of being competitive in the future.

Notes

Some of the material in this chapter originally appeared in the article, "Carpé Futurum" by the author in *Industrial Engineer*, August, 2008. Reprinted with the permission of the Institute of Industrial Engineers, 3577 Parkway Lane, Suite 200, Norcross, GA 30092, www.iienet.org. Copyright 2009 by Institute of Industrial Engineers.

Some of the material in this chapter originally appeared in *Business Horizons*. Reprinted with permission from *Business Horizons*, vol. 43, issue 1, by Stephen C. Harper, "Timing-The Bedrock of Anticipatory Management," 75–83, (Copyright 2000), with permission from Elsevier.

1. Gary Hamel and C. K. Prahalad, *Competing for the Future* (Boston: Harvard Business Press, 1994), 4.

2. Christopher Cerf and Victor S. Navasky, *The Experts Speak* (New York: Villard Press, 1998), 237.

3. Ibid., 52.

4. Ibid., 208.

5. Ibid., 231.

6. Laura Lee, *Bad Predictions* (Rochester: Elsewhere Press, 2000), 108.

7. Ibid.

8. Peter Lewis, "A Perpetual Crisis Machine," *Fortune* September 19, 2005: 62.

9. Karl Albrecht, *The Northbound Train* (New York: Amacom, 1994), 62.

10. Gary Hamel and C. K. Prahalad, "Competing for the Future," *Harvard Business Review* 74, no. 4 (1994): 128.

11. Warren Bennis and Burt Nanus, *Leaders* (New York: Harper & Row, 1985), 166.

12. Ibid., 172.

13. Maya Angelou, "Inaugural Poem," January 20, 1993, Washington, D.C. at the inauguration for President Clinton.

Chapter 4

Guidelines for Visioning and Positioning Your Company

Executives with a clear vision invent excellent futures for their companies; those who lack it set their companies adrift in dangerous waters.[1]

—Craig Hickman and Michael Silva

It has been said that companies that fail to prepare for the future will have no future. In a sense, companies can be categorized as:

Those that live in the past and reminisce about the good old days.
Those that live in the present and make the most of the present.
Those that prepare for the future and position themselves for different times.
Those that create their future by changing the possibilities, probabilities, payoffs, and states of nature.

The last type of company has a vision for what it wants to be and develops the corresponding strategy, culture, and systems to make the vision a reality.

The classic question, "where do we go from here?" challenges even the best executives. There was a time when companies could "do more of the same." Companies that continue a linear-incremental strategy today need to recognize they have chosen a "self-destruct" strategy.

This book has stressed the need for your firm to be an ever-evolving enterprise, yet the question needs to be raised, "What should the enterprise evolve into?" Being an ever-evolving enterprise should not be seen as an end or as a goal in itself. To be ever-evolving is the *means*; the goal is to become an exceptional enterprise.

Lewis Carroll's classic book, *Alice's Adventures in Wonderland* captures the dilemma faced by many executives today. When Alice asks the

Cheshire Cat which path to take, the cat asks where she wants to go. When Alice indicates she does not really know where, the cat states, "Then it doesn't matter which way you go."[2] Over the years, the Cheshire Cat's response has been transformed into the popular saying, "When you don't know where you're going, any road will take you there—nowhere!"

One of the primary roles of a leader is to position the firm so its future is better than the present. Executives and managers at all levels of the enterprise must be able to answer the questions, "What is the firm striving to become?" and "How does it plan to get there?" If management is not able to answer these question, then it has failed its employees and investors.

This chapter focuses on two areas. It focuses on crafting a compelling vision so everyone in the firm knows what the firm is striving to become. It also focuses on positioning the firm so it can fulfill the vision.

Bifocal Management: Vision and Execution

Organizational success is contingent on the extent to which executives demonstrate bifocal management. Executives need to craft a shared and compelling vision. They also need to make sure systems are in place to ensure that little or nothing falls through the cracks on a daily basis. Some executives relish the opportunity to think on a strategic level. They look forward to running scenarios and contemplating possible competitive strategies. Other executives enjoy developing detailed action plans and monitoring ongoing performance.

Few executives have the ability to blend both proficiencies. A fixation on operational matters without a sense for the big picture is like a mechanic tuning the engine of a car that will never leave the garage. Leaders of ever-evolving enterprises combine a strategic orientation with a precise operational focus. Executives who want to create their company's future need to be like champion archers. They need to identify the bull's-eye of distant targets and have the ability to focus their company's efforts to hit the bull's-eye.

It is easy for executives to get caught up in immediate issues. People who do not meet short-term expectations may not be kept on the payroll to do the things that enhance long-term performance. Yet thinking only about the short term may keep people from developing innovative products and game-changing strategies that may take a few years to produce significant results.

Executives need to be able to blend short term and long term. By doing so, they will then have a framework for approaching middle-term issues. Middle-term issues become the "fill in the blanks" efforts that link short-term and long-term endeavors. The following section profiles how the five-stage strategic management process can extend your time horizon as well as open your mind to new possibilities, identify new initiatives, and operationalize them into ongoing actions.

Fundamentals of Strategic Management

Strategic management encourages executives to adopt a "long-term backward" perspective. This approach is quite different from the short-term forward incremental approach used by most firms. When visionary executives are asked the question, "How do you climb a mountain?" They respond, "From the top down." They know that by mentally envisioning what it would be like to stand on the summit, they can see the best path for climbing the mountain. If they were to climb the mountain from where they currently stand at its base, then it would limit them to the path immediately in front of them.

Visionary executives realize that there may be many paths to the summit and that the best path may not be the easiest, shortest, or even the one they are currently on. With the long-term backward approach, executives identify where they want the firm to be in five to seven years. Then, they work backward from that date by asking, "If we want to be there in the year 20XY, where will we need to be the year 20XY-1?" The process of identifying each of the preceding year's prerequisite positions is calculated until it is brought back to the present.

The long-term backward approach has four distinct advantages. First, it recognizes five to seven years of an incremental approach may lead to a completely different and probably less advantageous position. It takes time to identify, cultivate and capitalize on emerging opportunities. The short-term forward incremental approach may miss emerging opportunities altogether. Second, when executives use the long-term backward approach, they often realize they are already at least two years behind schedule. Their timetable may indicate a seven-year "critical path" to achieve the desired five-year strategic position. This creates a sense of urgency and a bias for action to initiate plans that might otherwise be postponed or never implemented. Third, this perspective unleashes people's minds throughout the firm to find innovative ways to compress the critical path to meet the firm's

FIGURE 4.1.   The Strategic Management Process

Thinking → Learning → Positioning → Planning → Controlling

Stage One: Strategic Thinking:
  Accepting the need for strategic thinking
  Undertaking "Strategic Inquiries"
  Developing contingency scenarios
Stage Two: Strategic Learning:
  Gaining "Strategic Insights"
  Clarifying strategic opportunities and threats
  Identifying possible strategic positions
Stage Three: Strategic Positioning:
  Crafting a unified and compelling vision
  Selecting the target strategic position
  Identifying "Strategic Initiatives"
Stage Four: Strategic Planning:
  Formulating the corporate strategy including comprehensive long-term plan and
  specific performance goals
  Insuring the corporate strategy and all management systems support the
  corporate vision and long-range plan
  Managing the implementation of the plan
Stage Five: Strategic Monitoring and Controlling:
  Checking the assumptions that served as the basis for the plan
  Monitoring the effectiveness of the plan and making appropriate changes
  Reviewing the effectiveness of the plan and the planning process so planning and
  performance can be improved in the future

desired date of arrival. Fourth, it encourages executives to consider entering new markets and emerging industries instead of treading water in
mature markets and declining industries.

The strategic management process profiled in Figure 4.1 has five
important stages. It includes thinking, learning, positioning, planning,
and controlling. The first three stages are the crux of the strategic management process. They emphasize the need for executives to extend their
time horizons and to recognize the contextual nature of planning. Stage
Four represents the generally accepted long-range planning process.
Stage Five looks like the traditional approach to controlling. Yet, strategic controlling is more future-oriented than the traditional "rear-view
mirror" approach used by most organizations.

The strategic management process indicates that formulating the
long-range plan must be preceded by strategic thinking, creating a
corporate vision, and selecting the desired future position for the firm.
It is important to note that strategic management does not attempt to

replace long-range planning. It is designed to improve long-range planning. Strategic management is a broader and more encompassing umbrella. The first three stages indicate numerous areas where strategic planning may encounter problems. Delineating the first three stages also indicates the need for different time horizons, perspectives, mental and technical skills, types of information, and reporting requirements.

The first three stages have not received as much attention by top executives as the more mechanical fourth and fifth stages. They are a bit "fuzzy" to most executives because they cannot be placed in mathematical models to produce the "best" answer. Most executives feel comfortable around the last two stages because they are more tangible and can be handled in a very logical manner. The last two stages represent the nuts and bolts of the "engineering" side of *managing* a company. The first three steps of the strategic management process represent the "imagineering" side of *leading* a company.

The last chapter profiled how strategic thinking via anticipatory management can provide interesting insights. This chapter provides a brief profile of the second and third stages of the strategic management process. Strategic planning—stage four—is not covered because it has received considerable attention in other books.

Crafting a Unified and Compelling Vision

The first two stages of the strategic management process are prerequisites for creating a unified and compelling vision. It may be helpful to start the discussion on developing a corporate vision by indicating what a vision is not. First of all, it should not be confused with a company's "mission" statement. For years, consultants have encouraged CEOs to develop mission statements for their companies. While mission statements have merit and every company should have one, they tend to resemble the back side of a tapestry. They may be colorful and may even inspire a few people to strive to new heights, but they tend to be too general to provide a clear sense of direction, to foster crisp decision-making, and to enable effective execution.

The following legend identifies the relationships between various components of the strategic management process and their trickle-down effect:

Mission: A general statement that reflects the company's reason for being.
Vision: A statement that identifies specifically what/where the company wants to be and by when.

Strategic Position: It targets the company's future competitive, market, and financial position.

Objectives and Goals: Identify specific targets that will lead to the fulfillment of the vision.

Key Values: Identify what is sacred to the company. These are areas that will not be compromised. They contribute to the firm's culture by aiding decision-making and guiding behavior.

Strategy: The company's basic game plan for fulfilling the vision and gaining competitive advantages.

Long-term and Operational Plans: The company's road map. Plans identify the resources, timelines, critical path, human resource requirements, and budget.

Tactics: Components of the plans that are subject to ongoing modifications.

While a company's mission indicates the type of business the company is striving to be in very general terms, the vision is intended to serve as the front side of the tapestry. It should provide a clear mental picture of where the company should be at a specific time in the next five to ten years. It represents the proverbial "x" marks the spot! Jim Collins and Jerry Porras, authors of *Built to Last*, note that if the vision is not clear, crisp, and gut-grabbing, then it will not galvanize people to put forth their best efforts.[3]

John F. Kennedy illustrated the difference between a mission statement and a compelling vision. After the Soviets launched Sputnik in 1957, NASA was created so the United States could be "the world's leader in space." This mission statement was nice and appealed to our patriotism, but it was not until John Kennedy's presidency that a true vision was articulated. Kennedy's vision, "To land a man on the moon and return him safely to Earth before the end of the decade," provided a sense of direction. It created a sense of urgency and a bias for action because it provided a benchmark to measure progress. Unfortunately, most of the presidents since Kennedy have failed to grasp the importance of having the crisp, time-based vision that Kennedy provided.

The vision should not be confused with the company's strategy or long-range plan. The vision represents a desired future destination for the company with a date of arrival. It should spell out what markets the company is expected to be in, its anticipated size in terms of employees and assets, and whether it will be a domestic or global enterprise. It should also indicate whether the company will be publicly traded and whether it may acquire other companies.

The vision serves as the North Star in every decision to be made by every manager at every level every day. Any time an issue comes up, the question can be raised, "Will this action move us toward the fulfillment of our vision?" Too often, when people are asked what the company wants to be, one or more of the following situations occurs: (1) no one can articulate the vision, (2) there is a wide range of responses, or (3) they quote a mission or vision statement that is nothing more than a string of esoteric platitudes. Each of the three situations may place the future of the company in jeopardy. The first situation resembles Alice's question to the Cheshire Cat. The second situation causes people to go in different directions and diffuses valuable energy and resources.

The third situation occurs because most mission statements sound like a corporate version of the national anthem. Let's face it: mission statements are so generic that they all sound alike. You might as well say the company's mission is, "To be the best that it can be!" Most mission and vision statements are so general that they seem to have been generated by a fill-in-the-blanks software package. They look like:

> XYZ Corporation *strives to be the most innovative, highest quality, employee empowering, corporate citizen that embraces diversity and customer responsiveness organization in the galaxy.*

When the vision is stated as a specific destination with a specific date of arrival, decision-making becomes a lot easier for everyone in the company. The vision not only clarifies what the company is trying to become, it also states what the company is trying "not" to become. A clear vision also minimizes the likelihood the company will be seduced by short-term opportunities.

Reality Check: While leadership has been described as the ability to transform the vision into reality, such a transformation cannot be the result of a one-person show. Organizational transformation takes more than rhetoric; it takes commitment from every person at every level. One of the features that sets excellent companies apart from the crowd is that every person has a keen awareness of what their companies represent and specifically what they are trying to accomplish. Hickman and Silva note, "Vision joins strategy and corporate culture together to achieve corporate excellence. Without vision to bind them, corporate strategy and culture tend to drift apart."[4]

Reality Check: Too often, top management is comprised of executives who are within a few years of retirement and are tired from their climb to the top. These executives concentrate their attention on making sure nothing goes wrong rather than laying the groundwork for the next decade. They see the "retirement" light at the end of the tunnel, so they adopt the attitude, "If I don't make any mistakes, I'm home free," or "I won't be around to benefit from a bold initiative, so why should I take the time or the chance?" The same executives also tend to look for quick fixes or cosmetic solutions for problem situations that require far more comprehensive action.

Selecting the Target Strategic Position: Make Sure the Firm Is in the "Right Forest"

The vision provides a basis for navigating the seas of change. It also serves as the basis for selecting the company's target strategic position. The firm's target strategic position identifies the markets to be served, the technological expertise it will need to develop or acquire, the resources it will need to have at its disposal, and the advantages it must have over its competition.

This may be a good time to differentiate short term, medium term, and long term. In the short run all you can do is play the hand you have been dealt. You must make the most out of your current products, processes, facilities, people, and so forth. In the medium term, you can add products and services to attract additional customers, expand your sales territory, modify various organizational processes, and the like. In the long term, you can change almost everything. You can explore new market spaces, develop revolutionary products, and develop new core competencies, among other initiatives.

The beauty of the long term is that you are not tethered to the present. You can transform the firm so that it is positioned to capitalize on emerging opportunities. In short, by having a long term perspective, management may be in a position to draw on the example presented in chapter one, where management makes a deliberate effort to make sure the firm is in "the right forest." If the firm is not in the right forest (markets and industry), then it will not be in a position to excel. If the firm is not in a position to offer what the market truly wants in a manner that is clearly superior in the target market's eyes, then nothing good can happen. The firm will become "irrelevant."

The company's target strategic position may place the company in a completely different industry. Executives must be prepared to reallocate the company's limited resources to reposition the company to capitalize on tomorrow's opportunities. Peter Drucker offered an interesting approach to addressing the appropriateness of the company's current position. He encouraged managers to take a good look at what the company is involved in doing and ask, "If we were not committed to this today, would we go into it?" If the answer is no, then the next question should be, "How can we get out—fast?"[5]

The market life cycle concept has direct application to this step in the strategic management process. Selecting the target strategic position is a deliberate effort to identify the markets or industries the company will/ should be in, where it expects to be in each market life cycle, the geographic territories it will operate in, and the configuration of the company in financial and structural terms.

Identifying Strategic "Initiatives"

The targeted strategic position clarifies where the company should be three to seven or more years into the future. Once the "where" has been targeted, attention can be directed to "how" to get to the desired destination. If the company plans to initiate a major repositioning effort, it should be apparent that fine-tuning existing products and processes will not be enough. If executives want to move their company from where it is to where it should be, then they must establish an atmosphere that encourages innovativeness and unleashes corpreneurial endeavors. Chapter six profiles corpreneurship—the process where firms can become more entrepreneurial.

Executives need to pay particular attention to efforts that require substantial lead time. If executives want to transform their companies, then new markets will need to be researched, new prototypes created and test marketed, new technologies adopted, new production and distribution capabilities developed, new skills learned, and financial reserves set aside.

Identifying strategic initiatives means the company will no longer do "business as usual." Executives must accept the need to plant the seeds for tomorrow's success rather than focus their attention solely on this year's bottom line. Most of these efforts will take at least two years lead time before they will provide significant returns. Savvy executives acknowledge the need to develop sinking funds for major capital acquisitions or for replacing expensive equipment when it wears out. The same logic needs to be adopted for the company's strategic initiatives. DuPont provides a good example of committing today's resources to tomorrow's markets. Instead of staying just in petrochemical technology, it invested a significant amount of money to position the company to be a leader in the emerging biotechnology field. This commitment is justified because biotechnology is expected to have at least as revolutionary an impact on the way people live as computer technology has had on the way people work.

For an organization to be future-oriented, its management systems must be designed to direct everyone's attention to doing the things that will move the company to its desired strategic position. Goals will have to be set for new product development, incentives must be established to reward people for being innovative, and performance reviews must focus on the extent each person has moved the company closer to its target strategic position.

Executives are encouraged to use the "Charting the firm's future course" matrix profiled in Table 4.1 to provide better insights into the need for the firm to evolve. The first step involves completing the yesterday's column that profiles the various dimensions for the firm three to five years ago. The next step involves completing the today's column. Completing these two columns fosters two things. First it illustrates how much things including the firm have changed, which indicates how it will need to continue changing. Second, it encourages them to

TABLE 4.1. Charting the Firm's Future Course

Factor	Yesterday's	Today's	Tomorrow's
Type of Business			
Customers			
Products			
Services			
Technology			
Competition			
Competitive Advantage(s)			
Competitive Disadvantage(s)			
Other			

TABLE 4.2.   Insights and Initiatives

Insight #1:
Insight #2:
Insight #3:
Insight #4:

Initiative #1:
Initiative #2:
Initiative #3:
Initiative #4:

explore how it may need to be different in the next three to five years as well. The basic premise is the firm will have to change more in the next three to five years than it has changed in the past three to five years.

Table 4.2 profiles how each insight may lead to one or more initiatives. The matrix helps executives document the insights and initiatives.

Table 4.3 profiles the various changes that will need to be made to enable the firm to achieve the desired strategic position.

Table 4.4 profiles the strategic milestones for the various activities or events that need to be made to enable the firm to achieve the desired strategic position.

Crafting the Vision: An Example

Developing the company's vision involves considerable time and thought. The process defies the "one-afternoon" strategic planning retreat when the executive team brainstorms a few "emotionally charged" words and then wordsmiths them into an eloquent statement. The roller-coaster nature of the vision development process is reflected in

TABLE 4.3.   Table of Strategic Priorities

Areas to Discontinue	Areas to Reduce	Areas to Continue	Areas to Increase	Areas to Initiate

TABLE 4.4.   List of Strategic Milestones

Activity or Event	To be Initiated by:	To be Completed by:
1.		
2.		
3.		
4.		
5.		

the following example. The example has been modified to provide anonymity. It also represents a simplified and abbreviated version of the actual situation.

The founder and chief executive of a successful manufacturing company contacted a consultant and asked him to meet with him to discuss a dilemma. The CEO was concerned that the company might not be positioned to capitalize on the opportunities on the horizon. He indicated that the executive team had spent two days in a corporate planning retreat a few months earlier. He said the retreat had been worthwhile because he and the other members of the executive team had successfully drafted the company's first mission statement.

The chief executive, however, expressed his growing frustration that the mission statement did not provide the focus, sense of urgency, and bias for action he had expected and the company needed. The chief executive then handed a copy of the statement to the consultant. Harper Manufacturing has been substituted for the real name of the company to maintain anonymity. The company's product line has also been disguised.

MISSION STATEMENT FOR HARPER MANUFACTURING

Harper Manufacturing *designs and manufactures fabrication machinery. We are dedicated to identifying customer needs and meeting those needs with innovative, high quality products backed up with outstanding service.*

While the mission statement put into words what the company did and its business strategy, it did not elicit the energy needed for the company to excel, nor did it provide specific enough guidance for the multitude of decisions that had to be made. After a few months of trying to use the mission statement as the company's North Star, the chief executive concluded that while it sounded nice, it just did not provide the specific sense of direction he needed. The consultant indicated the chief executive needed a "bridge" that could connect the company's general, value-laden mission to the various decisions that have to be made in identifying the company's priorities, drafting the company's strategy, and developing the company's critical time line.

The consultant told the chief executive that most chief executives echo the Peggy Lee song, "Is that all there is?" when they try to operationalize their company's mission statement. The consultant then suggested that the chief executive develop a specific vision statement. The consultant began the process for developing the vision by asking the chief executive what he thought the company should be, as well as his perceptions of the future of the industry. The consultant then asked each of the vice presidents the same questions. Next the consultant asked similar questions to a stratified sample of key employees. An effort was made to have the sample include some veteran employees as well as a selection of the people who had just joined the company. The consultant chose to conduct individual interviews because he wanted to learn each person's perceptions and maintain confidentiality.

The interviews provided the consultant with perspectives from various vantage points. The consultant was not surprised to find a lack of consensus on exactly what the future held and what the company should become. The usual functional mental silos existed for people in manufacturing, marketing, and finance. Their specific training, experience and orientation limited the breadth of their perspective. The interviews also provided a wide range of attitudes about risk, technology, and the company's human resources. A number of managers were very optimistic about the future. Other managers felt that the future would be filled with turbulence, more intense competition, and eroding profitability. The interviews also indicated that some people were truly team players, while others would rather do their own thing.

The consultant put together a report that highlighted the salient points generated in the interviews. The report was forwarded to the chief executive so he could see how his staff viewed the company and the world around it. A series of weekly Friday afternoon meetings was then scheduled for the chief executive and his executive team.

The first meeting focused on the need for the company to operate with a strategic perspective. The consultant presented various models that play an integral role in fostering visionary leadership and strategic management. The second meeting was designed to have the executive team identify key factors for the company's future success. The group went through a SWOT (Strengths, Weaknesses, Opportunities, and Threats) analysis for the company. Particular attention was directed to present SWOT as well as SWOT factors in the next five years. The future SWOT analysis was essential because it helped the team identify factors that might not exist today but could arise in the next five years. At various times, the consultant brought up points from the report so the team could see that there were varying views of SWOT-related factors.

The second meeting identified some general issues. The third meeting forced the team to be more specific in their discussions of SWOT factors as they closely scrutinized each one. The team members were encouraged to share their thoughts and perceptions. The group continued meeting weekly to analyze the company's future. They incorporated the quick environment scanning technique (profiled in chapter three) and ran scenarios for various possible situations.

The team followed the initial stages in the strategic management process and moved toward a consensus for what the future represented with each passing week. The strategic *inquiries* about the future led to strategic *insights* into the factors and forces that could have a beneficial or detrimental effect on the company.

Next the team analyzed windows of opportunity that would open as well as how the company could harvest the opportunities currently available. The team then identified the resource and capability requirements for each of the current and potential opportunities.

The team then directed its attention to developing a vision for where the company should be in five years given the favorable opportunities that existed and those that were expected to emerge. The consultant encouraged the team to state the vision as a destination in five years. The consultant also encouraged the team to identify a destination that could be achieved with innovation and stretch rather than simply adding five years to the company's current situation.

The chief executive encouraged the team to pay particular attention to what the stockholders wanted the company to be worth in five years. The team recognized that if the investment objectives of the stockholders were not met, the team would not be around to satisfy the other stakeholders' expectations—especially their own!

When the board of directors was asked where they wanted the firm to be in the future, the directors indicated the principal stockholders wanted the company to be worth at least $368,000,000 in five years so they could cash out. The team then estimated the company would have to generate $220,000,000 in sales with $66,000,000 in pre-tax profit and $46,000,000 in after-tax profit in the fifth year using an eight-to-one price/after-tax earnings ratio for the company to be worth $368,000,000. The company had generated $97,341,000 in sales with $29,202,300 in pre-tax profit and $19,565,541 in after-tax profit the year that just ended. The eight-to-one price earnings ratio put the present worth of the company at $156,524,320.

The management team realized the five-year valuation target and profitability target were challenging, but it also knew it had to start somewhere. The overall value and corresponding profit level permitted the team to investigate the conditions that would have to exist for the targets to become a reality. The board's two financial targets provided the basis needed for identifying the company's strategic planning gap. The strategic planning gap profiled in Figure 4.2 measured the difference between where the company needed to be in five years and where it would be if it did not change what it was doing.

The team adopted the "inquiries ... insights ... initiatives" format of strategic management. The team ran scenarios that reflected various market conditions. Particular attention was directed to economic, competitive, and technological conditions. The team then projected the corresponding level of sales and profits for the company's existing products and services to determine possible levels of sales and profits for those products in the next five years. It soon became apparent that even under the best conditions the company could not fulfill the financial targets with the company's current product and service offering.

FIGURE 4.2.   The Strategic Planning Gap

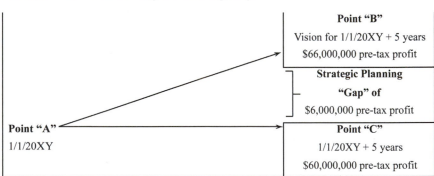

When the team combined the long-term backward approach with its projections for enhancing sales and profits for the company's three existing products and corresponding services, it concluded that the company needed to develop one or more products or services that would generate at least a $6,000,000 pre-tax profit in the fifth year. The $6,000,000 pre-tax profit represented the firm's strategic planning gap.

The team was faced with an interesting dilemma when it realized the company's current products and services—as successful as they have been—would not be able to fulfill the five-year valuation target. The team could either lower the valuation target so that it would conform to the team's projection of what could be achieved with the company's current products and services, or it could keep the five-year valuation target and find a way to make it a reality.

The team recognized it had to create its future by developing one or more products or services to bridge the strategic planning gap. The team devoted its next meeting to scanning the horizon for emerging opportunities. The team chose to look for unexploited and emerging opportunities rather than existing markets because these opportunities would offer higher profit potential than existing markets that were saturated with competition. The team also recognized that it had the time needed to develop new products and services if it used a five-year time horizon.

Both matrices encourage executives to view their companies as "customer problem solvers" rather than as producers of certain products or as providers of certain services. Customers do not really want to buy a product or service. Products and services are merely means to an end. Customers want to have their problems solved. Customers will be delighted only to the extent that the products and services meet or exceed their specific needs. It is easy for executives to get caught up in their company's existing markets, products, and services. It is also easy for executives whose companies are in highly competitive markets to get caught up in making sure their companies retain their current customers and maintain their market share. Gary Hamel and C. K. Prahalad noted, "However well a company meets the articulated needs of current customers, it runs a great risk if it doesn't have a view of the needs customers can't yet articulate, but would love to have satisfied. . . . Any company that can do no more than respond to articulated needs of existing customers will quickly become a laggard."[6]

Executives need to recognize that the company may need to change its target market(s) as well as its products, services, locations, and infrastructure. Hamel and Prahalad encourage executives to explore gaps that may constitute unexploited opportunities in the current market. They focus on two dimensions: needs and customer types. Needs can be divided into articulated and unarticulated categories. They define unarticulated needs as "needs customers can't yet articulate, but would love to have satisfied." Customer types can be divided into customers served and those unserved. Hamel and Prahalad noted that firms should explore the "unexploited opportunities" that can be found in the unarticulated needs of customers being served as well as the articulated and unarticulated needs of customers not being served.[7]

The difference between whether a company will experience moderate growth or significant growth may be contingent on the extent to which it explores uncharted areas. Hamel and Prahalad noted there are three kinds of companies: "Companies that try to lead customers where they don't want to go; companies that listen to their customers and then respond to their articulated needs; and companies that lead customers where they want to go but don't know it yet. Companies that create the future fall into the third category. They do more than satisfy customers, they constantly amaze them."[8]

Futuring, which was profiled in chapter three, enhances an executive's perceptiveness and sense of timing. It encourages executives to look beyond the present. Futuring reflects the Wayne Gretzky approach to managing described in that chapter by anticipating where the market will be rather than focusing exclusively on current market conditions. Executives should try to identify what their current customers will need in the future. Executives also need to identify who should be their future customers. The "Future Positioning" Matrix profiled in Figure 4.3 indicates three types of opportunities that should also be explored by the company. This lead time may help the company develop products and services for markets that are not being served. Executives who want to create their company's future should identify the "wide open" opportunities that may emerge in the future.

Sony's development of the Walkman provides a good example of having the product before the customer even recognizes the need. When Akio Morita realized that jogging was not just a fad, he explored the ways for Sony to get a piece of the action. Morita noted that if people were going to spend a lot of time jogging, sooner or later they would want to find a way for it to be more pleasurable. He also noted that a large number of the people who were jogging also liked listening to

FIGURE 4.3.   Future Positioning Matrix

Future Product/Service Needs	Future	Future product/service development opportunities	Wide-open future opportunities
	Current	Current product/service offering	Gaps in current product/service offering
		Current	Future
		Customers	

music on high-quality sound systems. Morita then set out to capitalize on Sony's core competence of miniaturization to create a high-quality, compact, and affordable tape player for joggers. The Walkman was an outstanding success because it made the time spent jogging more enjoyable. It also made the minutes or hours seem like they were passing more quickly. Years later, Apple capitalized on the market's desire for portability when it launched the iPod, iPhone, iPad, and a whole set of other product platforms that have changed the way people live by providing power and portability that was unimaginable not long ago.

The team at Harper Manufacturing then analyzed its current markets to determine if certain needs were not being met enough or at all. The "gap" analysis was not limited to the company's current customers. It also included companies that were buying products and services from the company's competitors. The team also did not restrict its analysis to the company's current market segments. It explored other market segments to see if other gaps existed.

If the team had adopted a three-year time horizon, it would have been relegated to developing one or more products that were no more than imitations of products offered by other companies. The team recognized an imitative strategy would not elevate the company to the "premiere" status set in the mission statement nor would it generate the profit margin needed to achieve the company's overall valuation target.

The team then took a mental leap forward and brainstormed a list of emerging markets that might offer lucrative and lasting opportunities. Attention was directed to markets that were near the edge of the company's five-year radar screen. The team did not want to direct its attention to markets where the window of opportunity would not open for at least five years. Instead, they were looking for windows that would be opening in about two years. The two-year window of opportunity was chosen because it would give the company two years to develop the product or service and three years to harvest that opportunity. The team also knew it should not get caught up in sales projections because profit was the bull's-eye of the target if it was to achieve the company's valuation target.

The team's brainstorming session went well beyond the company's current markets, products, processes, services, and technology. The team was even encouraged to test the outer limits of its industry and to see if related industries offered opportunities. The openness of the brainstorming sessions encouraged the team to "think outside the box." The executives were encouraged to think thoughts they might have been reluctant to consider if they had used traditional, shorter-term time horizons.

The team generated a number of emerging market gaps/opportunities and current gaps/opportunities in the first brainstorming session. The consultant suggested that they not try to analyze the gaps, rough-out product or service specifics/logistics, or determine funding requirements at that time. Instead, the consultant encouraged the group to stay "outside the box" for the next week when the team would meet again to continue its brainstorming. The consultant reminded the group that the two rules of brainstorming are (1) It is the quantity not the quality of ideas that counts in the beginning and (2) Criticism or evaluation of ideas is not allowed until the brainstorming session is concluded. The second brainstorming session produced new ideas as well as ideas that "piggy-backed" on some of the ideas generated in the preceding week.

Two things should be noted at this time. First, the team decided it should proactively solicit new product or service ideas from its customers and potential customers. The team sought to establish an alliance with potential and/or existing customers in the development of breakthrough products and services. This would reduce the amount of time, funding, and risk associated with the company's research and development efforts. It would also give the company at least one customer. Second, the team decided the company would not acquire or license the product or service in its effort to bridge the gap. The team was committed to being a "developer" of fabrication-related machinery or services.

The team's brainstorming sessions were very productive. Everyone was amazed at the number of opportunities they were able to identify. The list of market gaps/customer needs and the team's corresponding product and service ideas were impressive—and well beyond what the company needed to fulfill its vision. The next meetings were devoted to performing "reality checks." The team analyzed the various market gaps and their corresponding products and service logistics. Each gap/customer need was subjected to a preliminary analysis to determine if it had the potential to be a breakthrough opportunity. The team used a screening process similar to the one used by venture capital firms when they consider funding proposals. Attention was directed at the ability to develop a proprietary position, the opportunity to dominate the market, lucrative profit margins, and sustained growth. Additional meetings addressed whether the company would be able to enhance sales and profits for its present products and services to meet the target and whether the company had the talent and resources needed to actually develop the product(s) needed to bridge $6,000,000 fifth-year pre-tax profit gap.

The complete list of product and service ideas was also well beyond the company's available resources. The team then projected the financial, human, technological, informational, and infrastructure requirements associated with the most promising opportunities. A number of the opportunities were dropped from consideration because their requirements exceeded the company's available resources and the resources it could secure.

It was at this time that the team tightened up the company's vision statement so it would reflect the numerous iterations of weekly meetings that had followed the revision in the mission statement. The following statements and tables for Harper Manufacturing are calibrated for a five-year time horizon.

VISION FOR HARPER MANUFACTURING THE YEAR 20YZ+5

BY JANUARY 1ST, 20YZ+5 Harper Manufacturing is expected to generate $220,000,000 in sales with a pre-tax profit of $66,000,000 and an after-tax profit of $46,000,000. By 20YZ+5, the company will be positioned so it may be sold to another company, outside investors, or the management team for at least $368,000,000.

The visioning process produced a number of insights. Four insights were particularly noteworthy. First, there appeared to be enough lucrative opportunities in the fabrication machinery field that the company would not have to transform itself into a completely different industry. Second, management realized that its core competence was identifying customer needs and then designing and manufacturing fabrication machines that fit their needs. The process reaffirmed the company's mission statement that Harper Manufacturing should be a developer and manufacturer. Third, the company needed to develop at least one product or service that could generate at least $6,000,000 in pre-tax profit by the fifth year.

The fourth insight came as a direct result of the recognition that the company's current products and services would not be enough to fulfill the vision. The management team also realized there was a strategic planning gap in the management team. The company needed to have a Director of Research and Development if it was to develop the product(s) or service(s) needed to hit the five-year target. The team realized that if the company's journey for fulfilling its vision was mapped out in a PERT chart, then hiring a Director of Research and Development would be the first activity on the company's critical path. Table 4.5 profiles the insights generated during the visioning and positioning sessions.

TABLE 4.5.   Projected Product/Service Mix for 20XY+5

Sales Goal (Margin)	Sales Goal (Margin)			
	"Stretch" (35%)	"Target" (30%)	"Minimum" (20%)	Percent of Sales
Product A	$87,500,000	$70,000,000	$52,500,000	35%
Net	$30,625,000	$21,000,000	$10,500,000	
Product B	$87,500,000	$70,000,000	$52,500,000	35%
Net	$30,625,000	$21,000,000	$10,500,000	
Product C	$50,000,000	$40,000,000	$30,000,000	20%
Net	$17,500,000	$12,000,000	$6,000,000	
New Product "D"	$25,000,000	$20,000,000	$15,000,000	10%
Net	$8,750,000	$6,000,000	$3,000,000	
Total Product Sales	$250,000,000	$200,000,000	$150,000,000	100%
Net	$87,500,000	$60,000,000	$30,000,000	
Additional Revenue from parts and service	15% of Sales $37,500,000	10% of sales 20,000,000	5% of Sales $7,500,000	
Net	$11,250,000	$6,000,000	$1,500,000	
% Margin	35%	30%	20%	
Total sales for firm	$287,500,000	$220,000,000	$157,500,000	
Net	$100,625,000	$66,000,000	$31,500,00	

The management team then directed its attention in subsequent weekly sessions to articulating various factors and issues that would be critical in managing the company so that it would be positioned to transform its vision into reality. The CEO noted that the visioning and positioning process clarified what needed to be done to transform the firm. Yet he made an interesting comment when the management team was wrapping up its efforts. He noted, "None of this will have any value unless you have the guts to make it happen." This demonstrates that if the team could not convert its thoughts into actions, then the visioning and positioning processes were nothing more than "dreaming sessions."

Concluding Comments: Seize the Future!

Visioning must be an ongoing process where management regularly ponders what may be over the horizon, identifies and monitors key factors, conducts environmental scanning sessions, runs various scenarios, and does all the other activities to remain in tune with what is possible. It encourages you to take an objective look at where the best opportunities may be for your company in the years to come. Only then, will you be able to capitalize on the opportunities that lie ahead. It also encourages you to make a deliberate effort to lead the company in such a way that every person, every resource, and every moment in time are directed to moving the company toward its target strategic position.

The visioning process is not something that is done once every five to ten years. When Andy Grove, the CEO of Intel, was asked if it is possible for firms to have a five-year vision when things are changing so quickly, he responded, "It is necessary, but the five-year vision needs to be revised and modified systematically each year or twice a year. We look at our five-year picture and modify the second half of it so it is constantly a five-year plan rather than one that is prepared and then placed on the shelf."[9] Take the Visioning and Positioning Quiz in Table 4.6 to learn the extent your firm has a clear vision and is positioned to make the vision a reality.

Where there is no vision, the people perish.

—Proverbs 29:18

TABLE 4.6. Visioning and Positioning Quiz

How does your firm rate on the following dimensions?
*Scoring Level: 1 = not at all, 2 = rarely/barely,
3 = occasionally/somewhat, 4 = frequently/sufficient,
5 = ongoing/extensive

		Level*
1.	To what extent does your firm have a specific and challenging vision for its future that fosters a high level of energy and commitment in people at all levels to be engaged and stretch to their potential?	1-2-3-4-5
2.	To what extent is your firm searching for emerging opportunities in and outside its current markets?	1-2-3-4-5
3.	To what extent is your firm committed to strategic management?	1-2-3-4-5
4.	To what extent does your firm operationalize strategic management via effective execution . . . bifocal management?	1-2-3-4-5
5.	To what extent does your firm have a clearly articulated set of strategic initiatives for transitioning the firm?	1-2-3-4-5
6.	To what extent does your firm have a set of strategic milestones for planning and monitoring its strategic initiatives?	1-2-3-4-5
7.	To what extent does your firm do the strategic management process on an ongoing basis rather than a process that is done only once every few years?	1-2-3-4-5
8.	To what extent does your firm use a backwards to the present—using the strategic planning gap mental framework rather than a present into the future approach?	1-2-3-4-5
9.	To what extent does your firm identify its customers' unarticulated needs?	1-2-3-4-5
10.	To what extent does your firm identify its future customers' needs?	1-2-3-4-5
11.	To what extent does your firm solicit employee input in the visioning and positioning process?	1-2-3-4-5
	Total points	

Scoring Key

50–55	Congratulations, your firm demonstrates most of the qualities of a visionary and proactive firm.
45–49	Your firm has many qualities of a visionary and proactive firm, but still has areas that can be improved.
40–44	Your firm has some of the qualities of a visionary and proactive firm, but there is a lot of room for improvement.
33–39	Your firm has some significant shortcomings that will impede its ability to be visionary and proactive.
11–32	Your firm is very short-sighted and reactive. It may be beyond hope. It will take a radical change in management, systems, and processes to have any chance of being competitive in the future.

Notes

1. Craig Hickman and Michael A. Silva, *Creating Excellence* (New York: New American Library, 1984), 150.

2. Lewis Carroll, *Alice's Adventures in Wonderland* (London: Oxford University Press, 1971), 71.

3. James C. Collins and Jerry Porras, "Organizational Vision and Visionary Organizations," *California Management Review*, 34, no. 1 (1991): 31.

4. Hickman and Silva, 156.

5. Peter F. Drucker, *Management* (New York: Harper & Row, 1973), 126.

6. Gary Hamel and C. K. Prahalad, *Competing For The Future* (Boston: Harvard Business School Press, 1994), 102.

7. Ibid.

8. Ibid., 100.

9. Interview with Andy Grove by the author via an America Online chat room, November 17, 1998.

Chapter 5

Establishing a Results-Oriented Performance Management System

The key to executing your strategy is to have people in your organization understand it—including the crucial but perplexing processes by which intangible assets are converted into tangible outcomes.[1]

—Robert S. Kaplan and David Norton

This chapter focuses on having a performance management system in place to help management make sure the firm is staying on track by doing the right things the right way at the right time with the right resources. Crafting a vision and identifying the firm's targeted strategic position will be an exercise in futility if systems are not in place for ensuring performance. Someone once noted that the purpose of planning is *not* to develop plans. The purpose of planning is to develop plans that *when implemented* lead to the achievement of the desired results.

In times of rapid change and uncertainty, no executive can afford to believe everything will go as planned. This does not mean executives should stop developing plans. Nor does it mean that planning should not be done. It is because of the rapidity of change and the corresponding uncertainty that executives need to develop plans. Planning is essential because it represents the process where management develops a set of choreographed actions to translate the company's vision into reality. This chapter highlights a number of ideas, concepts, and approaches that foster the development of a mental framework for establishing a performance management system that ensures the strategic perspective is not lost in the shuffle by the company's ongoing operations. Chapter ten provides a more in-depth profile of what it takes to have exceptional execution.

Off-site strategic "visioning retreats" are frequently devoted to identifying what the company should be doing—especially what it should be doing differently—to be positioned favorably for the years ahead. Unfortunately, the enthusiasm and energy demonstrated at the retreats are usually met with a corresponding lack of action following the strategic sessions. Too often, initiatives that were identified gather dust when executives return to the world of day-to-day management.

Reality Check: Without clear action plans and identified responsibility for their implementation, strategic initiatives that are needed to fulfill the company's vision are destined to die of neglect. To make matters worse, these initiatives are frequently forgotten by the time the executive team meets again a year later to contemplate the company's strategy. Ironically, subsequent "annual strategic planning sessions" have a tendency to raise the same issues that were raised in previous sessions. As Yogi Berra stated, "It's déja vu all over again."

Peter Drucker noted decades ago that a plan is not really a plan unless it produces actions. More recently, someone observed that strategic planning sessions often resemble two elephants mating—while there may be a lot of noise and energy, it takes at least two years to find out if anything productive came from the "interactive session."

Measurement and Control Are Integral Parts of a Performance Management System

The latest approaches for addressing the challenges of planning and control resemble "management by objectives" (MBO) systems developed years ago. The Management by Objectives system is built on a four-step foundation. Step one involves setting specific objectives. Step two involves developing action plans to achieve the objectives. Step three involves conducting periodic reviews of the factors that affect the achievement of the objectives within their corresponding timeline and budgets. Step four then compares what was actually accomplished with the objectives that were established in step one. The fourth step plays a key role in modifying the plans for the following year so the company will be on track in fulfilling its longer-term goals. Step four also provides the basis for conducting performance reviews and providing rewards, as well as improving future performance via training and development.

Effective control will only be possible if the planning processes provide it with a solid foundation. If the company's planning processes fail to identify specifically: (1) what the company is trying to accomplish, (2) the strategy to be used to achieve the objectives, and (3) the timeline and resource requirements for achieving the objectives, then controlling will be like trying to steer a ship without a rudder.

Someone once applied Murphy's Law to military situations by saying, "In combat, plans have to be adjusted as soon as the first shot is fired." Without effective monitoring and controlling processes, management will not know if the company's plans need to be adjusted. Management will just keep on going until it is too late to initiate change. The Contextual Change Model profiled in the introduction of this book noted that without awareness, there cannot be constructive change!

Controlling in its purest form is actually an ongoing effort to change the company's future. Controlling is most effective when it forces management to look ahead when there is still time to alter the company's course or strategy. By focusing on the company's current situation as well as any corresponding trends, controlling identifies the need to change early enough for the company to still operate in a proactive manner. Control processes that take a "rearview mirror" or "after-the-fact" approach relegate the company to a reactive stance.

Building a Strategic Measurement and Control System

The company's vision needs to serve as the cornerstone for the company's plans and strategies. The company's plans and strategies, in turn, need to provide the parameters for the allocation of the company's resources and serve as the basis for the company's timeline. The timeline, in turn, must identify and reflect key performance milestones. Monitoring and controlling the company's operations will be effective only to the extent that the processes incorporate the factors that contribute to the company's success.

Measurement plays an integral role in the strategic management process. The measurement system should ensure executives are practicing bifocal management. Management needs to be sure that the concern for meeting ongoing operational targets and staying within the period's operating budget do not keep people from addressing strategic issues. The measurement system will be worthwhile only to the extent it makes sure that short-term actions, targets, and milestones will lead to the accomplishment of long-term objectives.

> Reality Check: The measurement system must measure the right factors. Two of the facts of organizational life need to be considered in the development of the performance measurement system. The first fact of life is, "What gets measured, gets managed!" The second fact of life is, "If management wants something to happen, it needs to be encouraged, reviewed, and rewarded." If one of these three components is missing, then the desired behavior will not be exhibited or sustained.

Measurement works best when the factor to be managed can be put in quantitative form. Someone once said, "If you can't put it into numbers, then you don't know what you are talking about enough to manage it." Two notes of caution, however, need to be provided here. First, management needs to be careful that the measurement system is not composed solely of factors that are easy to quantify and measure. Second, management also needs to be sure that in its zeal to put together a measurement system that it does not merely monitor factors that are already being monitored. If management is truly committed to developing an effective performance management system, then it needs to call a time-out, deliberately step back, release its grip on the company's current system, and then identify the factors that are truly important to the company's long-term success.

Focus: Identifying the "Drivers of Success"

Although we might prefer to live in a world of facts, we must recognize we really live in a world of perceptions and assumptions. Every decision we make is the result of a "mental model" that reflects our perceptions of the world and our assumptions about what it takes for the company to succeed. Our mental models attempt to identify the factors and forces that affect performance as well as determine how the factors and forces affect each other.

Mental models reflect one's assumptions about current and future market conditions, how competitors will respond to the company's strategy, how the company's employees will respond to change efforts, and how long it will take to recalibrate the company's internal processes to implement the change efforts. One's mental models also reflect assumptions about price elasticity, customer response time in adopting a new product, and the company's cost-effectiveness in improving product or service quality. When the company's strategy has not produced the expected results as indicated by various interim metrics, milestones, and the like, then management needs to recognize that the assumptions that went into the strategy were inappropriate and/or the plan has not been executed well.

Identification of the factors that contribute to the company's success is essential if management is to be successful in fostering exceptional performance. Identification of the key causal or contributing factors represents the very foundation in developing the company's performance management system.

While a multitude of factors may contribute to the company's success, management must identify the factors that are the true "drivers of success." Pareto's "80/20 Principle" may be helpful here. It states that 80 percent of the gain usually comes from 20 percent of the factors. Management needs to identify the few factors that make the greatest difference in the company's long-term performance. Particular emphasis must be placed on identifying the "causal" factors rather than the "symptom" or "result" factors.

If management wants to achieve exceptional performance, then it should focus its attention on the identification of emerging markets that offer lucrative growth opportunities and the development of first-to-market products and services that will command considerable profit margins. The same reasoning also applies to the company's human resources. Management needs to recognize that all products, processes, patents, and profits come from people.

Developing the "Balanced Scorecard"

Tom Peters observed that if you are spending 100 percent of your time doing continuous improvement, then you are spending 0 percent of your time on innovation. The same logic can be applied to management's tendency to be preoccupied with the financial dimensions of the company. If management is preoccupied with monitoring cash flow and absorbed in fine-tuning daily operations, then it will be overlooking the enterprise's true drivers of success. Robert Kaplan and David Norton in their book, *The Balanced Scorecard*, provide a useful mental framework for managing the overall enterprise. Kaplan and Norton encourage executives to use a "balanced scorecard" that identifies, monitors and measures the company's drivers of success.

When management develops the company's performance management system it needs to be sure its corresponding scorecard differentiates the drivers of success from the factors that are the effects of the drivers. For example, should the scorecard focus on employee turnover, productivity, or satisfaction? Which employee factor is the cause, and which is an effect? The same question applies to financial measures. Should management focus on sales (and corresponding cash flow) or monitor the percent of repeat purchases?

The process of developing the balanced scorecard tends to be very frustrating for most executives because they must identify and articulate the drivers of success. The process of developing the scorecard usually brings different perspectives to the surface. Kaplan and Norton state, "In our experience with the design of scorecard programs, we have never encountered a management team that had reached full consensus on the relative importance of its strategic objectives. . . . When executives from different functional perspectives . . . attempt to work together as a team, there are blind spots—areas of relative ignorance around which it is difficult to form teams and create consensus because so little shared understanding exists about overall business objectives and the contribution and integration of different functional units."[2] The balanced scorecard has the potential to create a shared model of the entire business if top management—working as a team—develops it.

The process of identifying the true drivers of success presents another challenge for the members of the executive team. The development of the scorecard forces them to be specific in terms of performance expectations. The scorecard will be of little value if the performance expectations are merely a set of lofty platitudes. The scorecard needs to be composed of the drivers of success, and the drivers need to be stated in quantitative terms.

Imagine a thermometer with just six calibrations: hot, warm, tepid, cool, cold, and frigid. The lack of precision would make monitoring and management very difficult. The first step in developing the balanced scorecard is to translate the company's vision and strategy statements into an integrated set of objectives and measures that describe the long-term drivers of success. Kaplan and Norton note that despite the best intentions of those at the top, lofty statements about becoming "best in the class," "the number one supplier," or "an empowered organization" do not translate easily into operational terms that provide useful guides to action.[3]

The scorecard needs to be viewed as an organizational thermostat. While thermostats incorporate thermometers, it is the thermostat that initiates the changes needed to produce the desired results. The scorecard must do more than monitor the temperature of the company's drivers of success; it must serve as the springboard for modifying the company's operations and, in some instances, altering its strategy in the years ahead.

The Scorecard Needs to be Balanced and Holistic

The scorecard will be beneficial only to the extent that it is "balanced" and managers view the company with a "holistic" perspective. Future financial performance is the result of financial and nonfinancial decisions. The balanced scorecard does not devalue the role played by financial strategies and the need for financial measures. Instead, Kaplan and Norton emphasize a more holistic perspective by supplementing the financial factors with three sets of nonfinancial factors. They stress the need for executives to use a scorecard that also includes: (1) *customer factors*, (2) *internal-business-process factors*, and (3) *learning and growth perspectives*. These three additional perspectives, like the financial perspectives, are derived from an explicit and rigorous translation of the organization's vision and strategy into tangible objectives and measures.[4]

According to Kaplan and Norton, financial measures tell the story of past events. Financial measures are inadequate for guiding and evaluating the journey that information age companies must face to create future value through investment in customers, suppliers, employees, processes, and innovation.[5]

Financial indicators are not always the *leading* indicators of organizational performance. Customer and employee satisfaction factors influence cash flow. A drop in the repeat purchase rate will surely have an adverse effect on cash flow. Cash flow will deteriorate when the company has to spend more on advertising when market share drops. Cash flow will be affected when product quality fluctuates and the company has to spend more on process improvement efforts. In these instances, management will need to determine whether the company's products are in sync with market demands and whether work processes are being monitored. Cash flow may also deteriorate with a drop in the level of employee commitment, training, and experimentation.

If management wants to improve future cash flow, the company's strategy may need to be altered to attract new customers as well as foster customer retention. Analog Devices initiated a process to learn what its customers really valued. It surveyed its customers and did benchmarking studies. It found that its customers cared about things like delivery time and improved quality. Analog then built a model that would help its managers track and thus manage such things. Arthur M. Schneiderman, who developed Analog's balanced scorecard found, "Overall, there were about 15 nonfinancial measures that we identified as critical to the company's performance."[6]

Because customer satisfaction is a driver of financial success, management may need to direct its attention to establishing customer alliances, boosting new product development, reducing cycle time, improving response time, enhancing quality, reducing costs, and incorporating the latest information technology. The same logic also applies to enhancing employee satisfaction by creating a work environment that attracts the best talent, having management practices that enable employees at all levels to grow and contribute, and designing compensation systems that provide exceptional rewards when people turn in exceptional performances.

Management must make every effort to ensure that every component of the scorecard and corresponding business strategy are consistent with one another. The scorecard and strategy must reflect the cause and effect nature of the overall business. Major omissions or inconsistencies in the scorecard and/or strategy will not produce the synergistic effect needed to move the company ahead. Kaplan and Norton noted, "Once targets for customer, internal-business-process, and learning and growth measures are established, managers can align their strategic quality, response time, and reengineering initiatives for achieving breakthrough objectives."[7]

The Balanced Scorecard Can Foster Bifocal Management

The balanced scorecard addresses a serious deficiency in traditional management systems. Traditional management systems place so much emphasis on current financial metrics that the company's overall strategy does not get enough attention. The balanced scorecard is noteworthy because it links short-term actions and goal achievement to strategic milestones.

Kaplan and Norton believe the balanced scorecard has its greatest impact when it is deployed to drive organizational change. They note senior executives should establish targets for the scorecard measures three to five years out, that, if achieved, will transform the company. Managers must establish stretch targets for their customer, internal-business-process, and learning and growth objectives.[8] Breakthrough performances in the scorecard's nonfinancial dimensions should lead to breakthrough financial performance. The scorecard is instrumental in change efforts because it identifies what the company has to do well to succeed. Linking compensation to achieving stretch targets for the scorecard's measures also helps foster change.

The balanced scorecard's holistic nature also enables management to link organizational, departmental, team, and individual goals and actions together. The balanced scorecard helps management translate the scorecard into operational measures. The operational measures, in turn, become the focus for improvement activities in local units.

The balanced scorecard can also provide the basis for creating a "personal scorecard" for everyone in the company. The balanced scorecard does not have its full effect unless it translates into personal objectives, measures, targets, and initiatives. Once corporate targets and individual unit targets are established, then each employee establishes his/her corresponding goals. Every employee then identifies up to five performance measures and targets for the corresponding goals.[9] Each person's performance is then reviewed according to the extent that the targets were met and the extent to which that person contributed to the unit's and the company's goals. The company's compensation system helps reinforce the balanced and bifocal nature of the scorecard. According to Kaplan and Norton, individuals will not earn incentive compensation if performance in any given period falls below the minimum threshold.[10]

The Balanced Scorecard Can be Configured as an Organizational "Dashboard"

The concept of a balanced scorecard has contributed to the development of the "organizational dashboard." Executives cannot watch every dimension of the company's operations. The cockpit of an airplane provides an interesting example of the need for executives to translate the balanced scorecard into an organizational dashboard. It is physically impossible for the captain and the crew to watch every gauge during every moment of the flight. The same applies to executives at the helms of today's companies.

Spencer Ante of *Business Week* noted, "The dashboard is the CEO's killer app, making the gritty details of a business that are often buried deep within a large organization accessible at a glance to senior executives."[11] Ante also noted that dashboards are helping management become more of a science.

Executives need to identify the few factors that are essential to enhance current performance and future success. Executives then need to create an organizational dashboard that includes gauges for the factors that are the drivers of success. The dashboard needs to be calibrated so the gauges reflect the ongoing status of the drivers of success. The gauges must be displayed in a manner so executives can monitor them easily and frequently. Considerable thought goes into the design of aircraft dashboards; the same amount of thought should go into the configuration of the company's dashboard.

The dashboard must be configured so executives focus their attention regularly on a balanced set of gauges rather than just the ongoing financial metrics which tend to be located at the center of most organizational dashboards. The dashboard should include gauges that monitor the rate of new product development, the amount of time it takes to introduce new products, the overall cycle time, the on-time delivery ratio, and the customer retention index. Gauges that monitor employee satisfaction and organizational learning will also foster a more balanced perspective.

Verizon provides a good example of the role a dashboard can play in enhancing performance. Ivan Seidenberg, Verizon's CEO noted, "The dashboard puts me and more and more of our executives in real-time touch with the business. . . . The more eyes that see the results we're obtaining every day, the higher the quality of our decisions."[12] Seidenberg and other executives can choose from more than 300 metrics for their dashboards.[13]

If new product development is an important driver of success, then goals and strategies to enhance new product development will need to be developed. 3M's goal that "Thirty percent of sales four years from now should come from products that don't exist today" can serve as the basis for a new product development gauge that monitors the extent the company is making progress on an ongoing basis in meeting that goal. The gauges can monitor the rate of development and the introduction of new products. They can also monitor the revenue, profit and return on investment generated by new products.

Because human resources are considered drivers of success, goals and strategies need to be developed to ensure the company has the right number of people with the right capabilities in place. An Ohio-based company has a goal of always having at least one successor for every manager and other key employees. That company monitors the "key personnel with successors to key personnel" ratio to make sure the company has minimized the likelihood of having a management stockout.

If generating ideas for improvement and experimentation are considered drivers of success, then monitoring the number of employee suggestions may provide an indication of the level of employee involvement and learning. The average profit or savings per suggestion may also serve as a key indicator.

The organization's dashboard can play an integral role in fostering a shared perspective throughout the company. The dashboard enables people at all levels to read from the same set of gauges with the same set of metrics that are measured the same way. In too many companies there is little agreement on the metrics and/or how they are measured. Too often, the metrics are measured differently from one unit to the next. For example, employee productivity may be measured in terms of "labor cost per unit," while another organizational unit may measure employee productivity in terms of "sales per employee."

The Quality of the Company's Management Information System Is Critical

The company's performance management system can only be as good as the company's management information system. The company's balanced scorecard and corresponding dashboard will work only to the extent that executives have the right information, at the right time, and in the right format.

The company's management information system must be timely, selective, and efficient. It should measure the status of the company's drivers of success as well as ongoing performance. The information system should indicate milestones, trends, and variances. If the system is properly designed, it will function as an early warning system. It will also serve as the basis for correcting deficiencies and preventing problems.

If the system only monitors financial factors, then it may be dealing with results or lagging factors. Nonfinancial factors also need to be monitored. Management needs to decide whether market share should be measured and monitored more closely than customer satisfaction. Management must also decide whether it monitors the employee turnover rate or employee satisfaction more closely. The second factor in the preceding sets of factors is more causal than the first one. If the information system is not able to provide the right information, the company's scorecard and dashboard will be of little benefit.

Measurement frequency also plays a key role in the management information system. If the company is looking for continuous improvement, then the system needs to measure performance in those areas on a continuous basis. If continuous improvement depends on the "plan-do-check-act" cycle, then the "check" component needs to be continuous. Measurement frequency may vary with each factor being monitored.

Monitoring and Measuring Are Not the Ends

Performance management systems should be viewed as learning systems that constantly raise questions, test assumptions, probe for the real issues, analyze variances, and provide feedback. The balanced scorecard, organizational dashboard, and management information system should also foster insights, learning, and change. Conventional measurement systems are designed to answer questions like, "Are we meeting our targets?" "Are we on schedule?" and "Are we within our budget?" Performance management systems, however, place a lot more attention on learning, not just monitoring performance and modifying operations.

Most companies use "single-loop" learning. With single-loop learning, an adverse variation from expected interim results initiates actions until the variation is corrected. With double-loop learning, however, management deliberately steps back and analyzes the whole situation, including the objectives, strategies, plans, tactics, and timelines. Instead of the typical knee-jerk of "see a variance, fix the variance," that assumes the overall strategy is still the right path to take, management goes all the way back to ground zero and challenges the assumptions and objectives that served as the basis for developing the strategy being implemented.[14]

Double-loop learning encourages managers to reexamine their mental models and the corresponding cause-and-effect relationships. For example, if monthly sales for a product are falling below expectations, management should go beyond the usual single-loop learning response of increasing advertising or lowering its price. With double-loop learning, management steps back and reexamines the product's position in its life cycle and whether the resources invested in that product could be deployed more favorably in the development of a new product to serve an emerging market.

With double-loop learning, departures are seen as opportunities to learn, not just things to be fixed. If management really embraces the concept of double-loop learning, it will not wait for variances to raise the fundamental questions about whether the company is doing what it should be doing. If the company is truly a learning organization, then serious questioning of basic issues will take place on a regular basis. Learning organizations deal with strategic issues on a regular basis; they do not save them for annual planning retreats or major crises.

Cypress Semiconductor: Profile of Focus and Control

Having crucial information on a real-time basis permits real-time adjustments. State-of-the-art management information systems resemble the radar-interfaced flight control systems that enable jet fighters to fly closer to the ground at even faster speeds. Cypress Semiconductor, under the leadership of T. J. Rogers, embraced and operationalized a performance management system years ago that permits its top management to monitor what is happening throughout the entire organization.

Cypress Semiconductor has demonstrated a total commitment to identifying performance objectives and monitoring whether they are being accomplished. Cypress Semiconductor's comprehensive system sets and monitors over 6,000 performance factors on an ongoing basis.[15] Its system forces each manager to focus on the areas that make a difference. Cypress Semiconductor's system also provides an early warning system that activates quick response.

According to an article by Rogers in the *Harvard Business Review*, "The systems are designed to encourage collective thinking and to force each of us to face reality every day."[16] Rogers further noted, "At Cypress, our management systems track corporate, departmental, and individual performance so regularly and in such detail that no manager, including me, can plausibly claim to be in the dark about critical problems. . . . Our systems give managers the capacity to monitor what's happening at all levels of the organization, to anticipate problems or conflicts, to intervene when appropriate, and to identify the best practices—without creating layers of bureaucracy that bog down decisions and sap morale."[17]

Rogers noted, "All of Cypress's 1400 employees have goals, which is no different from employees at most other companies. What does make our people different is that every week they set their own goals, commit to achieving them by a specific date, enter them into the database, and report whether or not they completed prior goals."[18]

Cypress's computerized goal system is a detailed guide to the future and an objective record of the past. In any given week, some 6,000 goals in the database come due. Rogers noted that Cypress's ability to meet these goals ultimately determines its success or failure. Every month a Completed Goal Report is issued for every person in the company. At year end, managers have a dozen such objective reviews to refresh their memories and fight the proximity effect.[19]

Cypress Semiconductor's system does not focus exclusively on financial and operating factors. Its system incorporates the balanced scorecard's emphasis on human resource factors in addition to monitoring yields, costs, and cycle times for every manufacturing operation, and the average outgoing quality level for each of the company's leading product lines. Revenue and productivity per employee are also monitored on an ongoing basis because these metrics are critical to the company's competitiveness.[20]

Cypress Semiconductor's performance management system also fosters management by exception. T. J. Rogers indicated that collecting information, reviewing it regularly, and sharing it widely allows him to practice management by exception in the truest sense. He believes that if people use its systems, the organization will virtually run itself. Rogers intervenes only to solve problems and champion key projects.[21]

Management by exception gives Rogers the time to scan the horizon for blips on the radar screen and to focus on the things that really matter. He views his job to be *anticipating* problems. He does this by sorting through the goal system looking for patterns. He uses the system as a kind of organizational speedometer that not only tells him how fast the company is traveling, it also helps identify what is holding the company back.[22]

Cypress's system also enables Rogers to get a quick sense of reality. With a few keystrokes he can check on the performance of any one of his vice presidents. Rogers notes that his access to the details means vice presidents cannot snow him.[23] The company's performance management system is also tuned in to factors outside the company. Cypress's system constantly checks the company's performance against that of its best competitors.[24]

Concluding Comments: Proceed, but Proceed with Caution

If the performance management system is designed well, it will enhance performance, not just measure it. Like most things in business, it can become an organizational nightmare if it is not handled skillfully. Every effort should be made to keep the performance management system from being the fuel that lights the fires for bureaucrats or religiously measures the wrong things.

Effort should also be directed to making sure the performance management stays in tune with the times. For the performance management system to work well, it must be ever-evolving. Changing environments and business conditions frequently necessitate changes in business strategy. Such changes may change the drivers of success as well as their corresponding targets and metrics.

Your company's performance management system must identify what really matters. It must also make sure everyone knows how those factors affect performance. If properly designed and administered, it will also measure those factors on a frequent enough basis that deviations can be spotted early. This will give your company additional time to determine the cause for the deviation and the opportunity to take corrective action before it is too late or too costly. Take the Results-Oriented Performance Management System Quiz in Table 5.1 to learn the extent to which your firm is positioned to monitor and manage the drivers of success.

Change hurts. But indecision kills.[25]

—Avram Miller, CEO of the Avram Miller Company

TABLE 5.1. Establishing a Results-Oriented Performance Management System Quiz

How does your firm rate on the following dimensions?
*Scoring Level: 1 = not at all, 2 = rarely, 3 = occasionally,
4 = frequently, 5 = ongoing/extensive

		Level*
1.	To what extent does your firm practice bifocal management that integrates a long-term orientation and compelling vision with operational excellence?	1-2-3-4-5
2.	To what extent does your firm recognize that financial metrics are the results of nonfinancial (customer, internal processes, learning and growth) dimensions and drivers?	1-2-3-4-5
3.	To what extent does your firm have a balanced scorecard that incorporates nonfinancial (customer, internal processes, learning and growth) dimensions and drivers in addition to financial metrics?	1-2-3-4-5
4.	To what extent does your firm think long-term backward (focus on long-term objectives) and set intermediate milestones to guide and measure progress?	1-2-3-4-5
5.	To what extent do your firm's executives and managers use an electronic dashboard that can be monitored throughout the firm on a daily basis to monitor key performance areas?	1-2-3-4-5
6.	To what extent does your firm deliberately extend its mental time horizon to sense variances and possibly trends in key performance dimensions at the earliest possible time?	1-2-3-4-5
7.	To what extent does your firm operate with a *management by exception* system that includes various dimensions (in addition to the usual budgets) that sets parameters for various dimensions (customer retention, number and nature of customer complaints, delays and rework, employee attrition, etc.) that allows initial deviations to be identified early and then corrected?	1-2-3-4-5
8.	To what extent does your firm operate with a double-loop framework so deviations are not just fixed; they are analyzed to determine if that activity or process should even be done at all?	1-2-3-4-5
9.	To what extent is your firm's performance review and reward systems include nonfinancial (learning and growth, development of people, innovativeness, etc.) dimensions?	1-2-3-4-5

(continued)

TABLE 5.1.   (Continued)

How does your firm rate on the following dimensions? *Scoring Level: 1 = not at all, 2 = rarely, 3 = occasionally, 4 = frequently, 5 = ongoing/extensive	Level*
10. To what extent are people at all levels encouraged to, and able to, share their concerns (either candidly or anonymously) about assumptions, decisions, plans, practices, processes, and/or performance so problems can be prevented, surprises minimized, and bad news can be reported quickly?	1-2-3-4-5
Total points	

Scoring Key

45–50	Congratulations, your firm demonstrates most of the qualities of a results-oriented firm.
40–44	Your firm has many qualities of a results-oriented firm, but still has areas that can be improved.
35–39	Your firm has some strengths, but there is a lot of room for improvement.
30–34	Your firm has some significant impairments that impede its ability to improve its performance.
10–29	Your firm may be beyond hope. It will take a radical change in management, corporate culture, systems, and processes to have any chance of being competitive in the future.

Notes

1. Robert S. Kaplan and David P. Norton, "Having Trouble with Your Strategy?" *Harvard Business Review* 78, no. 5 (October, 2000): 167.

2. Robert S. Kaplan and David P. Norton, *The Balanced Scorecard* (Boston: Harvard Business School Press, 1996), 12.

3. Robert S. Kaplan and David P. Norton, "Using The Balanced Scorecard as a Strategic Measurement System," *Harvard Business Review* 74, no. 1 (1996): 75–76.

4. Kaplan and Norton, *The Balanced Scorecard*, 18.

5. Ibid., 7.

6. Joel Kurtzman, "Is Your Company off Course? Now You Can Find Out Why," *Fortune* 135, no. 3 (1997): 130.

7. Kaplan and Norton, *The Balanced Scorecard*, 14.

8. Ibid., 13.

9. Kaplan and Norton, "Using the Balanced Scorecard as a Strategic Measurement System," 81.

10. Ibid., 82.

11. Spencer E. Ante, "Giving the Boss the Big Picture," *Business Week*, no. 3971 (2006): 47.

12. Ibid., 48.

13. Ibid., 50.

14. Kaplan and Norton, *The Balanced Scorecard*, 16.

15. T. J. Rogers, "No Excuses Management," *Harvard Business Review* 68, no. 4 (1990): 84.

16. Ibid., 85.

17. Ibid., 84.

18. Ibid., 87.

19. Ibid., 89.

20. Ibid., 90.

21. Ibid., 86.

22. Ibid., 89.

23. Ibid., 90.

24. Ibid., 92.

25. Katharine Mieszkowski, "The Power of the Internet Is That You Can Experiment," *Fast Company*, no. 30 (1999): 162.

Chapter 6

Corpreneurship: Creating Your Company's Future by Maintaining the Entrepreneurial Edge

The best way to predict the future is to invent it.[1]

—Alan Kay, Founding Principal of Xerox's PARC and Apple Fellow

During the last two decades firms in almost every industry have developed a variety of strategies to improve their performance. Most firms have launched initiatives to reduce costs, provide better and more consistent quality, and so forth. Some firms have taken the "linear-incremental" approach where they just try to do more of what they have been doing. Some firms have taken the "related-extension" approach where they added a few products and services that are merely extensions of what they currently offer. Some firms have taken the "mergers and acquisitions" approach to broaden their product or service offering or to gain access to certain geographic markets. Some firms have expanded into foreign markets to gain additional customers.

It is becoming clear that "tweaking" and "acquiring" strategies rarely provide exceptional results. Tweaking strategies may seem like they minimize the firm's risk and R&D outlays, but they rarely provide firms with significant and sustainable competitive advantages. Tweaking strategies are particularly vulnerable to competitive breakthroughs that could make their products and services obsolete. Research shows that most acquisitions fail to live up to their expectations. Moreover, most acquisitions of small, emerging firms made by large firms are nothing more than acts of desperation by the larger firms to buy a future because they fell asleep at the wheel and did not create their own futures.

Gary Hamel and C. K. Prahalad note in their book, *Competing for the Future*, "A company surrenders tomorrow's businesses when it gets better without changing."[2] This chapter focuses on making entrepreneurial growth part of your firm's overall growth strategy. It profiles the numerous dimensions in which entrepreneurial initiatives can fit into your growth plan. It helps rekindle the entrepreneurial sparks that served as the basis for creating your venture. This chapter outlines guidelines for developing corporate entrepreneurship, or "corpreneurship" as it is termed in this book, in several core dimensions of your organization. "Corpreneurship" means creating an environment where entrepreneurial types of people in the company are encouraged, supported, and rewarded for their efforts to sense and seize market opportunities. Corpreneurship thereby represents a significant stage in the development and evolution of your firm.

More firms are recognizing that while conventional strategies may help them survive in the near term, conventional strategies may not be sufficient if they want to thrive in the long term. Corpreneurship captures the spirit of *Star Trek*. It encourages firms to go where they—and possibly other firms—have not gone before by introducing new products or services and/or entering different or new markets.

Too many firms take a *Field of Dreams*, "If you build it, they will come" approach to innovation. It is based on the premise that first you develop products and then you find people to buy them. Corpreneurship, however, starts with the marketplace. It starts by exploring the marketplace for situations where people's needs are not being met well enough or at all. It then uses innovation to exploit those opportunities.

Two points about corpreneurship should be made up front. First, it is not new. Numerous firms have embraced the ideas and techniques associated with corpreneurship. What is new is the extent that more and more firms are considering it as an integral strategy for fostering profitable growth. Second, corpreneurship is not the same as intrapreneurship. Gifford Pinchot III promoted the concepts of intrapreneuring and intrapreneurship in his book, *Intrapreneuring*, published in 1985. His book emphasized the need for executives to create an environment that supports innovation.

Pinchot's concepts are just as applicable today. The idea of being able to function as an entrepreneur in an established firm appeals to a lot of people. Firms that embrace corprenership provide the air cover, infrastructure, and resources to transform entrepreneurial ideas into profitable realities.

> Reality Check: A lot of people who want to be entrepreneurs are just dreamers. If they cannot bring their ideas to market, then nothing happens. There are plenty of people who go to their graves wishing they had followed through on their ideas. Firms should avoid the dreamers who do not have the ability to focus and the commitment to make things happen.

> Reality Check: A lot of people are fascinated by the idea of entrepreneurship or being entrepreneurial, but when they really understand what starting a venture involves and the possible risks—i.e., risks to their marriages, mortgages and MasterCard balances—they seek the shelter of an existing organization. Corprenership is not a sanctuary for people who are looking for a security blanket. There are no free lunches; there will be expectations and accountability for people who want to be intrapreneurs.

This chapter builds on Pinchot's ideas by emphasizing even more the need for firms to have an external orientation. Many of Pinchot's ideas promote unleashing the ability of people inside the firm to be innovative. This chapter, however, stresses the need to focus on market opportunities and then to develop and offer innovative products and services. Innovation plays a critical role in enhancing performance, but innovation is just a means to an end—the end being to create an exceptional enterprise by delighting customers.

> Reality Check: Innovation is of value only when it is targeted, approached in a systematic manner, and enhances profits.

Corpreneurship requires a commitment to explore the marketplace for emerging opportunities on a continuous basis. It involves probing what your current customers and noncustomers may need in the future, developing innovative products that make existing products (even your own) obsolete, exploring your market's fringe for customers who have problems that are begging for breakthrough solutions, and scanning the horizon for clues for markets and even industries that do not exist today.

This chapter focuses on ways firms can go beyond conventional approaches and make corpreneurship a central component of their business. Figure 6.1 shows the distinction between historical approaches to innovation and the next generation of corpreneurship. It profiles the differences between conventional growth strategies and corpreneurial growth strategies.

Corpreneurship may involve developing new products for your current target market, offering current products to different target markets, or doing both at once. Bolder levels of corpreneurship may involve developing breakthrough, first-generation products, and/or entering markets that are just materializing. Corpreneurship may be directed to serving unmet or even unarticulated needs for your firm's current customers and noncustomers. It may also involve focusing attention on future customers' needs as well as current customers' future needs. In short, corpreneurship involves developing new products or services and/or exploring new market space.

FIGURE 6.1. Conventional Growth Strategies and Corpreneurial Growth Strategies

Traditional Approach to Growth	Linear-incremental product strategy
	Expanding into related markets
	Mergers and acquisitions
	Expanding into foreign markets
Corpreneurial Approach to Growth	Developing innovative products and services
	Searching for un-met customer needs
	Exploring new target markets
	Redefining business models and strategy

Starbucks, Dyson, Apple, and Virgin have benefited from their efforts to offer innovative products and services and appeal to target markets that are different from their mainstream businesses. Starbucks found that its customers liked the music played in its stores so it developed a line of CDs. It even ventured into the movie business with *Akeelah and the Bee*. Starbucks also demonstrated its willingness to explore new possibilities by entering the ice cream and cold drink markets, providing a speed card, and forming alliances with the airlines and hotels. Starbucks' greatest achievement may be how it created a "third place" in people's lives. It created a place millions of people can *escape* from their home "place" and their work "place" each day for a few minutes and a few dollars. Howard Schultz got it right when he recognized that Starbucks should offer more than just an assortment of products and services—it should offer an "experience."

James Dyson looked at how conventional vacuum cleaners lost their efficacy because dust and other objects clogged the filters or bags. He developed the cyclone chamber that does not need bags or filters. Dyson then developed a wheel barrow that uses a sphere instead of the front wheel. More recently Dyson developed a revolutionary hand dryer that is much faster and more efficient than conventional hand dryers.

Apple demonstrated its willingness to explore new possibilities when it ventured into the music and communications businesses with its iPods and iPhones. Even though the management team at General Motors made numerous mistakes over an extended period of time, it did get one thing right when it encouraged the development of the OnStar system. General Motors demonstrated its willingness to explore new possibilities when it developed the OnStar system. General Motors recognized a growing number of people—especially older people—felt vulnerable in their cars. Cell phones and membership in AAA helped reduce people's vulnerability, but neither was able to provide a game-changing solution to the growing frustration for people who wanted a very user-friendly solution. OnStar demonstrated that many people are willing to pay a premium for a solution.

Virgin may be the best example of corpreneurship. What started out as a sheet music business has become a virtual cornucopia of businesses, including transportation, communication and numerous retail businesses. The Virgin Group includes over 300 businesses. Founder Richard Branson's never-ending quest for starting new ventures is evidenced by his keeping a book that lists problems to be solved or ideas in search of customers. Branson has noted that he is not driven by the potential for profits. He has stated that when he sees an industry that is not providing the products and services consumers deserve, he is driven to find a better way. It is his contempt for complacency that drives him.

Starbucks, Dyson, Apple, and Virgin demonstrate that established firms—if they embrace corpreneurship—may have advantages over startups. Established firms have brand identity, distribution networks, considerable talent, and sophisticated systems that can handle large-scale operations, as well as access to capital. The key is whether established firms can leverage their talent, systems, and resources in a "corpreneurial" manner.

Corpreneurship: The Confluence of Emerging Opportunities and Entrepreneurial Prowess

Entrepreneurship is typically thought of as an effort to establish a new enterprise. It requires foresight, creativity, drive and a willingness to take risks. With corpreneurship, the company operates like an entrepreneur by scanning the environment for lucrative and lasting opportunities. Corpreneurial firms also place a premium on innovation by streamlining internal processes to foster experimentation and the rapid transformation of ideas into actions. The combination of anticipating opportunities and being prepared to act on them quickly as they emerge is the heart of the corpreneurship model depicted in Figure 6.2.

Corpreneurship should continue to have appeal because the entrepreneurial revolution shows no signs of coming to an end. There has never been a time with greater challenges and opportunities in the world. People and organizations are seeking solutions to their problems. Consumers want products and services that make their lives better. Businesses want products and services that make their firms more competitive and profitable. The challenges and opportunities will increase even more in the future. Firms that develop corpreneurial capabilities have the potential to experience dramatic and profitable growth by sensing and seizing the right opportunities.

FIGURE 6.2. Corpreneurship Begins with a Market Orientation

	Step one: *Exploration*	
The Corporation ⟶	Step two: *Opportunities*	
	Step three: *Innovative solutions* ⟶	The Marketplace

Innovative products like iPods, iPhones, iPads, and OnStar have the distinction of being in the "I can't imagine what my life would be like without it" category of products and services. This happens when firms focus on what customers value and provide them with things that improve their lives.

Corpreneurship involves *taking* the road less traveled—or even *making* a road to be traveled. It involves operating at the edge. Success is defined as what happens when preparation meets opportunity. Corpreneurship incorporates anticipatory marketing. Anticipatory marketing is exemplified in how Wayne Gretzky played hockey. Chapter three profiled how Gretzky anticipated where the puck would be. Gretzky's success was tied to his ability to sense and seize emerging opportunities. Gretzky's approach illustrates how being the first mover can be advantageous when a window of opportunity is about to open.

Corpreneurship Must Be Viewed Holistically

Corpreneurship is multifaceted, and developing it requires taking deliberate steps in several major areas of the firm. The keys to developing corpreneurship are profiled in Figure 6.3.

Managers also need to recognize that a piecemeal approach to corpreneurship, such as attempting to change the firm's culture to be more corpreneurial but not its structure, is likely to fail. The benefit of becoming more corpreneurial in multiple dimensions, as illustrated in Figure 6.3, is that these changes will be mutually reinforcing. Corpreneurial firms thrive by approaching strategy, structure, culture, people, and transformational processes as well as the external environment as an integrated system. More corpreneurship in any single dimension will facilitate

FIGURE 6.3.   Corpreneurship Dimensions

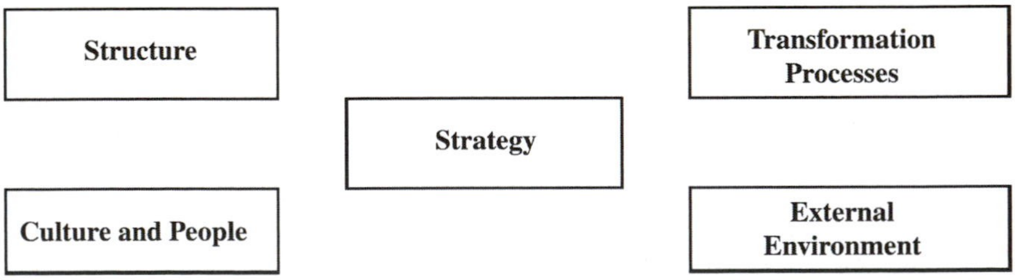

conditions for corpreneurship in the others, but resistance in any dimension may hinder corpreneurship throughout the firm.

Some firms embrace corprenerurship as their primary strategy. Some firms consider it a very small part of their overall strategy. Some firms may not even consider corpreneurship because it is not part of their DNA. They are so focused on fine-tuning what they are currently doing and are so risk averse that they are unable or unwilling to leave their comfort zones.

Corpreneurship should not be seen as the great panacea for every firm's problems or as the only way to grow. Instead, it should be seen as part of the firm's overall strategy. Numerous factors must be considered in determining the extent to which corpreneurship should be part of the firm's strategy. These factors are profiled in the next sections.

Formulating Corpreneurial Strategy

The core of a firm's competitiveness is its strategy. Too many firms have the strategy, "If you build a better mousetrap, then the world will beat a path to your door." This approach bets the firm's future on its R&D efforts. Corpreneurship, however, starts with a strategy for competing in the marketplace by sensing and seizing opportunities. To formulate a corpreneurial strategy, you should:

- **Craft a challenging and compelling vision.** Crafting a specific, compelling, and relevant vision can have considerable motivational value. People at all levels of the organization want to know specifically what the firm is striving to achieve, why it is important, and how fulfilling the vision contributes to their well-being. The last point—relevancy—rarely gets sufficient attention. Leaders need to create an environment where each person has a direct line of sight for how she can contribute to fulfilling the vision and how she will personally benefit from doing so.
- **Make sure you are in the right forest.** Chapter four profiled how executives need to make sure the firm is in the right markets. If your firm is in the wrong markets, offering products that do not meet customer expectations, and/or focusing on improving the wrong processes, then it is on a path to bankruptcy.
- **Determine the "corpreneurship gap."** The strategic planning gap profiled in chapter four that was developed by Peter Drucker encourages managers to ask the following three questions: (1) Where do we want the firm to be in "x" years? (2) Where are we now? and, (3) Where will we be in "x" years if we do not change what we are doing? Drucker noted that the difference

between the answers to the first and third questions is the "strategic planning gap." The greater the gap, the greater the need for, and magnitude of, change. The issue at this point is whether making modifications to the current product/service offering will be sufficient to bridge the gap. If not, then corpreneurial growth initiatives may need to be considered to bridge the gap. By determining how much of the strategic planning gap needs to be filled via corpreneurial efforts (the corpreneurial gap) the firm will know how great a role corpreneurial efforts will need to play in its strategy.

- **Set corpreneurial goals.** Consider establishing an innovation goal such as "Twenty percent of sales three years from now must come from products or services that your firm does not offer today." The goal can be raised in the future as your firm develops more corpreneurial experience and success. Setting a goal of having at least one new product ready to launch within nine months is an ambitious but reasonable way to get the corpreneurial processes going.

Designing a Corpreneurial Structure

The famous architect Frank Lloyd Wright popularized the principle "form follows function." An organization's form, or its structure, follows from, and must be compatible with, its function or its strategy. A corpreneurial structure requires, in part, that you:

- **Foster a collaborative atmosphere.** Your firm's structure should foster internal collaboration through teams of people charged with sensing and seizing opportunities. Taking a "skunkworks" approach that allows these teams to operate independent of your firm's normal rules and regulations can be very beneficial. 3M, Google, and numerous other innovative firms provide spaces where people from various organizational units can work together, either in person or electronically.
- **Support and reward corpreneurial efforts and successes.** The saying, "You only get what you encourage, review, and reward" applies to corpreneurial efforts. Encouraging it is nice, but if firms really want to implement corpreneurial strategies and processes, then they need to support them with sufficient resources and consider making them part of the reward system. Some firms provide cash prizes for ideas that make it all the way to launch. Some firms even offer a royalty based on new product or service sales. 3M has provided the opportunity for a few of the people who came up with great ideas to head the division or subsidiary that was formed to commercialize their ideas.
- **Develop a different managerial mindset.** Corpreneurship involves having a different managerial mindset and organizational systems. Corpreneurial

efforts cannot be managed with a tight grip. There is an art and a science to corpreneurial initiatives. They involve more openness and finesse—especially in their initial stages—than regular ongoing efforts. Corpreneurship involves planting a lot of seeds and recognizing that most of them will not be fruitful. It involves patience because it takes longer to develop and launch a new idea than it does to tweak an existing product in an existing market.

- **Use different metrics.** Corpreneurship involves using different metrics. Developing and launching new initiatives involves considerable uncertainty. Standard costing techniques, having fine-tuned schedules, and developing detailed plans do not apply as well to corpreneurial efforts. Corpreneurial efforts need to have goals, timelines, and budgets, but they have to be far more flexible than conventional efforts that do not involve exploring new territories and developing new products and services.

Developing Corpreneurial People and a Corpreneurial Culture

The adage "Our people are our most valuable resource" is particularly true in corpreneurial firms. Corpreneurship involves motivating employees to explore ways of thinking differently. Developing a corpreneurial culture, however, is not simply a matter of stating, "We are now a corpreneurial firm." It involves building consensus around corpreneurial values and uncovering assumptions in the firm's existing culture that do not support corpreneurship. To help achieve this, firms should:

- **Champion corpreneurship.** Every leader casts a shadow. Leaders who want to foster corpreneurship need to create a sense of urgency for corpreneurial efforts. People are more likely to embrace and pursue corpreneurial activities if they feel they are on a burning platform. When people realize there is no future if they just continue what they are currently doing, then they will demonstrate a sense of urgency and bias for action that will expedite corpreneurial efforts. Most organizations have processes that keep people from exploring corpreneurial opportunities. Leaders need to remove bureaucratic barriers that inhibit thinking and acting "outside the conventional growth box."
- **Set people free and encourage them to think corpreneurially.** People at every level and in every area should be encouraged individually and in groups to identify potential opportunities. 3M encourages its people to spend at least 15 to 20 percent of their time and possibly budgets (a process called bootlegging) on projects that are not part of their regular work. Google has a similar policy but limits it to its R&D people and employees

in a few other areas. Google encourages its people to explore ideas that may be outside current product/service/markets. Some of Virgin's businesses—including Virgin Bride—started when employees contacted Richard Branson about gaps in the market that represented potential business opportunities.

- **Create a culture that fosters corpreneurship.** Corpreneurship involves exploring and experimenting. Some experiments will not be successes. Some paths will lead to a dead end. People must be free to look for new possibilities and to develop new solutions. Failures are not encouraged, but they need to be expected. The key is to learn how to increase your batting average from each experience. People must be willing to leave their comfort zones. Like entrepreneurs, people in the firm must have contempt for maintaining the status quo.

- **Create a corpreneurial virus.** Leaders should focus their attention on developing the corpreneurial mindset throughout the firm so others can become champions and project leaders. The more people gain corpreneurial skills and experience, the greater the multiplier effect and the sooner leaders can pass the corpreneurial baton to them. You should develop your employees' confidence to the point where they want to lead corpreneurial efforts and are no longer dependent on you to lead them.

- **Develop a corpreneurial team.** Leaders must recognize that all products, processes, patents, and profits come from people. You want leaders to have a team of people who sense and seize opportunities. Look for people who are open-minded, market-oriented and have considerable mental dexterity when you select people to be part of a corpreneurial team. You may need to bring in a few people from outside your firm who can provide a fresh perspective in looking at the marketplace. While top leaders should be actively involved in fostering corpreneurial initiatives, they also need to delegate more key decisions to the team as it gains momentum.

- **Recognize corpreneurship takes time.** Adopting the corpreneurial approach to growing your business cannot be done by just flipping a switch. It may be best to start by taking baby steps. Corpreneurial skills need to be developed, and systems that support corpreneurship need to be established. Small projects should be pursued before larger, higher-risk projects are undertaken. A few early victories will also help develop momentum.

- **Expect resistance.** Some people will exhibit overt and/or covert resistance to corpreneurial efforts that markedly change what the firm has been doing. They may have serious reservations about the time, attention, and resources that are being committed to new initiatives. It is easy for the people who have helped get the firm to where it is to be concerned that what they are doing is no longer at the center of attention. They may challenge corpreneurial efforts with a "Why mess with success?" attitude. A few early victories will help silence the people who are skeptical about the value of corpreneurship.

- **Recognize that some people get it; others do not.** Some people like living at the edge. They like exploring and innovating. Other people are more incremental. They are improvers. Leaders need to make sure corpreneurial people are given corpreneurial opportunities and incremental people are brought in to fine-tune corpreneurial activities. Too often the best and brightest are assigned to try to save product/service areas where the situation is deteriorating. Corpreneurial people need to have challenges to keep their entrepreneurial juices flowing. Every effort needs to be made to avoid losing them. If they leave they may go out and start their own ventures—and possibly become your competitors.

Guidelines for Fostering Corpreneurship

Every organization includes a core set of processes for transforming inputs into outputs. Corpreneurial firms, however, also develop processes that generate innovative ideas and transform them into actions. Corpreneurial processes add value by fostering growth and enhancing profits.

- **Establish processes that expedite the deliberate consideration of ideas.** It does not take much to kill ideas before they have a chance to grow. One of 3M's guiding principles is, "Thou shalt not kill an idea before its time." Creating an environment that encourages people to think in a corpreneurial way is important, but processes need to be put in place to move their ideas forward. Rumor has it that 3M has a policy that two or three phrases scribbled on the back of a cocktail napkin will be considered. The processes for evaluating ideas should be known, easy, fast, and able to provide feedback. Attention also needs to be directed on a continuous basis to keep corpreneurial processes from becoming bureaucratic. Leaders need to make sure that the idea suggestion system does not become a black hole where things that enter it are never seen again. Establishing an "idea review committee" is one way of addressing this issue.
- **Use the stage-gate framework to screen ideas.** Robert Cooper developed the stage-gate process for evaluating new product ideas.[3] Each stage has criteria that determine which ideas continue to get attention, which ideas are put on hold, which ideas are recycled back to the beginning for a new review, and which ideas are killed. This system helps reduce the risks associated with developing new products. It also keeps the firm from investing significant resources until a product concept has demonstrated sufficient merit.

- **Set aside new venture funds to provide critical seed money.** As people develop a more corpreneurial mindset, your firm may consider establishing an "ideas to explore fund" to invest in submitted ideas that warrant further consideration. The fund would provide seed money for individuals or groups that have identified a gap in the market, a way to apply technology in an innovative manner, a new technology, or a new product, service, or process idea. As your firm develops even more momentum, you may consider establishing an internal venture fund to provide a second round of support for ideas that demonstrate considerable financial merit. Funding at this stage would be more substantial and may allow one or more people to work on the idea on a full-time basis. It may also provide sufficient funds for the development of a prototype and market tests.
- **New venture incubators.** Some firms have established new venture incubators to help transform new business concepts into new ventures. New venture incubators have designated space—possibly in a separate facility—so one or more projects can move forward with minimal distraction from regular operations. When Steve Jobs saw the potential for the Mac computer as a radical departure from Apple's existing line of personal computers, he put the Mac team in a separate building so they could work freely on their innovative computer system. The Mac team reveled in their freedom and raised the skull and crossbones on their building's flag pole to symbolize their maverick culture. The Mac team was so excited about the Mac that their signatures were engraved on the inside of every Mac unit.

Reality Check: Even if you choose not to create a facility for a new venture incubator, you should create an incubator-without-walls environment and culture in your firm so every person is free to explore corpreneurial opportunities, get financial and infrastructure support, and be recognized for their efforts, even if their ideas do not make it to market.

Leveraging Resources in the External Environment

Corpreneurial firms recognize and take advantage of the many resources in the broadening landscape. They avoid the trap of relying exclusively on either internal or external resources and/or practices, such as having a policy of unconditional promotion from within or the wholesale outsourcing of activities. Instead, they search for the best ways to meet emerging opportunities.

- **Encourage out-of-company/out-of-industry cross-pollination.** People in and outside the firm can be a source of ideas. People throughout the firm should be encouraged to read magazines and journals, attend trade shows, and interact with people in other industries to learn more about trends and gaps in the marketplace that may represent corpreneurial opportunities. Every person in the firm should be encouraged to ask people they meet (not just customers) about areas where their needs are not being met well or at all. Blogs and social networks may be an excellent sources of ideas. Every person has the potential to be a customer problem identifier and/or solver.

- **Not-invented-here can be an effective strategy.** Most firms have an "It if was not developed in our R&D lab, we will not consider it" mentality that inhibits the free flow and consideration of ideas. They believe that any idea that does not come from their R&D labs or their marketing people should not be considered. Yet, open-minded and proactive firms consider there to be an open market for ideas in their firms. They welcome and even solicit ideas from people inside and outside their organizations. Some firms have used a technique called crowdsourcing. They sponsor contests where people outside the firm compete in offering innovative ideas or solutions to problems.

- **Foster external collaboration.** Some firms put together special groups that are composed of people with certain backgrounds to identify problems and/or brainstorm ideas that have the potential to be solutions. If people from outside the firm are involved in the firm's corpreneurial processes, then caution needs to be used with intellectual property and competitive issues.

- **Realize that partnering can foster symbiotic benefits.** Consider partnering or doing a joint venture with another firm that has similar interests. There may be considerable synergy when you leverage and/or combine competencies, talent, and resources.

- **Consider acquiring another firm to be a catalyst to corpreneurial efforts.** You may consider buying other firms that have innovative products, technology, and/or processes to speed corpreneurship and to avoid spending time and resources reinventing the wheel. Bill Gates noted that he sometimes bought companies just to get the company's talent. He indicated that, in some cases, it cost less to buy the company than to try to hire the people. You may not be Microsoft, but there may be merit in acquiring a small firm if its people can cross-pollinate your firm with innovative ideas and accelerate your efforts to provide innovative products and to enter new markets.

- **Do not ignore your current customers.** It is easy for firms to get so caught up in improving their products that they take their eyes off their current customers' true needs. Firms need to make sure their marketing offerings are synchronized with what their customers really want. It is also easy for firms to get so caught up in meeting their future customers' needs that they ignore their current customers. Revenue from current customers usually plays an essential role in funding the development of solutions for future customers, and cannot be forgotten.

Corpreneurship Can Take Your Firm to the Next Level and Beyond

Firms that merely make minor changes in the present are destined to fail in periods of rapid change. Doing more of the same with more sales-people, more advertising, and price discounts will not cut it. Firms that are fixated on cost cutting and fine-tuning operations will miss out on the numerous opportunities that lie ahead. The traditional linear-incremental approach to doing business will not provide high-growth, high-profit opportunities. The marketplace is changing too rapidly for firms to operate from a reactive stance by responding only to today's needs and relying on today's technology. The firms that will thrive in the years ahead will be the ones that develop and offer innovative solutions to pressing problems.

Firms that can incorporate the various corpreneurship dimensions will be in a better position to create their futures. The following guidelines help foster corpreneurship:

- **Look for "growth platform" opportunities.** If you want to foster significant growth, then consider directing your attention to developing one or more growth "platforms" rather than individual growth products. A growth platform can be seen as a launch pad for numerous related products. Apple's iPod, iPhone, and iPad represent new growth platforms. Each product represents the foundation for a whole family of related products. Each product also represents a new growth platform for smaller firms that develop numerous products for the various iPod, iPhone, and iPad models. For them Apple's "i" products are like the abdomens of a spider—except in this case, each abdomen may be able to support far more than eight legs.
- **Scan the environment for "Blue Oceans" where you can create new market space.** W. Chan Kim and Reneé Mauborgne, the authors of *Blue Ocean Strategy*, provide a fascinating way of looking for untapped market opportunities. They characterize markets as being either *red oceans* or *blue oceans*. They note that most firms are in red oceans because most markets are mature, and the firms in them are competing for market

share. The competition for a limited number of customers makes the market red (figuratively) from the bloody zero-sum struggle where intense price competition hurts firms.[4]

Kim and Mauborgne encourage firms to look for "blue ocean" opportunities. Instead of modifying an existing business model, a blue ocean strategy usually involves the creation of a business model that provides "value innovation"—a new alternative or experience for customers. This strategy is designed to provide a leap in value. In short, blue ocean strategy tries to create new and uncontested space either by creating a new industry or expanding industry boundaries.

A blue ocean strategy incorporates the irreverence associated with most entrepreneurial endeavors. It looks for what current firms in the industry take for granted. It looks for industries where firms are arrogant and complacent. It looks at every factor in the industry and challenges conventional wisdom and every assumption. It then looks for ways to provide a brand-new experience and ways to make possible what consumers and competitors consider impossible. It encourages each firm to compete against itself in serving the market, rather than competing against other firms. In short, it encourages firms to develop strategies that make competition irrelevant.

Southwest Airlines, Dell Computer, eBay, Yellow Tail wine, NetJets, and Cirque du Soleil created new business models that opened up all new possibilities and left established firms in their dust. Southwest Airlines brought the price down to the point where everyday people who had to take the bus or drive could fly from one major Texas city to another. Southwest Airlines did for flying what Henry Ford did for the automobile when he developed the Model T. He was able to drive the cost of car ownership down via the assembly line to the point that regular people could afford an automobile. By instituting no frills, no first class, and no reserved seats in advance, as well as simplifying operations by using only Boeing 737's, Southwest made it possible for people who would not have flown to fly. By deleting meals, they were also able to lower their costs and speed the turnaround of planes at airports.

Dell computer's Dell Direct allowed people to customize their computers and have lower prices because the middleman was eliminated from the business model. eBay provided an entirely different way for people to buy and sell products all over the world. Yellow Tail wine provided a user-friendly way to convert beer drinkers and other people into wine drinkers. Yellow Tail illustrated that a whole new space can be created even in a mature industry by providing value to people who were not consumers. NetJets changed the conventional business of having people or firms either purchase a jet or charter a jet. NetJets provides the opportunity to purchase a fractional ownership of a jet. NetJets now has the United States' largest private fleet of jets. Cirque de Soleil captured a lot of the excitement of the circus and refinement of Broadway to provide a unique form of entertainment.

Each of these examples represents the creation or recognition of a potential blue ocean. These firms created a whole new market space that brought customers into the marketplace who were not there before instead of competing for customers via price competition and modest product differentiation. Each firm used a value innovation strategy that provided a quality experience at an affordable price. Even Cirque du Soleil—with its tickets selling for over a hundred dollars—is considered a value to consumers. Cirque du Soleil has developed over a dozen themed shows that are offered at various venues to keep up with the demand for its extraordinary offering.

Each of the examples also shows that blue oceans are not limited to small boutique, niche markets. They can be large oceans if you can drive your costs down while maintaining high quality. Each firm stood out because it also focused on driving its costs down via economies of scale, diligent management, and effective execution. The firms also benefited from word-of-mouth advertising from customers by the value innovation. When you "wow" customers by providing value they have not experienced before, then you do not need to spend as much on advertising as firms operating in red oceans. Firms operating in blue oceans also tend to pass the cost savings on to customers because their costs are lower. This, in turn, makes their prices even more appealing for even more potential customers. The additional demand produced by turning noncustomers into customers (expanding the overall market) provides more economies of scale which allow for even lower prices.

Blue ocean strategy is very customer-centric. Most firms have been seduced into believing that adding all sorts of whistles and bells will differentiate their products and allow them to charge higher prices. Blue ocean strategy, however, focuses on what customers really value and are willing to pay for. It differentiates benefits from features. In the consumers' eyes, benefits add value to the purchase and consumption experience. Features do not add value; they simply add to the price.

Blue ocean strategy uses an "eliminate, reduce, raise, and/or create" grid to determine what customers value and are willing to pay for. Firms using blue ocean strategy recognize that more is better only if the customer values the "more." Firms using blue ocean strategy may actually enhance value by eliminating and reducing features. Firms using blue ocean strategy increase or even create the dimensions that will provide value. This is part of value innovation that separates blue ocean strategy from red ocean strategy.

Reality Check: Do not confuse high growth or even high tech with high profit. Almost all of the firms that have capitalized on blue ocean and other opportunities have done so without using breakthrough technology. Amazon, eBay, and numerous other less-well known companies capitalized on various opportunities by using existing technology in innovative, customer-centric ways.

Reality Check: It would be very easy to say, "Well, those blue ocean examples are very interesting, but they do not exist in my industry." Step back and ask, "What do consumers consider to be impossible?" and "What would it take to change nonconsumers into consumers?" You may think that these areas may not represent opportunities, but most of the firms that positioned themselves to explore blue ocean opportunities totally underestimated the tsunami of interest. 3M had no idea about the phenomenal success Post-its would have. GM had no idea that it would also offer OnStar to competitors. The creators of YouTube had no idea that they would sell their firm to Google for over $1.6 billion. They thought that maybe a few people might load their videos on their Web site. Who would have thought that microwave ovens would be used to prepare more meals than conventional ovens? Who would have thought that millions of preteens would have their own cell phones?

Formulating a Corpreneurial Strategy

It is easy to get caught up in your company's existing markets, products, services, and territories. It is also easy for you to get caught up in trying to maintain your customers and market share if you are in a highly competitive market. These two preoccupations limit a firm's ability to explore the marketplace for emerging and untapped opportunities.

The core of a firm's competitiveness is its strategy. Most firms rely on their R&D labs to come up with new product ideas. Yet most R&D labs have an internal orientation that bets the firm's future on a "product push" strategy where R&D operates with the attitude, "Let's make this product and hope that the sales team can sell it."

Corpreneurship, however, starts with a "demand pull" strategy where the firm explores the marketplace for needs that are not being met well enough or at all. Corpreneurship is rooted in Peter Drucker's belief that within every problem lies at least one disguised business opportunity. It starts, in most cases, with customers searching for a solution rather than the firm developing products in search of customers.

Companies that embrace corpreneurship recognize that opportunities exist in many areas. Three particular situations may provide lucrative opportunities. First, *frustrating* situations cause people to exclaim, "There must be a better way!" Second, where there is *pain*, people are motivated to reduce the pain. Third, every time *government regulations change*, people have to change in order to comply with the new regulations. All three situations prompt people to search for businesses that solve their problems.

The most successful firms recognize that customers tend to be the best source of ideas. Many of their problems (articulated and unarticulated as well as current and future) may have the potential to provide lucrative and lasting opportunities. If you want to go the corpreneurial route, then you should focus your attention on identifying problems and developing solutions that may provide appealing risk-return ratios.

Chapter four profiled how Gary Hamel and C. K. Prahalad—two of the best minds on corporate strategy—made the distinction between articulated and unarticulated needs. While most firms focus on what customers say they want, they stressed the need for firms to probe deeply to discover people's unarticulated needs. They noted that if you ask consumers what they want or need, they will provide rather obvious improvements—features like additional colors, different sizes, lower costs, and so forth. Hamel and Prahalad stressed that what you really want to find out is what people need but cannot articulate.

This reasoning goes back to Henry Ford's observation about what people would say at the beginning of the twentieth century. He noted that if you asked people who rode horses in the early 1900s what they wanted, they'd probably say, "A faster horse that doesn't require as much maintenance." How many of the people who rode horses would have responded,

"An automobile"? How many people would have responded with the desire to not have a horse at all? That was an unarticulated need.

Clayton Christensen, in his book *The Innovator's Dilemma*, profiles the advantages that disruptive innovation provides. He discusses three particularly interesting ways of looking at the marketplace. First, too many firms add too many features to products. These features increase the price, add to the product's complexity, and increase the likelihood that the item will break. Second, if you offer the most basic product without all the whistles and bells, then the major players in the market are not likely to consider your firm to be a threat. Third, the key is to find ways of transforming nonconsumers into consumers.

Nintendo's Wii may be the best example of how a group of people who are not consuming a product can be transformed into consumers. If your firm can find out what is holding them back and offer them what they really want, then they may become consumers. Christenson noted that Nintendo realized that it would be in a head-on battle if it tried to take on Sony and Microsoft's gaming consoles. Their systems were extremely sophisticated and appealed to serious gamers who had very high and ever-increasing expectations. Many of them also had high brand loyalty. Nintendo probed what kept nonconsumers from buying gaming consoles altogether. Nintendo found that the complexity of the games and their corresponding consoles—particularly the handsets—were overwhelming, especially to older people and young kids. Nintendo developed the Wii so people could enjoy playing games right away and eliminated the need for considerable manual dexterity to manipulate the handsets.

Reality Check: The best way to find out if people really want something is to ask them, "If we could develop a product that could . . . would you pay for it right now?" If they respond, "Wow, if you can do that, then here is my money," that is a sign that your product may have the potential to delight them and to pass what is called the "dog food test."

Reality Check: Most focus groups and interviews do not provide a good indication of a customer's *intent* to buy. The more that you can put them in a situation that approximates the actual buying situation, then the better you can predict the actual level of consumer interest. If you want to know if dogs will eat the dog food, do not ask them, let them see, smell, and taste it.

Reality Check: If you really want to know how people behave and what they want, observe them in their actual settings. What people say and what they do are often not the same things. Some firms make an effort to see consumer behavior first hand. A hospital supply firm actually has its people in the surgical theater so they can hear doctors and nurses complain about medical equipment and procedures. That firm has found that consumers may be the best source for new product ideas.

Reality Check: We need to balance the emphasis on having R&D come up with new ideas with the need to get ideas from consumers. Corpreneurship is not about shutting down R&D. We need R&D to focus on what may be over the horizon and to explore breakthrough technology that has the potential to provide game-changing products and services. But for the intermediate term, we should spend just as much time sensing and probing the marketplace for what people really want, as well as emerging opportunities.

The moral to the story is to get to know your target market better than they know themselves and then develop products and services that will delight them. You need to be able to distinguish between what customers: (1) feel they must have, (2) consider *nice to have*, (3) view as *no big deal*, and (4) *do not want at all*. In short, what you offer must pass the "dog food test." You have to offer your target market products and services that customers want to tear the box open to get, rather than ones you have to bribe them to eat. In short, firms like Dell Computer get it and base their strategy on the old Burger King ad, "Have it your way." Dell Computer began by doing what the major computer firms did not do—it offered customized computers at a fraction of the cost of traditional PCs.

Reality Check: You need to be constantly vigilant that you do not fall prey to the "Have it 'our' way" mentality where you believe you know what is best for your target market. Such arrogance may be fatal.

Reality Check: There is a big difference between features and benefits. Beware of the engineers who like to add various whistles and bells to make the product even better. Customers want benefits and to pay only for things that they value.

Reality Check: When you offer what people want, you will rarely have to lower your prices or provide rebates to attract customers. Years ago Volvo ran an ad when most car companies—particularly American car companies—were trying to generate sales by offering significant price rebates and financing terms with low or almost zero interest rates. To paraphrase the Volvo ad, "When you offer what people want, you don't have to pay them to buy your product." If you are having to drop your prices, then ask yourself, "Have we confused features and benefits?" and "Are we truly offering what they want to buy?"

Every strategy involves certain conditions. Three particular conditions must exist when you develop your strategy:

1. A market must exist where people want to buy your products and services.
2. Your firm must have the ability to provide the products and services.
3. You must be able to do so for a sufficient profit to justify the risk and the investment.

All strategies involve risks and returns. Your strategy should provide the best risk-return ratio. You would think that the linear-incremental strategy of making minor modifications to your current product/service offering would involve little risk because it requires limited change. Ironically, it may have considerable risk. If the market changes dramatically or a competitor comes up with a game changing product or service, then you may be out of business. Peter Drucker noted that if you stay in one business long enough, then you will go out of business.

The related-extension strategy of broadening your product and/or service into closely related products and services has similar risks. In both cases, the short-term risks may be modest, but the returns may also be modest. The growth by acquisition strategy has merit in some cases if it is handled well, but in many instances it produces culture clashes that inhibit synergy. Also, if the acquired firm's products or services are vulnerable to competitive threats or consumer shifts, then you may not have improved your risk-return ratio.

Firms that can incorporate the corpreneurship strategy will be in a better position to create their futures. The following guidelines help firms adopt a corpreneurial strategy:

- **Corpreneurship begins with searching for opportunities "in all the right places."** Every new venture has its own story for why it was created. Some ventures were started because the entrepreneur saw an opportunity at the firm where he/she worked that the firm was not willing to pursue. The person may have been told, "We are not in that business," or the firm may have been so caught up in what it was doing that it did not have the time, talent, or resources to pursue that opportunity. Some firms were started by people who bumped into a situation in their personal lives when they or someone they knew exclaimed in frustration, "There has to be a better way to . . ." Both of these situations demonstrate what is known as the proximity effect. The vast majority of firms started today are the result of entrepreneurs encountering a gap in the market at work or in their personal lives.

- **Assign "A" people to "A" opportunities.** Identifying "A" opportunities and developing an "A" team to capitalize on them will increase the odds for success. Entrepreneurial efforts are often described as a horse race where both the horse and the jockey are important. Some people say that the horse (opportunity being pursued) is more important than the entrepreneur (jockey) because they have never seen a jockey carry the horse across the finish line. Other people say the jockey is more important because the horse needs to be guided, and that the best jockeys can sense which horses have the potential to win. The corpreneurial leader's job is to make sure the firm has an "A" team and is pursuing "A" opportunities.

- **Distinguish between "innovators" and "improvers."** There are two types of people. Some like living at the edge—exploring and innovating. Others are more incremental; they are improvers, not explorers. Assign explorers and innovators to high-potential opportunities. You need to provide your really innovative people with projects that challenge them and get their entrepreneurial juices flowing. Do not lose them; they are rare. Assign the improvers to projects that will benefit from incremental improvements. In some instances, improvers may transition into explorers with additional training, encouragement, and mentoring.

- **Do not fixate on your products.** It is easy for firms to get so caught up in improving their products that they take their eyes off their customers' true needs. Firms need to make sure they are in sync with what their customers really want. Focus your attention on developing capabilities to solve customer problems. When you focus on products, you may take your eyes off what the customer values.

- **Leaders must reduce/eliminate barriers.** Every firm has barriers that keep people from exploring entrepreneurial opportunities. Leaders need to make sure people in the firm do not create bureaucratic barriers that inhibit thinking and acting "outside the conventional growth box."

- **Corpreneurial efforts need resources.** You need to make sure the various initiatives have the necessary resources and infrastructure.
- **Do not start your corpreneurial efforts from scratch.** Leverage your talent, resources, and competencies as much as possible. As you develop momentum and move up the learning curve, you can expand your boundaries and explore new areas. For example, capitalize on your brand identity. Richard Branson is a master at leveraging Virgin's brand and notoriety when launching new business ventures.
- **Bury the dead.** Some products should be allowed to die when the market no longer values them. Too often creative people are assigned to postpone product death. Instead, their time should be invested in creating the future rather than trying to revive something that should be phased out or sold to a reactive firm that is trying to buy a future rather than creating it. Jon Vincent of JTV Business and Management Services noted, "Don't attempt to ride a dead horse in hopes that it will come alive again."[5]

The Portfolio Approach to Corpreneurial Strategy

Corpreneurship will be more successful if it uses a portfolio approach. The following guidelines may be helpful:

- **Do not be a one-trick pony.** Few firms experience sustained growth if they offer just one product or service. You are at risk if you have all your eggs in one basket. If the market changes or a competitor introduces a superior product, then you may go out of business. The key to sustained growth is to develop a portfolio of products and/or services that evolves.
- **Your portfolio needs to be contingent on the firm's situation.** Your product strategy will be contingent on your firm's vision, capabilities, time horizon, resources, talent, and so forth. If your firm has an ambitious vision, it will need to be more innovative and venturesome. If it does not have resources in reserve, it may need to be less venturesome. Saying you want your firm to be corpreneurial will not make it corpreneurial. Each corpreneurial dimension must be there, and they must be synchronized for corpreneurship to occur.
- **Not every idea can make it to commercial launch.** Use the stage gate process to identify the best new product ideas and focus your attention on them. If you have the right metrics for each stage of the new product development process, then early in that process you should be able to weed out the projects that do not have sufficient merit to warrant additional funding. The key is to identify the best projects and to focus your time and resources on them.

- **Use the venture capital model.** If you are ambitious, then you may need to approach new product development initiatives in a similar fashion to how venture capital firms approach their investments. They understand the 20-60-20 rule. They recognize that if they invest in ten firms, then 20 percent may do very well, 60 percent will be the "living dead" which just get by, and 20 percent will go down in flames as total losses. Most new product ideas never make it to launch. Many that make it to launch do not generate the desired level of return. The key is to approach the process with both eyes open and to increase the odds for success by being proactive, customer-centric, and diligent.

- **Consider cash flow.** Your portfolio should be balanced between offensive products that explore new opportunities as well as products that generate cash flow from current endeavors. New products often take considerable time and money to get on their feet. Having some established products generate considerable positive cash provides a good balance. The Boston Consulting Group divides products into question marks, stars, cash cows, and dogs.[6] Its model stresses the need to have some cash cows so you have the funds to develop new products and to carry them until they can pay their way.

- **Develop a pipeline that balances time horizons.** Some people say that cash is the oxygen of business. If you run out of cash, you die. Your product/service offering is like the blood in your body that carries your oxygen. Make sure your product development efforts are designed to provide a rich bloodstream—or pipeline—for years. Your product/ service portfolio should have a balanced time line. It should foster growth and reduce revenue valleys. This can be done by balancing products that have short, medium, and long-term launch dates. It can also be done by balancing products that have short, medium, and long-term life expectancies. The new product/service pipeline should also have projects that are in various stages of development. Some should be in the idea stage. Some should be in the concept-testing stage. Some should be in the prototype stage. Some should be in the market testing stage. Some should be in the pre-launch stage. Some should be in the launch stage.

- **Balancing breakthroughs with improvements.** A portion of your firm's product development strategy may be invested in developing breakthrough products, but balance these efforts by improving your existing products. General Electric divides product efforts into four categories. They are categorized in terms of effort and yield. Low-hanging fruit provide quick yet modest returns. Jewels provide a fairly high return in a fairly quick time with a modest investment. High-hards may have the potential to produce a very high return, but they also take considerable time and risk. Then there are the "drops." They involve large risks in terms of time and money, but they do not have the potential for high returns—so they should be dropped from consideration. Most firms will focus their attention on jewels and low-hanging fruit. Firms that are very ambitious, that can commit the resources, and have a long-term time horizon, may consider investing a small portion of their funds in one or two high-hards.

- **Balancing current and future customer needs.** Your product development efforts should balance your current customers' needs and your future customers' needs.
- **Sometimes product line extensions are the way to go.** Some of your product development efforts should be directed to extending your product line and continuing to differentiate your products from the competition's. While product modification and extension are not as sexy as developing breakthrough products and entering virgin markets, efforts to differentiate your products from your competitors' may offer the best risk-return ratio in the short and medium term.
- **Not every firm can be a first mover.** Some of your products may be targeted to be first movers. Some may be developed as fast followers. Few emerging firms have the skills and resources to be the first mover with all of their products. There is a big difference between a first mover and a fast follower. Being a first mover requires different skills, capabilities, and resources. First movers have to spend time and money to educate prospective consumers. They also have to be patient. First movers run the risk of trying to offer a product before the market materializes. Fast followers get to learn from the first mover and the first customers. Remember, the second mouse often gets the cheese. The real issue is to be the "first to the finish line," not the first out of the starting blocks. You want to use the strategy that produces the desired profit and return on investment; it does not have to be "first to sales."
- **Make sure you are providing value.** If your target market wants the bare essentials, then give them what they want. Numerous firms are seduced by cool technology. If your customers want to kill flies for $2.00, then offer them a fly swatter, not a $29.95 fly evaporator.
- **Do not take your eyes off the bottom line.** Do not get so wrapped up in increasing the top line that you lose sight of the bottom line. 3M asks three critical questions with each initiative it is considering. It asks: "Can we make it?" "Will they buy it?" and "Can we make 3M margin with it?"[7]
- **Transform the ordinary into extraordinary.** Corpreneurship often involves finding innovative ways to improve the performance and/or design of a common product. Numerous industries have products that have been on the market for years, to the point where existing firms have

almost taken them for granted. On the other hand, numerous innovative firms have transformed the ordinary into the extraordinary. James Dyson may be the best example of how innovative designs can transform everyday products. None of Dyson's innovations is very sexy, but each one improved the overall customer experience (vacuuming, moving heavy objects, hand-drying) by approaching customer frustrations from a different perspective. Sherwin Williams's Dutch Boy changed the way paint is packaged with its all-plastic, one-gallon "Twist and Pour" paint can. It will not rust, has an ergonomic handle, can be closed like a jar, and reduces the tendency for paint to drip down the side. None of these innovations is very sexy, but each improved the overall customer experience by approaching customer frustrations from a new angle. Both firms also captured Orison Swett Marden's philosophy, "Don't wait for extraordinary opportunities. Seize common occasions and make them great."

• **Manage risks.** Corpreneurial initiatives can be a rather intuitive process. Each project involves risks. You run the risk of killing an idea that may actually have merit. You also run the risk of letting a project go forward that lacks merit. The key is to generate a lot of good ideas initially and then to use the stage gate process to screen them quickly to identify the ones that may have the most merit and to drop those that require too many resources, have limited return on investment, or are too nebulous to be considered at the present time. The portfolio approach is helpful in determining the number and nature of projects you should consider and move forward. The whole process can be described as patient persistence with a little sense of urgency and paranoia thrown in as well.

• **Balance good and great.** Corpreneurial initiatives involve balancing good and great. Firms that have been successful first movers or even fast followers, recognize that when speed to market is crucial, then you cannot afford to be a perfectionist. There are times when good (the first mover) is good enough. There is a difference between leading edge and bleeding edge. There is also a difference between introducing a new and improved generation of a product and just hyping a product with a media blitz to get consumers to buy something that has already lost its edge. There are times where you will need to offer a wow product or service, and there are times when being a little bit better, quicker, or more convenient makes better business sense. The key to success is knowing the difference.

Reality Check: Few firms have the skills and resources to be the first mover with all of their products. There will be times when you may be better off being a fast follower.

Reality Check: If you are striving to develop and launch a blockbuster product, then guard against the tendency to water it down by cutting costs and trying to have it appeal to everyone. Getting a product to market always involves compromises, but make sure you are not eliminating the WOW.

Corpreneurial Leadership Issues

Creating the company's future through corpreneurial efforts is not the same as leading a company. Leadership involves creating a vision and then developing the strategy, culture, systems, structures, infrastructure, funding, and people to make it a reality. Corpreneurial leadership involves exploring new terrain, entering new markets, and/or introducing new products or services. It tends to be more venturesome and involves more risk. The following issues reflect the challenges corpreneurial leaders face:

- Having the ability to focus on monitoring trends as well as sensing and seizing opportunities without getting too caught up in operational matters.
- Being venturesome but not falling prey to reckless funding of speculative new product ideas or being seduced by short-term opportunities.
- Having the optimism, energy, and enthusiasm to explore new areas and the resilience to be cool under fire in order to handle the inevitable surprises, delays, and setbacks.
- Ensuring various corpreneurial initiatives have the necessary resources and infrastructure.
- Making sure people in the firm do not create bureaucratic barriers that inhibit thinking and acting "outside the conventional growth box."

Corpreneurial Strategy Tips

Your business strategy should have strategic, corpreneurial, and operational dimensions. Each dimension is designed to help the firm develop sustainable and profitable competitive advantages. The following suggestions are provided to develop an effective corpreneurial strategy:

- Make sure you are in the right markets while looking for emerging opportunities. If your current market is not the right market, then you will have to plan an exit strategy as well as a growth strategy.

- Identify the adoption hurdles you are likely to encounter and develop ways to minimize the downside risk.
- Test new product ideas when they are in the "concept stage" on prospective customers.
- Test and learn. Get prototypes into the hands of prospective customers as soon as possible. Learn from them, make modifications quickly, and then get it into their hands again. Reduce the "test, learn, modify" cycle so you can accelerate the launch date or drop the product if it does not demonstrate sufficient potential.
- Launch and learn. By getting your new product into the market as soon as possible you have the opportunity to learn if other types of consumers want it and if consumers use it in other ways. This is known as the corridor effect. Look for other uses and other users that may be even more profitable.
- Look for opportunities that will enable your firm to cross-sell customers by developing additional products and services. Ask your customers what else they need.
- Avoid having too much of your business tied up in one customer or one product.
- Do more than offer conventional solutions to existing problems—look for newproblems that are looking for new solutions.
- Look at various stages in the value chain to find opportunities to add value for the consumer and to avoid being a commodity.
- Look for areas in the marketplace that are commodities. Create competitive advantages that allow you to enter that market space and give you a chance to charge higher or lower prices.
- You cannot be all things to all your customers. Remember the Pareto 80/20 Rule. Pay particular attention to the 20 percent of your customers that generate more than half of your profits. Your bottom 10 to 20 percent of your customers may actually be costing you money. You may have to fire some of your customers to position your firm for growth.
- Go with the flow with new technology. Do not fight it by trying to cling to out-of-date technology. Offering old technology at discount prices usually does not work.
- If your firm invents a new product or technology, then remember that inventors tend to fall in love with their products. Most inventors are also reluctant to take their products to market. They want to make them better and better. If a product never leaves the lab, regardless of how great it may be, it is like a boat that sits in its slip. As some boat owners say, it is a product that you just keep pouring money into.
- Make sure the product solves a real problem and customers are willing to pay for it. You do not want to have a solution when there is no problem. If the market does not say "Wow," then it is not a wow product.

- Do not over-engineer the product. Engineers and marketers often add whistles and bells that enable the product to do even more things or to do things better. Customers have their own expectations. If you offer them more than they are willing to pay for, then you are undermining the product—not enhancing it. Almost all software has capabilities that the vast majority of consumers will never use. Years ago, Eli Lilly spent millions developing an ultra-sterile saline solution. Few doctors were willing to recommend it because the price difference far exceeded the purity difference of the existing saline solutions.
- You do not have to develop innovative technology. Find innovative ways to use cutting-edge technology that exists elsewhere in a value-added way to offer customers what has not been possible.
- Look for ways to apply your technology to solve problems in other markets.
- Find innovative ways to improve and/or to simplify processes so you will be able to execute your strategy and provide consistent quality at a lower price. Business process reengineering may enable you to reduce time, costs, and prices, as well as improve service and convenience.
- Recognize that when you target a different group of customers, you will have to change some of your processes to meet their needs.
- Do what you do best and outsource the rest.
- Speed is important, but you also need to be pointed in the right direction.

The Innovation Portal: A Symbiotic Relationship between Providers and Users

Most corpreneurial firms are "customer problem-solvers." They use the Gretzky anticipatory marketing strategy so they can position themselves to: (1) anticipate what customers will want, (2) develop timely solutions to the problems, and (3) offer customers what they will want when they want it.

The "Innovation Portal" reflects the fertile situation that arises when a leading-edge provider interacts with a leading-edge user. The innovation portal illustrates a relationship of mutual discovery that may arise between a leading-edge provider and a leading-edge user. Some corpreneurial firms approach the symbiotic relationship in more formal ways. Some corpreneurial firms have formed alliances or joint ventures with other companies to capitalize on emerging opportunities and corresponding needs. Sometimes they are larger, more established firms that have an interest in having a firm develop a product or service for them. Sometimes they are emerging firms that are trying to find a firm to do their R&D work.

Corpreneurial firms often develop an especially close relationship with one or more current or prospective customers. If your company wants to be the "leading-edge provider" of products or services, then it should try to develop symbiotic relationships with "leading-edge users." Leading-edge users serve as a source for new product/service ideas. By working closely with leading-edge users, corpreneurial firms have the opportunity to experiment with real customers in real settings in real time. This situation is superior to conventional marketing research techniques that merely ask potential customers about their "intentions."

A leading-edge user that acts as the beta site may provide valuable insights as the prototype is developed. The firm may also be the firm's first customer when the product is ready to be launched. Some leading-edge users may even be in a position to supply key resources including funding for leading-edge providers.

Corpreneurship Questions

The "Three I's" concept profiled in the chapter on anticipatory management indicates that before you can have *initiatives*, you have to have *insights*. Yet to have insights you must first make the right *inquiries*. The following questions help frame your firm's situation and judge whether it is positioned to be corpreneurial:

- Are we in the right business?
- What business should we be in?
- What are the best near-term opportunities for our core competencies?
- What are the best long-term opportunities for our core competencies?
- What core competencies should we develop to seize future opportunities?
- What changes can we make to change the way the game is played?
- What can we do to reinvent the market/industry?
- What areas have the potential to be game-changing and make it difficult for competitors to match our offering?
- How can we make our competition's products and services obsolete?
- What will it take for our firm to gain a temporary legal monopoly?
- What changes can we make that will bring new customers into the market?
- What changes can we make that will convert our competitors' customers into our customers?

- Are we spending enough time looking at the horizon for emerging opportunities?
- Are we spending enough time looking for what competitors may have in their pipeline?
- Are we really probing our customers to know their unarticulated and future needs?
- Are we really probing our noncustomers to know why they are not buying from us, as well as their unarticulated and future needs?
- What keeps us from being even more corpreneurial?
- What percent of our sales in three years should come from products and services we do not currently offer?
- Do we have enough products in the development pipeline to meet future growth and profit goals?
- Who are the people on the fringe who may be the lead users for new products and services?
- What will it take to get to the tipping points where we will go from serving a small set of lead users to having a large set of consumers?
- What type of time frame and return on investment margin, payback period, etc. do we expect for new products and services?

Reality Check: Almost every chapter in this book stresses growth should not be a goal in itself. The goal should be making the firm stronger and more profitable. There are occasions when it may be possible to increase the firm's strength and become even more profitable by being smaller. If you offer products with a strong proprietary position that wow customers, then you may be able to charge premium prices. Gross profit is determined by multiplying the number of units sold by their profit margins. It is possible to increase overall profitability and ROI with a lower level of sales (in units) than you generate with more generic products—especially if they are perceived as commodities by the marketplace.

Conclusion: Corpreneurship Can Take Your Firm to the Next Level and Beyond

Firms that want to create their future should consider including corpreneurship in their growth strategies. Most industries and markets are in their maturity stage where growth only comes from taking market share from other firms. Firms that merely make minor changes in the present are destined to fail in periods of rapid change. Doing more of the same with more salespeople, more advertising, and more price discounts will not cut it. Firms that are fixated on cost cutting and fine-tuning operations will miss out on the numerous opportunities that lie ahead. The traditional linear-incremental approach to doing business will not provide high-growth, high-profit opportunities. The marketplace is changing too rapidly for firms to operate from a reactive stance by responding only to today's needs and relying on today's technology. The firms that will thrive in the years ahead will be the ones that develop and offer innovative solutions to pressing problems, that enhance your customers' profits, and that make a significant difference in people's lives.

It is clear that trying to be the low-cost provider is not the best strategy for most ventures. There will always be some firm that has a lower cost structure or is so desperate that it will almost give its products away. Your firm will still need to focus attention on being efficient, but your future should be tied to sensing opportunities and seizing them by offering innovative value-added products, services, and processes.

The strategic planning gap raises two of the most profound questions a leader can pose in business. The first profound question is: What do I want my business to be like in five to ten years? This question leads to the following questions: (1) How much do I want it to grow? (2) To what extent will it involve corpreneurship? and (3) What areas should we focus our corpreneurial efforts on to get the best risk-return ratio?

The second profound question is "Are we in the right business?" If the answer is no from a risk-return perspective, then you have a choice of either: (1) selling your business while there is something left to sell, (2) doing nothing and watching your firm go down in flames, or (3) embarking on a new—possibly corpreneurial—path. Take the Corpreneurship Quiz in Table 6.1 to learn the extent that your firm has the qualities that will enable it to create its future.

You must have the freedom to look beyond what has been done before ... I couldn't find quite the car I dreamed of: so I decided to build it myself.

—Professor Dr. Ferdinand Porsche

TABLE 6.1. The Corpreneurship Quiz

How does your firm rate on the following dimensions? *Scoring Level: Rating: 1 = not at all, 2 = slightly true, 3 = somewhat true, 4 = mostly true, 5 = completely true	Level*
1. Your firm's top executives are really in tune with emerging opportunities in the marketplace, including opportunities in related fields.	1-2-3-4-5
2. Top management has identified the "corpreneurship gap" that indicates the extent to which corpreneurial initiatives are needed to bridge the strategic planning gap. It has established corpreneurship goals, metrics, and milestones.	1-2-3-4-5
3. Your firm demonstrates future-oriented, anticipatory marketing. It is continuously exploring the marketplace for additional entrepreneurial opportunities including new problems to be solved, new technology to be developed, new markets to enter, and new customers to serve.	1-2-3-4-5
4. Your firm's time and resources are being spent trying to develop innovative solutions to emerging problems rather than trying to get more mileage from your current products.	1-2-3-4-5
5. Your firm is truly customer-centric. It constantly probes for areas that may provide new value for its current customers and potential customers.	1-2-3-4-5
6. Management at all levels is actively involved in soliciting and rewarding employee ideas for how the firm can be more corpreneurial.	1-2-3-4-5
7. Management encourages all types of experimentation (bootlegging, skunkworks, etc.) beyond each employee's immediate responsibilities.	1-2-3-4-5
8. Management makes a deliberate effort to hire, encourage, and reward people who have diverse perspectives and provide breakthrough ideas.	1-2-3-4-5
9. Management makes a deliberate effort to encourage the cross-pollination of ideas across units in the firm.	1-2-3-4-5
10. Top management frequently challenges the merit of prevailing business models and practices.	1-2-3-4-5
11. Your firm either has a new business incubator or a designated unit that focuses on new avenues for organic, corpreneurial growth.	1-2-3-4-5

(continued)

TABLE 6.1.   (Continued)

How does your firm rate on the following dimensions? *Scoring Level: Rating: 1 = not at all, 2 = slightly true, 3 = somewhat true, 4 = mostly true, 5 = completely true	Level*
12. Your firm has an internal venture fund or sets aside specific funds each year for corpreneurial initiatives and experiments.	1-2-3-4-5
13. Your firm systematically screens ideas to determine which ideas should be considered and moved forward to commercialization.	1-2-3-4-5
14. Your firm monitors the success of corpreneurial and conventional initiatives to determine if they should be continued or abandoned.	1-2-3-4-5
15. Your firm openly solicits ideas—including crowd-sourcing—so it does not fall prey to the not-invented-here syndrome within and outside the firm.	1-2-3-4-5
16. Your firm has a variety of products in its pipeline that will foster growth for the next three to five years.	1-2-3-4-5
17. Your firm has a balanced portfolio in terms of risk, reward, and time horizon of products in its pipeline.	1-2-3-4-5
Total points	

Scoring Key

68–75	Congratulations, your firm demonstrates the qualities of a corpreneurial enterprise.
60–67	Your organization has many qualities of a corpreneurial enterprise, but has areas that can be improved further.
52–59	Your organization has some qualities of a corpreneurial enterprise but has a lot of room for improvement.
44–51	Your organization either has some significant impairments or is weak in many areas. Tweaking your firm's activities will not be enough to make a real difference.
15–43	Your organization may be beyond hope. It will take a radical change in management, in corporate culture, systems, and processes to have any chance of being competitive in the future.

Notes

Some of the material in this chapter originally appeared in the article, "Corporate Entrepreneurship" by the author and David J. Glew, and Jonathan D. Rowe in *Industrial Management*, September/October, 2008. Reprinted with the permission of the Institute of Industrial Engineers, 3577 Parkway Lane, Suite 200, Norcross, GA 30092, www.iienet.org. Copyright 2009 by the Institute of Industrial Engineers.

1. Alan C. Kay, "Predicting the Future," *Stanford Engineering* 1, no. 1 (1989): 1.

2. Gary Hamel and C. K. Prahalad, "Competing for the Future," *Harvard Business* Review 72, no. 4 (1994): 126.

3. Robert Cooper, *Winning at New Products* (New York: Basic Books, 2001).

4. W. Chan Kim and Reneé Mauborgne, "Blue Ocean Strategy," *Harvard Business* Review 82, no. 10 (2004): 76–84.

5. Stephen C. Harper, *The McGraw-Hill Guide to Managing Growth in Your Emerging Business* (New York: McGraw-Hill, 1994), 70.

6. www.bcg.com/about_bcg/history_1968.aspx.

7. John Nathan, *In Search of Excellence* video (South Easton, Massachusetts: Nathan Tyler Productions Inc., 1987).

Chapter 7

Fostering Speed and Agility

"Time is money" may have been true in Ben Franklin's time, but "Speed is profit" is the new business axiom that will make people and companies rich for the foreseeable future.[1]

—Michael LeBoeuf, *Fast Forward*

We live in a world of new realities. What was considered fast a few years ago is now considered painfully slow. The terms: *breakneck speed, Internet speed, real-time speed, warp speed,* and *lightning fast* characterize the accelerating rate of change. The terms: *hyperkinetic, whiplashed, blurred, dizzying,* and *head spinning* characterize its effects on people who are not prepared to handle the ever-accelerating rate of change. The need for firms to be even more agile applies as well if they want to be in sync with changing market conditions.

Consumers want more variety, and they want it faster. What firms had weeks to do must now be done in days. What took days must now be done in minutes. What took minutes must now be done in seconds. Technological innovations have conditioned people to expect immediate response. The Internet makes information about anything in the world available instantly. Fast customers require fast companies. To be analog in a digital world is certain death. Firms that are not agile will become irrelevant. Firms that do not change fast enough and in the right ways face extinction.

The physical sciences tell us that "open systems" are far more in tune with changing conditions and that "closed systems" fail because they do not evolve quickly enough or at all. The term "adaptational breakdown" describes what happens if you cannot keep pace with rate and nature of change. A Far Side comic panel provides a humorous example of how being slow to react can have detrimental consequences. The comic panel shows an outhouse that has been engulfed by a glacier. The occupant must have been oblivious to the changes taking place around him. While it is highly unlikely that someone could be encased by a glacier, it does provide an interesting wake up call for firms that are not swift and agile.

Every change presents opportunities for firms that are positioned to sense and seize them. This places a premium on speed and agility. Every change may also create threats for firms that are blindsided by them. Firms that can anticipate and prevent threats will thrive; firms that cannot will not survive. Michael LeBoeuf noted, "With massive change comes incredible opportunity . . . those who are aware of what's happening and prepared to act fast will be those who will enjoy unprecedented success . . . when change is the problem, speed is the solution."[2] The breakneck pace of competition is particularly evident in the comments made by Craig Barrett when he was President of Intel. He stated, "We are going down the road at 150 miles per hour, and we know there's a brick wall someplace, but the worst thing we can do is stop too soon and let somebody else pass us."[3]

The accelerating rate of change along with its associated discontinuities have forced managers to learn how to drive in the fast lane. The days of placing the company on "cruise control" and going with the flow of surrounding traffic are gone. If you are not the first mover or a very fast follower, then you are dead. Companies that fail to be at the leading edge will look like another Far Side comic panel that shows sloths trying to cross the Autobahn.

Timing can also make a real difference in corporate success. Companies need to have the sense of timing displayed by the cliff divers of Mexico. Executives who hesitate will miss the waves of change and crash in the shallows.

Today, being a day late means more than being a dollar short; it leads to bankruptcy. To operate on an eight-to-five, five-day schedule in a world that has gone to a 24/7 clock is corporate suicide. Ever-evolving enterprises recognize that competitive advantages are fleeting, so they are constantly creating ways to provide the right type of value at the right time for their targeted customers. They also recognize the role anticipation, speed, timing, perceptiveness, positioning, decisiveness, and agility can play in creating their future.

Ever-Evolving Enterprises "Get It"

There is a story about a student at Princeton who was taking a class from Albert Einstein. The frustrated student approached Einstein, saying that the questions on the exam were the same as the ones on a test in a previous course. According to the story, Einstein responded, "You're right, but the answers are different this year." This story captures the need for organizations to evolve, and to evolve quickly.

The phrase "Change or die" may be used often in the corporate arena, but it is not correct. A firm can change in many ways and still die. The key is to change in the right way and in the right time; that is what *evolving* is all about. Like the classic line, "Failure is not an option!" in *Apollo 13*, not evolving is not an option; procrastination is not an option, slowing down is not an option, delays are not an option, calling a time-out is not an option, and waiting for a convenient time to make the *right* changes is not an option. In nature, species have generations to evolve to meet changing conditions. Market realities require rapid evolution—real-time evolution.

Firms must tailor their evolution to the rate and nature of changes in the marketplace. Different conditions pose different challenges. Different challenges require different approaches. For example, a certain design of plane and engine were needed to exceed 300 miles per hour. A different design and engine were needed to exceed 400 miles per hour. Breaking the sound barrier required a different design and propulsion. The film *The Right Stuff* profiled how it took a different type of pilot to break the sound barrier, and to be an astronaut. The ability to make quick decisions and react quickly in situations no one had experienced before explains why NASA selected test pilots for the Mercury program.

Charles Darwin promoted his concept of "survival of the fittest." In today's marketplace, though, it may be survival of the swiftest and most nimble. Firms that are "quick learners and quick responders" can capitalize on the unexpected. They are able to zig when the competition is still zagging. The days of bigger is better are over. The days of fast and agile have arrived. Speed and agility are particularly valuable in a time of chaos. Firms that can combine innovation with speed and agility thrive when lesser firms are still wondering what hit them. There is a distinction between uncertainty and ambiguity. Times of uncertainty are easier to handle than times of ambiguity, because with uncertainty at least you have some idea about possible courses of action and their corresponding probabilities. In times of ambiguity—which are happening with increasing frequency—the possible courses of action are not clear, and the likelihood that certain things could happen is unknown.

Reality Check: Firms that can sense sooner, analyze more quickly, learn more quickly, decide more quickly, innovate more quickly, implement more quickly, and make adjustments to plans as they are being implemented more quickly will evolve more quickly and get favorable results more quickly. As we venture into the future, there will only be two types of firms: the quick and the dead.

Firms can be classified in one of four ways. There are laggard firms, reactive firms, proactive firms, and visionary firms. Laggard firms are fatally slow in their ability to sense the need to change. By the time they see the need to change, their efforts are too late; they are destined to be among the dead. Laggard firms miss the indicators that their product/service offering or even the whole market is waning. Reactive firms recognize sooner that their product/service offering or even the market is waning. This gives them more time to change than laggard firms, but their delayed actions place them in a precarious position; they are among the "living dead." Proactive firms realize earlier that no product, service, or market lasts forever. They are committed to providing successor products and service offerings so they will be available when a window of opportunity opens. They are in sync with market changes. Visionary firms operate with a longer time horizon. This gives them the opportunity to have a head start over even proactive firms in creating and capitalizing on emerging opportunities.

The ability to think ahead and be prepared to create the firm's future is captured in the concept of playing one or two markets ahead. This concept was developed by observing pool players decades ago. When the top pool player was asked how he plays the game, he noted that he "plays two racks ahead." While this may sound like Wayne Gretzky's comments about what it takes to excel in hockey, the master pool player made his comment well before Gretzky put on his first skates. When the interviewer asked the pool player what separated him from all the other players, he stated that he was like other pool players who focused their attention on "clearing the balls currently on the table" and then having the cue ball positioned to break the next rack of balls so that he might be able to run clear the table again. Yet he said that while his opponents played "one rack ahead," he played two racks ahead. His comment sounded almost metaphysical. Yet it did make sense when it was seen in the context of market opportunities. In market strategy terms, firms that think two markets ahead will be in a position to sense and seize

TABLE 7.1.   Four Types of Firms

| Type of Company | Percentage of Management's Time and Resources | | | |
	Yesterday's Breadwinners (%)	Today's Breadwinners (%)	Tomorrow's Breadwinners (%)	Tomorrow's Tomorrow Breadwinners (%)
Laggard	100	0	0	0
Reactive	80	20	0	0
Proactive	0	80	20	0
Visionary	0	70	25	5

emerging opportunities. Proactive firms think one market ahead. Visionary firms think two markets ahead. Ever-evolving enterprises are a synthesis of proactive and visionary firms. They capitalize on their current markets while developing successor products. They are also committed to developing a continuous pipeline of products that are two or more markets ahead. Table 7.1 profiles the distinction among the four types of firms.

Peter Drucker had an uncanny sense for what was truly important as well as foresight into the types of challenges executives would face in the future. He noted, "There are three dimensions to the economic task: (1) The present business must be made effective; (2) its potential must be realized; (3) it must be made into a different business for a different future. Each task requires a distinct approach. Each asks different questions. Each comes with different conclusions. Yet they are inseparable. All three have to be done at the same time today."[4] If Peter Drucker were alive today, he might stress that all three of these areas must now be done faster and better.

> Reality Check: Conditions change in large and small ways. In the short term, firms may have to improvise to adjust to changes. Yet ever-evolving enterprises are committed to being innovative in their efforts to capitalize on markedly different conditions.

Evolving may go beyond just introducing new products and services. It may include introducing new business models. Dell changed the way the game was played when it introduced customized computers with incredible turnaround time. Progressive Insurance changed the competitive landscape when its people could cut a check at the scene of an accident. Southwest Airlines changed the game when it showed that it could turn a plane around at the gate in just a few minutes. This saves time and money. It also enhances customer satisfaction.

Dell has fine-tuned its operations so that it can ship an order within two hours. Dell's ability to coordinate with its suppliers also reduces Dell's need to carry inventory. Dell's billing strategy enables it to get the customer's money well before it has to pay its suppliers for the components.

Achieving world-class speed and agility will only be possible if they are built-in at every level—the divisional level, the departmental level, and the individual level. Achieving world-class speed takes more than just being fast at the big things; you also have to be fast at the daily things that make a difference. Dell, Progressive, and Southwest Airlines demonstrate the value of making significant changes in a firm's processes and illustrate how firms with the quickest response time win.

Enhancing response time can also apply to even smaller business processes. Two retail chains provide good examples of how to adjust operations on a daily basis to changes in daily demand. One retailer uses real-time data from each store's cash registers to determine daily sales. By midmorning if sales are not meeting expectations, some of its employees are sent home to keep payroll costs in line with volume. Another retailer takes a more proactive approach to less-than-expected sales. It sends e-mails to its customers indicating specials. The e-mails also include special coupons for that day.

Reality Check: The phrase "Don't be 'Delled'" applies to almost every industry. How can you learn from Dell, Southwest Airlines, Progressive Insurance and other "fast companies" so that your competitors do not leave you in their dust? How can you learn from the best practices of the fastest in other industries? One firm even studied a pit crew in a NASCAR race to see what they did to give them an edge.

The Role of Strategy in Fostering Speed and Agility

For years the marketplace has been seen as a battle between the Davids and the Goliaths. In this case the Davids are smaller, entrepreneurial firms, and the Goliaths are larger, more established firms. Large firms gained their strength through their economies of scale size and having plentiful resources in reserve to explore large market opportunities. Smaller firms relied more on guerrilla tactics to seize market niches and/or attack larger firms' weaknesses. Today's market realities have changed almost everything. Economies of scale require stable markets that no longer exist. Major strategic initiatives require considerable resources and patient expectations by investors, which are rare today.

Reality Check: More firms are focusing on enhancing short-term performance, even if it is at the expense of long-term performance. In baseball terms, they are focusing on getting singles rather than having a balanced portfolio that includes attempts to hit occasional triples and home runs.

Ever-evolving enterprises are designed to be as close to their customers as possible so they are in tune with their customers' changing expectations. Firms with speed and agility have a competitive advantage over firms that are more distant and bureaucratic. Their speed and agility are often reflected in their use of flexible design and manufacturing techniques, their aversion to reinventing the wheel, and their commitment to partnering, forming alliances and outsourcing.

Reality Check: Speed is relative in the competitive marketplace. There is a story of two guys who were camping. When one of the guys screamed, "Run, there's a bear coming this way!" the other guy sat down and started putting on his shoes. The first guy exclaimed, "You can't outrun a bear!" The other guy replied, "I don't need to outrun the bear; I just have to outrun you." In many cases, you do not have to have breakneck speed; you just need to be sufficiently faster than your competitors.

Reality Check: Your firm's success is tied to helping your customers be more successful. Do not let your preoccupation with speed limit your focus to how *your* firm can be faster. You should also direct your attention to how you can help save your customers' time, help them be faster. Increasing speed does not have to be a zero-sum proposition where increasing your firm's speed has to be at the expense of your suppliers and customers.

There Is More to Speed Than Speed

Speed can give a firm a decided advantage in the race to win customers. The phrases, "You are either fast or last" and "If you are second, then you are the first of the losers" stress the need for speed. Intel may have captured the need for speed when it said to its competitors, "You'd better run as fast as we are, because we're destroying the pavement behind us as we move along."[5]

Yet there is more to speed than how fast the firm is moving. Speed is unidimensional. It does not include direction. It does not matter how fast you are going if you are not pointed in the right direction. As a matter of fact, misdirected speed can be more devastating than being slow. The concept of momentum combines speed and mass. Momentum can be beneficial, and it can be detrimental. Momentum provides strength. Momentum helps a rocket leave the atmosphere. Yet momentum can make it hard to change direction or to slow down if the situation requires change. Many large firms are like aircraft carriers which take miles and many minutes to turn around. Smaller firms that are agile may be able to turn on a dime.

> Reality Check: Speed does not mean doing the same things faster. It means figuring out what the firm should be doing and identifying which things will make the biggest difference if they are done faster.

Most people would suggest that rapid-growth firms should slow down. While there may be some merit in slowing down, there is an alternative: learning how to travel fast without being out of control. This is what anticipatory management is all about. Executives should try to extend the company's headlights or—better yet—equip the car with radar to see distant objects sooner. If the company cannot extend its headlights (to anticipate what the future holds), then it needs to enhance its agility by improving its steering system so it can make adjustments along its path without careening out of control. It also means improving the braking system if it has to stop to avoid hitting them.

Ever-evolving enterprises feel comfortable at even faster speeds. They have people, systems, and resources in place to handle increased size and speed before you need them. In a sense, they welcome a variety of driving conditions and challenges.

Learning how to grow fast also involves having monitoring and control systems in place to let you know when to slow down. William Sheeline, as a journalist for *Fortune* magazine stated, "Prudence sometimes indicates easing back on the corporate throttle to give employees and internal systems time to adjust."[6]

Reality Check: When you are going fast, you cannot make radical change. The faster you go, the more difficult it is to make even minor changes without jeopardizing the firm. A KPMG ad asks, "How important is your steering wheel when you are traveling at 150 m.p.h.?"

Reality Check: Speed to market is only of value if gets your firm to positive cash flow, profit, and ROI sooner. Projects that recover their investment quickly reduce the firm's vulnerability to changes, consumer desires, and competition offering a superior product.

Reality Check: Speed does not have to cost more. If it is handled properly, it can save your firm money. Phillip Crosby showed that quality was "free" when it reduced defects, overtime, and decreased customer ill will. Smart speed may enable the firm to charge premium prices to "first-buyers." It may also deter other firms from entering the market if your firm has a substantial head start.

Reality Check: If market speed were to go from 70 miles per hour to 100 miles per hour, could your firm take 100 miles per hour in stride? What areas could not handle the faster speed? Going faster is like lowering the water level in rapids; it makes certain things vulnerable that were not vulnerable with a higher water level. Where is your firm vulnerable? What will it take to get your company into the express/passing lane and to stay there?

Reality Check: Speed can undermine agility. Firms need to recognize when agility is more important.

Speed is like a fast computer processor. Without the right software, no matter how fast it is, a computer cannot do anything productive. It is the software that provides focus and agility. This is similar to a question raised at a time management seminar. A participant asked if he should take a speed reading class. The instructor responded, "I can teach you to read one million words a minute right now." The instructor then stated that if you know what *not* to read, and do not read it, that is better than reading one thousand words per minute. The instructor noted that the trouble with speed reading is that by being able to read quickly, people will read almost anything.

Reality Check: Woody Allen noted, "I took a speed reading course and read *War and Peace* in 20 minutes. It involves Russia." Speed reading is of little value if there is minimal comprehension.

Reality Check: Speed often prompts multitasking behavior, yet some things should not be done at all. Peter Drucker suggested asking, "If we were to start the firm today, would we do this activity? If not, then drop it."

Reality Check: Do not let speed be an obsession; put it into perspective. Speed counts only if you are pointed in the right direction and in the right forest (markets). Speed is irrelevant if your firm is in the wrong forest. Stephen Covey observed, "Doing more things faster is no substitute for doing the right things."

Reality Check: Undue or rash quickness can be detrimental. If you do not have the time to get it right in the first place, you will not have the time to fix it later.

The old saying, "Please engage your brain before you engage your mouth" seems to apply to the relationship between speed and decision making. Executive time can be divided into numerous categories. In the overall scheme of things, there is a time to think, a time to analyze, a time to reflect, a time to decide, and a time to act. While executives need to guard against paralysis by analysis, they also need to recognize that there are times when reflection may be more important to the company's future than swift action. While it may be easier and quicker to implement last year's strategy again this year, to do so could spell disaster. Some things do take time and should not be rushed too much. Creativity and the development of people are crucial to the company's success. They should be done on a continuous basis, but they should not be rushed.

Speed Should Be Targeted to Various Organizational Processes

Technological innovations are now challenging the proverbial "speed barrier." Recent advances in technology have made "rapid prototyping" a reality. It is now possible to go directly from the computer-aided design to the manufacture of actual products. Rapid design and rapid prototyping have been combined with rapid manufacturing technology to speed the idea to product cycle. When these are done concurrently with effective prototype testing, then engineering change orders—which require a change in product features/design/manufacturing—may be reduced.

Rapid prototyping allows firms to have multiple iterations of prototype testing. Rapid prototyping enables fast feedback, fast learning, and fast modifications. With rapid prototyping, customers serve as beta sites and have the opportunity to become codevelopers with the firm. This is important because potential customers can distinguish between benefits and features. Benefits add value in the customers' eyes. Features are things they may not be willing to pay for because their cost exceeds their value.

Reality Check: If prototypes are used to learn what customers really like, then make sure your research techniques get valid data. Testing a prototype is like testing a hypothesis. Doing focus groups and interviews may have some value, but real insights will only be possible if you do anthropological/ethnographic research that studies what people actually do with the product (rather than what they say about it).

Reality Check: Prototyping often experiences the law of diminishing marginal returns. Firms that do too many iterations run the risk that the market may change more than the product to be offered when it is offered. There is a time to think, and there is a time to act. There is a time when products need to move to production.

Reality Check: Guy Kawasaki cautioned firms against trying to launch "perfect" products. When firms are preoccupied with making sure a new product is perfect, they lose valuable time and timely feedback. His advice to firms is, "Don't worry, be crappy." This is his way of emphasizing the need to get new products into the hands of prospective customers so you can get feedback on suggested changes. While Kawasaki's point has merit, if you launch a product with a lot of problems you may be pressing your luck.[7]

Sony is one of the masters of the quick prototyping process. Today it is not unusual for a company to take up to a year to transform a concept into a prototype. Sony is committed to having a prototype ready within a few days. This capability gives Sony the opportunity to get a number of versions of a new product into the hands of potential consumers. Sony is then able to quickly turn the prototypes that garner the most favorable responses into actual products.

Reality Check: To function at higher speeds, you have to transform your company, not just push down on the accelerator pedal more.

Reality Check: Management's efforts to enhance speed should not be restricted to new product development. Management should also review the company's ongoing operations and processes to see if corporate performance can be enhanced by doing them more quickly.

Reality Check: Creativity cannot be forced. It takes time for things to fall into place. Your subconscious needs time to make connections, to provide insights, and to provide the "aha" moment. You may be lucky in some instances and come up with a creative breakthrough, but it will not happen a lot or often. Someone once noted, "You cannot have a child by having nine women pregnant for one month." Your mind needs time to incubate.

Preoccupation with Speed Can Have Detrimental Consequences

Some people are addicted to speed. Yet people need to take a moment frequently to stop and smell the roses. People need to pause and reflect, to build relationships, and to recharge their batteries. People need to learn to turn off their computers, Blackberries, cell phones, and the like occasionally, so their minds are able to run free and be reenergized.

Reality Check: You want to be faster at the things that matter—the things that truly add value to your firm's stockholders and other stakeholders.

Reality Check: A preoccupation with speed often causes a greater concern with the short term, with now. This keeps firms from sensing and seizing future opportunities as well as anticipating and preventing future threats.

Reality Check: A preoccupation with speed often causes firms to seek "quick fixes" rather than develop lasting solutions.

Reality Check: A preoccupation with speed causes firms to act superficially to not do an in-depth analysis and to reflect on the situation. Sometimes you need to slow down to get the real picture, to reflect on the situation, to sleep on it. Too much haste is like standing too close or too far from a Pointillist painting. If you stand too close, then all you see is a bunch of dots; you are too close to see how they fit together to form whole images. If you stand too far away, you cannot see and appreciate the details.

Reality Check: Make sure that your reward system rewards the right things; do not compromise quality by cutting corners. Dell made a mistake a few years ago when it tried to speed things up and measured the number of calls handled per hour rather than the extent to which its customer service reps solved each customer's concern. Its mistake caused considerable ill will with its customers and a drop in its stock price.

Reality Check: Mistakes are inevitable. The real the issue is how quickly you fix them and how many people even knew about them. Ironically, in some instances, rapid recovery may actually strengthen a customer relationship. Rapid resolution shows your commitment to making sure your customers' needs are met.

Timing and Perceptiveness Can Make a Real Difference

Speed is important, but timing is vital. In a world of rapid change, timing is everything. Timing is an essential part of anticipatory management. The ability to sense changes early and to make quick adjustments are essential competencies in a world of rapid change. Perceptiveness and foresight are critical parts of timing because they give the firm the ability to time corporate initiatives. Anticipatory enterprises are more successful than real-time enterprises because anticipatory management enables you to deal with problems before they become crises.

Timing allows the firm to enter the window of opportunity when it opens and to have a competitive advantage longer. Competitive advantages are usually fleeting, so the sooner you sense an opportunity, the more time you have to capitalize on it before competitors enter the scene or the market shifts again. When Richard Karlgaard was the publisher of *Forbes*, he noted, "Today, any idea can be cloned within days or hours."[8] He also noted, "Jump late through that window and it's glass shards and blood."[9]

Competition is quick to jump on the bandwagon for markets that show promise. The challenge is amplified by the fact that it may take more lead time to develop competencies to meet the needs of a more sophisticated market. If this is the case, then companies either need to be more perceptive and start sooner, or they have to be more agile so they can respond more quickly. The marketplace will show no mercy to late responders.

Numerous ventures fail, not because they do not have good ideas; they fail because their executives do not have a good sense of timing. The timing of initiatives continues to play an integral role in the evolution of an enterprise. There are at least five types of "offensive timing initiatives" that need to be addressed during the life of a venture. They include:

1. When to start the venture.
2. When to introduce a new product.
3. When to introduce a new process.
4. When to enter a new territory.
5. When to initiate major expansion.

Timing corporate initiatives, however, has defensive dimensions. There are at least four "defensive timing initiatives" that entail reducing or phasing out certain corporate activities. They include:

1. When to drop a product.
2. When to exit existing markets.
3. When to consolidate operations.
4. When to sell part or all of the venture.

Windows Open and Close More Quickly

Windows of opportunity are like waves. Firms need to be like surfers. They need to sense the wave early, position themselves to catch the wave at the earliest time—before it gets crowded, make the most of the wave, and then kick out before it crashes so they can catch another wave as soon as possible. Yet today's windows of market opportunity are opening and closing more quickly than at any time in the past. Yesterday's era of everlasting mass markets has been replaced by an era where market niches and micro-markets appear on the radar screen only for a finite period of time. Firms with perceptive timing are (1) able to sense the window being formed, (2) able to position themselves to serve the market when the window opens, (3) able to capitalize on the opportunity, and (4) perceptive enough to exit before the window closes on them.

While firms may want to be "first to market," management needs to ensure that their firms are not so far out in front that they outdistance or lose sight of the marketplace. For example, Corning Glass developed fiber optic cable ten years before the market was ready. Panasonic's strategy of being "slightly ahead of its time" is less risky than being "way ahead of its time." Firms that are way ahead of the market are also vulnerable if the market changes what it values.

It is said that the first bite of the apple is the sweetest. First-to-market firms accept numerous risks, but they also have the whole market to themselves if they are in tune with market needs. By the time laggard firms arrive, there may only be table scraps left for them. Staying too long also has its risks. Product managers are usually the last to acknowledge the market is waning and that it is time to move on.

A keen sense of timing may make the difference between people accepting a revolutionary idea and their considering its developer a complete fool. Fred Smith had his timing right when he created Federal Express. He launched his overnight delivery service at a time when the world was speeding up, and people were willing to pay a premium to have items delivered the next day. He saw a gap in the market and had the courage to go ahead, even though most people said it could not be done or few people really needed overnight service. When Nolan

Bushnell reflected on his life as an entrepreneur, he indicated that while his ideas were good, his timing was off. He noted that he got out of Atari too soon and that he got out of Pizza Time Theatres too late.

Firms that want to focus on the future have to slough off the past and the present. Sony and Mitsubishi actually set "sunset" dates for the abandonment of products so they do not get complacent. In a sense, they compete against themselves. One firm has the policy that it wants to create three new products for every product it phases out. Its three-fold strategy involves doing the following for each product it phases out: (1) developing one incrementally improved product from the original product, (2) developing a new product that is a spin-off from the original product, and (3) developing an entirely new product.

Agility: The Ability to Turn On a Dime

Agility can give a company a decisive edge over companies that fail to grasp its importance. The need for agility applies to entrepreneurial companies as well as established ones. Companies that lack perceptiveness and agility are destined to fall prey to the "here today, gone tomorrow" syndrome. Nicholas Murray Butler observed, "There are three types of people in the world: those who make things happen, those who watch what happens, and those who wonder what happened." If failed corporations were given funerals, many of their tombstones would read, "Here lies XYZ Corporation; its managers never knew what hit them!"

> Reality Check: Agility is of little value if the company is continuously blindsided. While the company may be able to adjust quickly, agility works best when the company has lead time. The company that sees the future first has a head start over companies that are preoccupied with what they are currently doing. Lead time determines whether the company will be a leader or a loser.

The show, *Stop the World—I Want to Get Off*, may have been popular on Broadway years ago, but trying to call a time-out when the world today is in a sea change is not a viable competitive strategy. Yet agility should not be viewed as a survival skill. Instead, it should be seen as a means for thriving in the years ahead. Just as companies recognized the need to continuously improve the quality of their operations to remain competitive in the 1990s, companies today must recognize the need for agility in the years to come.

Reengineering business processes can foster speed and agility. Reengineering can play an instrumental role in reducing and deleting activities that encumber value-added processes. Reengineering can reduce bureaucratic constraints and remove speed bumps that cause delays. Instead of just finding ways to do something faster by reducing the time required for an activity, reengineering may find a way to eliminate that activity or a series of activities altogether.

Reengineering also reduces handoffs between people when something needs to be handled within the firm or when a customer needs to have a situation addressed or resolved. The employee involved becomes a "case worker." Customer goodwill is generated when a well-trained case worker has access to real-time information and has the authority to do whatever needs to be done to resolve the situation promptly.

Increasing speed and agility may be beneficial in the human resources area as well. Companies that do not have the right number of people in the right place with the right capabilities will be passed by companies that are able to meet their human resource needs in a more timely manner. While a company may lose a customer because it did not have a certain item in stock, not having the right person in a mission-critical position can jeopardize the company altogether.

The firm should hire people who have the ability to hit the ground running. If people are hired who are accustomed to fast—where fast is no big deal, where they will not be whiplashed—they will be able to take fast in stride. General Electric looks for people who have a lot of mental and physical energy. Their energy gives them the adrenaline rush needed to rise to the occasion when faced with a challenge. Jeff Bezos of Amazon looks for people who are willing to change directions and to admit mistakes.

While it may be cheaper to hire less experienced people, such a practice means more time will have to be invested in training. People with less experience are more prone to learn by trial and error. They will not have the confidence and mental dexterity that comes from experience to be cool under fire when faced with trying challenges. Competent and confident people do not pause or freeze up when faced with a challenge. They are able to go from thought to action without hesitation. They pass the "match test," which tests whether the person can make a decision before they burn their fingers.

When US Airways Flight 1549 lost power in both of its main engines at 3,000 feet right after taking off from LaGuardia on January 15, 2009, Captain Chesley B. "Sully" Sullenberger realized he could not return to LaGuardia or make it to land at Teterboro airport in New Jersey. He then decided to glide the plane into a water landing in the frigid Hudson River. To do this with no power and no loss of life is truly amazing. Captain Sullenberger stated that his whole professional life prepared him for the challenge. He noted that his years of experience (being a fighter pilot, a commercial airlines pilot, safety instructor, and accident investigator) gave him the confidence and ability to do what he had never done.

The firm's processes need to foster fast hiring and fast firing. Most companies encourage slow hiring and fast firing. Mike Maples, cofounder of Motive Communications based in Austin, Texas observed, "Our really high hiring standards and slow hiring practices got us in trouble . . . we lost our competitive advantage. So we carefully started tracking our hiring process. We coined the term 'perfect hiring' which meant hiring 'A players on time.' Then we held a contest in which each team (engineering, marketing, etc.) would lose a point for every week a position remained open past the target hiring date. Now we treat our hiring forecast as seriously as our revenue forecast, and there's hell to pay for missing either one. . . . You need to be fully staffed to attack a market."[10] The firm's culture must be designed to make the firm the employer of choice where people will drop what they are doing to join the firm.

Cross training people also fosters speed and agility. Cross training and a willingness to take on any challenge help people function in various situations. Cross-functional teams build on this notion by bringing people together who are able to look at a situation from various vantage points at the same time.

Reality Check: Having a diverse group of people working on a problem may have merit, but it usually takes more time to reach a consensus with a diverse group. Make sure that everyone involved has a clear understanding of the priorities, expectations, and company's values.

Reality Check: Micromanaging slows things down. Micromanagers are like straitjackets to good people who want to manage themselves. Managers who micromanage cause good people to leave.

Reality Check: Perfection takes twice as much time as excellence . . . and some things just need to be done. Make sure you do not assign a perfectionist to a task where "good enough" is good enough.

Reality Check: Procrastination kills change. Some people just have a "put it off" mental framework. It's not that they are thorough and diligent. They just do not have a sense of urgency that is needed today. People who are not hard-wired to seize the day by making decisions and implementing them on the spot have no place in a fast company. You want people who, when asked, "Is that your final answer?" say, "Yes, let's roll."

Reality Check: The people serving on the board of directors need to get the need for speed and agility. Too often they have a legacy mindset or do not have an in-depth feel for the evolving situation. This causes them to be cautious and slow.

Every firm has a distinct culture. The firm's culture can affect its speed and agility. Some firms exhibit a sense of urgency that gives them a bias for making things happen "now." They are like sharks that have to keep moving to breathe. Some firms exhibit a sense of paranoia where they feel they have to move quickly to keep their competitors from catching them. The firm's culture must embrace change for the firm to be fast. People in firms with a strong set of values know what to do without having to ask their supervisor or check the policy manual before making a decision. The company's culture must also embody a constructive attitude about making mistakes, where mistakes are recognized as part of the learning and evolving process. The fear of making a mistake can freeze companies and people.

Reality Check: The days of walking the talk are over; leaders must run the talk. Lee Iococca noted the speed of the boss is the speed of the team. Fast companies need fast leaders, and fast-track projects need fast team leaders.

Executives Must Have the Ability to Focus on What Really Matters

Just as it is clear that no firm can be all things to all people, it is clear that no firm can pay attention to everything going on around it and within it. You cannot be fast if you are focusing on too many things. For a firm to be agile, it must be able to focus on what really matters.

Focus enables people to do split-second awareness, split-second deciding, and split-second action. Focus involves knowing what the yes's are and what the no's are. Triage involves more than just knowing what to do. It also involves knowing what not to do. Focus involves minimizing distractions. When you are traveling fast, you cannot afford to have distractions. Focus also involves having a clear sense of priorities. Firms with a clear sense of mission and a clearly articulated vision for where they want to be in the next three to five years are far less likely to be distracted or seduced by short-lived opportunities.

Focus enables management to direct its attention to the truly important issues. It also enhances the firm's ability to respond quickly when variances occur. Focus is enhanced by management systems that incorporate managing by objectives, time-activity networks, and sensitivity analysis. Managing by objectives forces the firm to identify what it is striving to accomplish. Time-activity networks like PERT and CPM help identify the most critical path(s). Sensitivity analysis like the "Pareto 80/20 analysis" helps identify the few (20%) actions that will make the greatest (80%) difference. Edwin Bliss, who wrote *Getting Things Done*, recommends using a five-category system that classifies endeavors in terms of their importance to long-term success and their urgency. He noted that executives need to direct their attention to endeavors that have high importance and high urgency. He also cautioned executives against falling prey to the "tyranny of the urgent" where their preoccupation with urgent issues with nominal importance keeps them from also focusing on longer-term issues that have greater importance.[11]

These techniques identify in advance the factors that need to be monitored closely. While these techniques have been around for years, today's online, real-time information technology makes it possible for people at all levels of an organization to monitor even the smallest variances. Information technology thereby permits management to focus its attention on exceptional variances. The sooner a variance is recognized, the quicker the firm can respond. The need for timely feedback is reflected in the Merrill Lynch ad, "It's not what you know that matters, it's when you know it that matters."

Jon Carlson, as CEO of SAS Airlines, stressed the need for everyone in the firm to consider every point of contact with a customer to be a "moment of truth" for the airline. He noted that each contact either reinforced or undermined SAS's commitment to customer service. Monitoring the quality of the moments of truth with your customers can play a significant role in whether you get repeat customers and whether your current customers recommend your business to others. One cruise line analyzes its customers' comment cards within a few hours after they disembark. The line provides the data to key people before the ship leaves on its next cruise later that day. This may sound impressive, but a real-time cruise line would have an ongoing system to get customer input *during* the cruise so some of the issues could be corrected while the passengers were still on the cruise, not after the cruise.

Focus is also reflected in Cypress Semiconductor's total commitment to managing by objectives which was profiled in chapter five. Under T. J. Rogers's leadership, Cypress established a system that sets and monitors over 6,000 performance factors on an ongoing basis.[12] The system was established to foster a "no surprises" environment. Cypress's performance dashboard provides timely performance information on mission-critical activities. Objectives are set on Monday, reviewed for progress on Wednesday, and reviewed again for completion on Friday. While Rogers's "Turbo MBO" system may seem too tight, it forces each manager to focus on the areas that make a difference. If awareness of the need to change is prerequisite to initiating a change effort, then Rogers's system provides an early warning system that enables quick responses. Having crucial information on a real-time basis permits real-time adjustments. State-of-the-art management information systems now resemble the radar-interfaced control systems that enable jet fighters to fly closer to the ground at even faster speeds.

Alan Solomon of Ford observed, "When things are already running fast . . . you have to give the right people the right information at the right time."[13] You also need to have an environment where people are not left in the dark or blindsided—especially with bad news. Harold Geneen, as CEO of IT&T years ago, insisted on operating with a "no surprise" environment. He was known for his policy, "I want to hear bad news and I don't want to hear it late!"

Reality Check: Even though this chapter has stressed the value of speed, the best firms rarely have to be that fast. Speed is less important if you start earlier. If you start earlier, then you can get to your destination with time to spare. By starting earlier, you are not rushed. This enables you to be cool under fire and to keep your head when your competitors are in a "red alert" condition.

Concluding Comments: Timing Is a Multidimensional Competency

The good old days of stability, linearity, and predictability are gone forever. Turbulence and discontinuity are no longer occasional occurrences. There will be times when the company's agility, speed, anticipation, perceptiveness, innovativeness, and decisiveness will provide the company with the ability to seize opportunities and gain formidable advantages.

Speed is not an option. If you snooze, you lose. Agility is not an option. If your firm is not changing as much as the world around it in the ways it needs to change, then it is facing extinction. It's no longer carpe diem, "seize the day," it's seize the second, in such a way that you also are positioned to seize the future. That's quite a challenge.

Raw and unbridled speed can kill a firm. Firms need "smart" speed. There will be times when the firm should put the pedal to the metal, but there will be times when it will have to slow down. Firms need to have a keen sense of timing so they do not hit the market too soon or too late. They will also need to be perceptive enough to know when it is wiser to be a fast follower rather than a first mover.

Your company's future will be contingent on whether it has the ability to quickly: (1) sense the need for change, (2) learn what needs to be done differently, (3) develop innovative approaches for providing value to the marketplace, and (4) commit resources to initiate changes. Your company will capitalize on emerging opportunities by developing opportunistic strategies and having an innovative corporate culture. Quickness and agility can be competitive advantages. If your firm is able to do things your competitors cannot do, at least at that time, then it will have an edge. With increasing discontinuity, the ability to adapt and improvise will also be valuable competencies.

If you want to increase your firm's speed and agility, then you need to make a deliberate and continuous effort to eliminate or reduce the red lights that slow people and processes down. You will also need to provide the green lights that enable people and processes to accelerate to their potential. And when your people get comfortable operating at an elevated pace and with greater agility, you will need to raise the bar again so they will have the ability to be even faster and more agile. To be an ever-evolving enterprise, your firm will need to keep pace—if not just a step ahead of the ever-accelerating rate of change. Ever-evolving enterprises also recognize that as they improve their speed and agility, they also need to make sure they are in the right forest and improve the other competencies as well.

While it may not be possible for management to sense every opportunity and to prevent every problem, every effort should be made to create an environment where the firm is able to operate from an offensive stance. In either case, management should embrace the following U.S. West ad. Take the Speed and agility quiz in Table 7.2 to learn the extent to which your firm is positioned for speed and agility.

You either make dust or you eat dust!

—U.S. West ad

TABLE 7.2.   Speed and Agility Quiz

How does your firm rate on the following dimensions? *Rating: 1 = not at all, 2 = slightly true, 3 = somewhat true, 4 = mostly true, 5 = completely true	Level*
1. Top executives get the need for and personify speed and agility.	1-2-3-4-5
2. Your firm recognizes when it is time to plan and when it is more appropriate to respond to change.	1-2-3-4-5
3. Your firm has ongoing efforts to reduce the constraints that impede speed and agility.	1-2-3-4-5
4. Your firm recognizes when speed is crucial and when it is not.	1-2-3-4-5
5. Your firm avoids paralysis by analysis.	1-2-3-4-5
6. Your firm consistently finds ways to reduce cycle times.	1-2-3-4-5
7. Your firm's people are cross-trained to foster change and adaptability.	1-2-3-4-5

TABLE 7.2. (Continued)

How does your firm rate on the following dimensions? *Rating: 1 = not at all, 2 = slightly true, 3 = somewhat true, 4 = mostly true, 5 = completely true	Level*
8. Your firm is decentralized so people closer to the action are authorized to make and implement decisions.	1-2-3-4-5
9. People at all levels in your firm have the confidence and confidence to make timely decisions on their own.	1-2-3-4-5
10. Your firm does SWOT analysis so it can identify potential opportunities and threats/vulnerabilities.	1-2-3-4-5
11. Your firm has a management information system that provides early warning indicators that indicate the need for change.	1-2-3-4-5
12. Your firm has systems and people in place who are ready to respond to various types of crises.	1-2-3-4-5
13. People throughout the firm have a clear sense of the firm's values and priorities which enable them to make decisions without having to refer to policy manuals or their supervisors.	1-2-3-4-5
14. Your firm handles strategic adaptation well.	1-2-3-4-5
15. Your firm handles tactical adaptation well.	1-2-3-4-5
16. Your firm is very customer-centric. It senses the need for change when your customers change.	1-2-3-4-5
17. Your firm capitalizes on the Internet and intranet to foster speed.	1-2-3-4-5
Total points	

Scoring Key

73–85	Congratulations, your firm demonstrates the qualities of a fast and agile organization.
60–72	Your organization has many strengths, but still has areas that need to be improved.
48–59	Your organization has some strengths, but there is a lot of room for improvement.
35–47	Your organization either has some significant impairments or is weak in most areas. Tweaking your firm's speed and agility will not be enough to make a real difference.
17–34	Your organization may be beyond hope. It will take a radical change in management, in corporate culture, systems, and processes to have any chance of being competitive in the future.

Notes

Some of the material in this chapter originally appeared in *Business Horizons*. Reprinted with permission from *Business Horizons*, vol. 43, issue 1. Stephen C. Harper, "Timing—The Bedrock of Anticipatory Management," 75–83, Copyright 2000 with permission from Elsevier.

1. Michael LeBoeuf, *Fast Forward* (New York: G.P. Putnam's Sons, 1993): 12.

2. Ibid., 207, 208.

3. Andy Reinhardt, "Intel," *Business Week*, no. 3558 (1997): 73.

4. Peter Drucker, *Managing for Results* (New York: Harper, 1993).

5. 1990 Intel publication.

6. William E. Sheeline, "Avoiding Growth's Perils," *Fortune* 122, no. 4 (1990): 58.

7. Guy Kawasaki, *Rules for Revolutionaries*, Stanford Executive Briefings video (Mill Valley, CA: Kantola Productions, 1999).

8. Rich Karlgaard, "Digital Rules," *Forbes* 164, no. 1 (1999): 43.

9. Ibid.

10. Rekha Balu, "Hiring Right Means Hiring Fast," *Fast Company*, no. 35, (2000): 396.

11. Edwin Bliss, *Getting Things Done* (NewYork: Time Warner Paperback books, 1993).

12. T. J. Rogers, "No Excuses Management," *Harvard Business Review* 68, no. 1 (1990): 84.

13. Gina Imperato, "SDRC Wants You to Go Faster," *Fast Company*, no. 28 (1999): 92.

Chapter 8

Becoming a Learning Organization

The ability to learn faster than your competitors may be the only sustainable competitive advantage.

—Arie deGeus, of Royal Dutch Shell

The primary responsibility of business leaders is to develop their firms so they will be more successful tomorrow than they are today. Fulfilling that responsibility will involve finding new things to do and new ways to do things. Organizational learning is one of the first steps towards achieving superior performance. Some firms even hire people to be their Chief Learning Officer or Chief Knowledge Officer. Firms that fail to recognize and eliminate obstacles to learning will not be able to make the changes necessary to create their future. This chapter focuses on how to create a learning organization.

Arie deGeus's observation should be amended in two ways, First, learning faster than your competitors is only of value if you are learning the right things and you are able to operationalize what you learn. Being smarter is of little value if you do not act on what you know. Learning may seem like a noble endeavor, but businesses need to get a return on what they learn. Second, the word "evolve" should replace the word "learn." Learning is important, but it is the extent to which the firm evolves that determines whether it succeeds. This chapter profiles how learning plays an integral role in helping the firm be an ever-evolving enterprise.

We live in a world where we can be suffocated by the incredible amount of information that surrounds us. Yet we gasp for the knowledge needed to enhance our firm's performance. One of the challenges of a learning organization is to be able to differentiate information and knowledge. Knowledge can be defined as information that can make a difference.

Learning is far from a given in most firms. Many firms get stuck in habitual ruts that prevent them from reaching their true potential. This causes considerable frustration for executives all the way down to first-line employees. Some firms make the same mistakes over and over, sometimes without even realizing it. Countless firms have missed opportunities for competitive success because they were unprepared for them or—worse—were simply unaware of them.

Someone once stated, "The firm with the smartest people wins." The observation is only true if the team is smartest in the areas that will give it a competitive advantage and if it *applies* what it knows. Being the smartest is of little value if you cannot apply what you know. Brain matter is nice, but if it is not converted into perceptive, value-added action, then learning is of little practical value. It is like having a fast car that does not leave your garage.

Learning organizations recognize that true learning is evident when behavior changes. The chapter on anticipatory management profiled how inquiries may lead to insights which may then lead to initiatives. Inquiries and insights are important, but they are the means to the desired end; they are only of value if they foster initiatives that enhance performance.

Peter Senge, who wrote *The Fifth Discipline*, defined learning organizations as, "Organizations where people continually expand their capacity to create the results they truly desire, where new and expansive patterns of thinking are nurtured, where collective aspiration is set free, and where people are continually learning to learn together."[1] Many executives resist the term "learning organization" despite the popularity of Senge's work. Yet if you ask executives, "What will it take for your firm to succeed?" most will say that they need to be better than their competitors at the things their customers value. Being better requires learning. Knowing what your customers truly value requires learning. How can you have continuous improvement without continuous learning?

While many executives have a negative stigma with the term "learning organization," they openly advocate the need for and value of market intelligence, customer intelligence, and competitor intelligence. These executives will embrace the concept of "learning organization" if they mentally substitute the term "intelligent enterprise" whenever they hear the term "learning organization."

Reality Check: There is no guarantee of success in today's competitive business environment. For your firm to have its best chance, it will need to be smarter and learn faster than its rivals. It will have to generate better ideas, develop more effective strategies, and make better decisions than competing firms. It will also have to be better at executing what it learns.

The Role of Learning in Achieving Superior Performance

When a firm executes what it has learned, it is by definition implementing a change. Figure 8.1 profiles how learning sets the stage for superior performance. To excel, firms must be able to create and sustain significant competitive advantages. To have a competitive edge, they must be able to offer better products and services than their competitors. They also need to find ways to offer more value to their customers by being faster, achieving higher quality, being more efficient, and so forth. Developing competitive advantages requires making changes that foster innovation and continuous improvement. Thus the firm's success is directly related to its ability to learn.

How Learning Organization Concepts Apply to Organizational Success

This chapter focuses on value-added learning and the ability to apply what you learn. It focuses on how to create an organizational environment where people grow, ideas flourish, and performance is enhanced. The next chapter focuses on to how to create your company's future by fostering innovation, which is one of the benefits associated with being a learning organization. Learning organizations provide a platform for enhancing their competitive positions by:

- Knowing where to go and how to get there.
- Making the right changes at the right time.
- Having the mental dexterity to think thoughts no one has thought before.
- Knowing what you need to know when you need to know it.
- Knowing what you do not know so you can be positioned to learn it.
- Looking for things others do not look for by continually scanning your external and internal environments.

FIGURE 8.1.   The Path to Achieving Superior Performance

Learning → Processes	Change → Programs	Competitive → Advantage(s)	Superior Performance

- Having a kaleidoscopic perspective to see things others do not see.
- Seeing things before others see them via strategic learning.
- Doing what your firm and possibly no other firm has done.
- Having the courage to challenge the status quo and conventional wisdom.
- Finding new things to do and new ways to do things.
- Finding innovative solutions to problems through breakthrough thinking.
- Modifying what you are doing by being adaptive when others do not see the need to change.
- Executing your plans more effectively through operational learning.

If your firm embraces, internalizes, and operationalizes these ideas and approaches, then it will be in a position to become an ever-evolving, and exceptional, enterprise.

Two of the critical components of learning organizations are intelligence and knowledge. Intelligence is an indication of mental capacity. It is like aptitude. It reflects the person's ability to learn quickly and to understand. Knowledge is what you know. Just as an individual has an Intelligence Quotient (IQ), each organization has an IQ. Organizational performance and success are contingent on the ability to learn quickly what needs to be learned and the extent to which the organization has the knowledge it needs to perform better than its competitors in providing value to its target market. The most successful organizations learn quicker and better than their competitors.

Reality Check: If your firm is to win in the marketplace, then it must strive to be an expert in the areas that make the greatest difference.

The Contextual Change Model Reflects the Role of Learning in Enhancing Performance

The contextual change model in Figure 8.2 profiles the situational nature of decision making. It also demonstrates the role learning plays in achieving desired results. Firms that learn, decide, implement, and gain

FIGURE 8.2.   Contextual Change Model

Step One—Results Orientation: Identifying the desired results.

Step Two—Awareness: Becoming aware of the factors and forces at play in the unique situation.

Step Three—Pre-action Learning: Identifying and reviewing available information and practices that provide insights into the situation.

Step Four—Understanding: Developing a model that reflects the relationships among the factors and forces.

Step Five—Management: Identifying and then evaluating the alternative approaches for addressing the situation. Making decisions about what needs to be done to achieve the desired results. Having an open mind helps in developing innovative solutions.

Step Six—Change: Implementing an action plan for achieving the desired results. Monitoring the degree of success as it is being implemented and making adjustments when and where appropriate.

Step Seven—Results: Achieving the desired results.

Step Eight—Post-action Learning: Reviewing what was learned from the experience and making the learning available to others in the organization so that you and/ or others will be even more successful if your firm is involved in a similar situation again.

sustainable competitive advantages more quickly, will achieve superior results more quickly.

Learning Organizations Embrace Curiosity, Inquiry, and Contempt for the Status Quo

John Kotter, author of *Leading Change,* stresses the need for brutal honesty. He indicates that managers need to have the courage to seek the truth, to challenge assumptions, and to face the truth in order to gain a sense for the true realities that need to be addressed in leading a firm.

Learning often begins with a set of attitudes that prompt a mental journey from the known to the unknown. Questions like, "Why does it have to be done that way?" get people to explore different possibilities and to come up with innovative ideas. People in learning organizations know that coming up with the right answers (an integral part of competitive strategy) involves asking the right questions. Learning and innovation often involve challenging what people have taken for granted.

Learning organizations develop processes so that people can ask perceptive and probing questions. Yet the best learning organizations also create an environment where people can ask "dumb" questions. Dumb questions can have value because they keep things from being taken for granted. Children often drive their parents crazy by asking, "Why, why, why?" about even the simplest things. Yet their questions often do not get much of a logical response from their parents other than, "That's the way it has always been done."

Dumb questions may lead to the development of smart answers. An example may illustrate the value of what some may consider a childlike question. Decades ago when a father took a picture of his daughter, the child asked why she could not see the picture right away. The father told her that was not possible because cameras cannot do that. As the story goes, the father Edwin Land, went on to develop the Polaroid camera that would develop pictures on the spot. It is ironic that years later Kodak missed the initial "digital photo wave" which introduced cameras without film that permitted the user to see what the pictures would look like immediately, delete the ones that were not wanted, modify and enhance the pictures on their computers, print them at home, send them to others electronically, and archive them for future use.

Learning organizations are never satisfied. They have contempt for the status quo and cannot tolerate mediocrity. If the firms that made cameras that used film had raised the question, "Why do cameras need film?" they might have been willing to catch or even invent the digital camera wave. This is why it is so important for firms to hire and interact with people who have different backgrounds and perspectives. New employees often ask the types of questions that regular employees no longer ask.

Reality Check: Suppliers, customers, and the public at large are also in a position to ask questions that may keep the firm from taking things for granted and accepting things as they are. Does your firm have processes in place that encourage people outside the firm to share their thoughts and suggestions with you?

Sony provides a good example of the need to approach a situation with a fresh perspective from the very beginning. When Sony entered the music business, top management decided to staff its music venture team with people from outside the music industry. Top management recognized it would be difficult to gain a competitive advantage if it staffed the team with people who had spent their careers in the music business. Sony wanted its music division to be innovative, so it put together a team of people from various fields including its video game business. Sony believed "outsiders" would ask probing questions, challenge prevailing wisdom, and offer innovative approaches, which would separate its music business from the pack.

Learning organizations also ask "What if ... ?" questions and run "What if ... ?" scenarios on a regular basis. The questions may involve identifying possible opportunities. They may also involve identifying possible threats. The chapter on anticipatory management provided a more comprehensive discussion of the role scenarios can play in enhancing performance. "What if ... ?" scenarios can broaden one's imagination. They can encourage people to think the unthinkable.

Two of Albert Einstein's observations reinforce the role that questions and imagination play in learning. He noted, "I have no particular talent. I am merely inquisitive." He also noted, "Imagination is more important than knowledge. Knowledge is limited. Imagination encircles the world."

Albert Einstein captured two other points about learning. He noted, "The significant problems we face cannot be solved at the same level of thinking we were at when we created them." Too many firms have like-minded people who have legacy mindsets. They are unable to think outside the box to come up with innovative or even different approaches to addressing their problems. If they had had mental dexterity, asked probing questions, challenged critical assumptions, and been proactive, they would not have been confronted by many of the challenges that could have been prevented or reduced.

Einstein defined insanity as, "Doing the same thing over and over again and expecting different results." His definition of insanity may be humorous, but it also reflects some of the problems firms are experiencing today Too many firms continue doing the same things the same way in a world that is experiencing incredible change. Too many firms are either unable to come up with new approaches or lack the courage to make the changes that need to be made. For decades, top executives at General Motors did not make the changes they knew they needed to make, and by the time they made the changes, it was too late to really help them to solve their problems and to capitalize on emerging opportunities.

How Do You Create a Learning Organization?

Just as superior performance (in Figure 8.1) reflects the true value of developing competitive advantage(s), so does effective change mirror the firm's ability to learn. Executives who want to take their firms to the next level and beyond will only be able to do so if they successfully initiate appropriate and timely changes. Recent research, however, indicates that about 80 percent of change efforts fail. Another way to think of this is that the vast majority of firms have learning impairments. To be successful, executives need to understand why most of their change efforts do not produce the results they desire. In other words, they need to understand why their organizations are unable to learn what they need to learn, when they need to learn it.

Kurt Lewin may have captured the reasons most change efforts fail. He developed two simple, yet powerful, models to explain the dynamics of change. Lewin's force-field change model—which was profiled in chapter one—profiles that change efforts are more likely to succeed when certain factors are incorporated in the change process. He identified dual sets of forces that are present in every change effort. One set of forces drives the change, and a competing set of forces restrains the change. His three-step change model—which was also profiled in chapter one—indicated that most change efforts fail because change is usually approached as a one-step process rather than as a three-step "unfreezing-change-refreezing" process.[2]

So what does all this psychological mumbo jumbo mean? First, it means that management's efforts to bring about change will not be successful if the restraining forces are stronger than the driving forces. At a more fundamental level, if the things that impair the firm's ability to learn are greater than the factors that support learning, the desired change will not occur as effectively, as quickly as desired, or at all. Second, before any change can be implemented, the firm must discontinue what it has been doing. Stated simply, the firm must experience the initial stage of change—the unfreezing stage—by recognizing it should not and cannot continue doing what it has been doing. This stage is a critical learning period for the firm. When employees understand the need for change—that they are on a "burning platform"—they will be more receptive to change efforts. Third, after the change has been implemented, a "refreezing" must take place in which newly learned behaviors that enhance performance are reinforced. Unfortunately, learning impairments inhibit change at each of these stages.

Eric Hoffer, author of *The Ordeal of Change*, noted, "In times of rapid change, the learners will inherit the future."[3] Executives who want to take their firms to the next level cannot continue doing what they have been doing, or merely try to keep up with their competitors. Someone once noted that if your firm is not changing as much as the world around it is changing, then you are on the road to bankruptcy. More of the same simply will not cut it.

Creating a learning organization requires a two-dimensional game plan. First, management must reduce and/or eliminate the factors and forces that impair learning. Second, management must provide an environment that enables the firm to be ever-evolving. This section focuses on some of the most common learning impairments. Other sections focus on creating an environment that fosters innovation and develops the firm's human resources to their fullest potential.

To be successful in the years ahead, your firm will need to be smarter, quicker, more innovative, and more adaptive. As you reduce and eliminate the forces that impair learning in your organization, you can begin to take those actions that will enhance your ability to learn.

A Closer Look at the Nature of Learning Impairments

John Gardner, the founder of Common Cause, described the propensity for organizations to be learning impaired. He noted in his essay *The Life and Death of Institutions*, "Most ailing organizations have developed a functional blindness to their own defects. They are not suffering because they can't solve their problems but because they won't see their problems. They can look straight at their faults and rationalize them as virtues or necessities."[4]

This section identifies factors that impair learning and keep firms from being more successful. In our research[5] 250 people were asked to describe factors that impaired learning in their organizations. The respondents were from a diverse set of organizations. Their positions ranged from senior executives to first-line supervisors. Some of the respondents were entrepreneurs. Some held staff positions. Some worked for Fortune 500 firms. Some worked for emerging ventures. Overall, they represented a variety of industries and types of businesses.

The respondents provided more than a thousand examples of factors that blocked learning in their organizations. Most of their responses could be grouped into the three broad categories of learning impairments:

managerial factors, organizational factors, and external and future factors.

Each of these three main categories includes a few related dimensions of learning-impaired organizations. For instance, the managerial factors category is composed of leadership failures, a lack of employee inclusiveness, inappropriate mental models, and poorly handled change efforts. In turn, within each of these narrower dimensions, specific examples of learning impairments are provided. The basic characteristics of each learning impairment are provided to highlight the corresponding obstacle.

Managerial Factors That Impair Learning

A. Leadership Failures

- **Leadership not setting the example for learning** Characteristics: Failure of top management to champion learning, to embrace the latest technology and to incorporate the lessons learned from previous experience and events.
- **Insular management** Characteristics: Management operates in a vacuum and is isolated from the rest of organization and the external environment. Top management is not able to provide a fresh perspective because it came up through the ranks.
- **Management arrogance, ignorance, and complacency** Characteristics: Strong egos and previous success cause managers to refuse to recognize and/or admit their mistakes. Management is unwilling to explore the best practices of other firms.
- **Poor top-down communication** Characteristics: Management's lack of concern or empathy for employees keeps employees in the dark. Information is provided on a "need-to-know basis."

B. Lack of Employee Inclusiveness

- **Not soliciting ideas** Characteristics: Management does not interact with employees and/or is unwilling to seek employee input. Employees have good ideas, but they are not being sought.
- **Lack of upward communication** Characteristics: Upward communication is ignored or channels are blocked. Management considers suggestions and constructive criticism to be an insult to the existing processes.
- **Lack of empowerment to learn and change** Characteristics: Lower level employees are not encouraged to think "outside the box" or to experiment with new approaches, and they are not empowered to initiate change.

C. Inappropriate Mental Models

- **Ineffective mental models** Characteristics: Management has a "legacy" mindset. It is not in sync with current realities and is unwilling to unlearn, to consider new possibilities and try different approaches.
- **Preoccupation with the short-term and the bottom line** Characteristics: Management focuses too much on the here and now. It focuses on cutting costs to enhance current profitability rather than taking the time to learn and invest in the future. Downsizing may be jeopardizing performance by reducing the talent pool.
- **Quick fix mentality** Characteristics: Management is unwilling to make the commitment to change the things that may take considerable time and resources.

D. Poorly Handled Change Efforts by Management

- **Lack of holistic approach to change** Characteristics: Changes are often approached on a "flavor-of-the-month" basis. Changes are either too few or too many. Changes are too late or not implemented well.
- **Lack of top management commitment to change** Characteristics: Management does not have the guts to do what needs to be done or to follow things through when problems are encountered.
- **Lack of communication about change** Characteristics: Management does not provide sufficient communication before, during, or after change. The lack of communication causes coordination problems among units.
- **Fear and anxiety about change** Characteristics: Change threatens management. Management's fear of looking bad causes it to not ask for help or advice from others. Employees are afraid of making mistakes and being fired.
- **Change in leadership** Characteristics: Turnover, rotation, restructuring, and the general lack of continuity cause employees to be uncertain and to resist change. Employees demonstrate a "Let's wait things out" or "Why bother?" attitude.

Organizational Factors That Impair Learning

A. Lack of Support for Learning

- **Inadequate training** Characteristics: Top management fails to support lifelong learning and does not provide sufficient time and funding for job-specific and advancement-related training.
- **Inadequate system for knowledge acquisition and sharing** Characteristics: There is no common database to contribute, store, access, and

disseminate information. People keep reinventing the wheel because they are unable to learn best practices and lessons learned from others.

- **Unwillingness to use the appropriate technology** Characteristics: Managers and employees do not embrace new technology, including capitalizing on the full value of the Internet. Changes are often made without sufficient preparation and debugging.
- **Lack of multidirectional communication** Characteristics: Top management is not indicating what is happening and why it is happening. Departments are not communicating with other departments. Departments operate as "silos."

B. Organizational Inertia and Dosed-Mindedness

- **The culture does not foster learning and change** Characteristics: The norm is for everyone to do the same thing again and again. People are reluctant to explore, to innovate, to take risks, and to challenge the status quo.
- **Organizational bureaucracy and rigidity** Characteristics: Deviations from standard operating procedure are not tolerated. Multiple layers for approval and bureaucratic processes impede learning, decision making, and taking the initiative.
- **Politics** Characteristics: People are more concerned about their own self-promotion and protecting their territory than doing what is best for the overall organization. Game playing and power brokering drain valuable energy that could be directed to finding ways to improve performance.

C. Reactive Approach to Human Resources

- **Lack of diversity and good old boy mentality** Characteristics: There is a tendency to hire similar people and to promote from within. This reduces the diversity of perspectives and reduces the chances people will make waves by thinking different thoughts.
- **Lack of performance measurement and accountability for poor performance** Characteristics: Performance issues are not addressed. People who do exceptional work are not rewarded. People who do poor work continue doing poor work and may still be rewarded.

External and Future Factors That Impair Learning

A. Organizational Lethargy

- **Lack of a future orientation** Characteristics: Management is not anticipating where the market will be in the future. It is too caught up in what is happening now.

- **Lack of anticipatory learning** Characteristics: Management is not focusing on trends, monitoring leading indicators, or pondering potential discontinuities.
- **Reactive management—lack of proactivity** Characteristics: Management tends to wait for a crisis before taking action. It has an, "If it becomes a problem, then we'll deal with it" mentality.
- **Clinging to the ways things have been done** Characteristics: There is a preoccupation with how things have been done rather than how they could be approached in a more innovative way. There is an "If it isn't broke, don't fix it." mentality.

B. Lack of Mindfulness

- **Lack of customer-centricity** Characteristics: Management exhibits arrogance toward customers. Customers are not the primary concern. Management does not focus on customer wants and does not actively solicit customer input.
- **Lack of contextual or holistic decision making** Characteristics: Management has symptoms of attention deficit disorder. It fails to look at situations from multiple vantage points or to think things through.
- **Lack of proactive problem solving** Characteristics: Problem analysis is superficial. Root cause analysis is rarely done, lessons learned from previous experience are not used, and post-project reviews are almost nonexistent.

Creating a Culture for Learning

Becoming a learning organization involves making a deliberate effort to reduce and prevent learning impairments and creating an environment that enhances learning. The following sections provide insights into how to become a learning organization and enhance performance.

Importing Best Practices Can Be a "Catch-22"

Few people would contest the need for companies to study the best practices of companies in and outside their industry. There will be times when utilizing existing business practices may be quite useful. Adopting best practices and benchmarking against other firms play a key role in learning organizations. Learning from other firms may speed the learning process because it may keep you from reinventing the wheel.

There will be times, however, when adopting the practices of other firms has drawbacks. There are at least four situations when borrowing existing solutions may not be appropriate or beneficial:

First, companies that want to be at the leading edge must come up with new insights and develop new answers. They need to be able to explore uncharted markets rather than just harvest existing markets. They also need to develop innovative products, services, and processes rather than just recycle existing knowledge and offer imitative solutions. Changing times call for new ideas, new approaches, and new solutions.

Second, executives should not become too infatuated with the benchmark companies, especially in their industry. They need to remember that the most radical challenges to established companies usually come from newcomers who do not play by the rules and who do not have legacy systems to slow them down mentally or physically. Newcomers that break the rules may become breakthrough companies.

Third, when you adopt best practices and benchmark against existing firms you are adopting what is currently being done. You must aim for a moving target, not a stationary target. If you try to match what the leading firms are doing now, then even if you can match their standard, you will still be behind them because they will most assuredly be moving forward and getting better.

Fourth, you need to know when to borrow and when to develop your own best practices. There will be times when you will need to develop unique solutions or practices to deal with your own unique situations. Just because one firm has been successful with its approach does not mean that it will work as well, or at all, in your firm. Its approach may have worked because it fit that firm's culture, readiness for change, goals, and reward structure. The goodness of fit also applies to adopting "off-the-shelf" or generic solutions and practices. They may not fit your firm's unique situation. Existing solutions may take less time and money, but they will be effective only to the extent that they match your company's unique situation. You need to recognize that, like humans, organizations can experience transplant shock when the receiving organization rejects the new part.

Executives need to step back and look at their company and their industry through irreverent glasses. They need to take a fresh look at every situation, every practice, and every assumption. Business process reengineering, when coupled with corpreneurial business strategies, enables companies to look for new opportunities and to develop revolutionary ways to delight customers who are not having their needs met well, or at all.

Creating a Learning Organization Involves Killing Bureaucracy and Sacred Cows

Learning organizations incorporate processes that resemble "tough love." Top management must encourage introspection, multidirectional communication, and constructive criticism throughout the company. When the company is confronted with a problem or performance falls below expectations, people must be free to challenge the key assumptions, prevailing perceptions, and the way things are done. For substantive learning to take place, there can be no sacred topics, no sacred practices, and no sacred cows.

The company's overall environment may play an even more important part in creating a learning organization. Numerous conditions must exist before a company can be considered a learning organization. Few companies demonstrate the internalization and operationalization of a learning organization better than General Electric. Jeff Immelt, as GE's CEO, captured the need for GE to be a learning organization when he noted that GE must experiment with new approaches, to accelerate the evolution of its processes, and to ensure his team has the right tools to "look around corners."[6]

GE's Management Development Institute is in the John F. Welch Leadership Center. It has been noted for its unprecedented candor. The no-holds-barred environment in the Institute's "Pit" enables new recruits to challenge any idea regardless of who presented it.[7] At the Welch Center, people regularly come up with ideas and action plans that foster higher levels of corporate performance. It also provides an environment where managers achieve personal breakthroughs that enable them to change.[8] The Welch Center's environment where present practices, policies, and strategies can be challenged has produced several ways to bust bureaucratic practices.

One particularly noteworthy technique GE developed is a CRAP Detector. The acronym stands for "Critical Review Appraisal." The CRAP detector takes a look at organizational processes and classifies them according to the degree of difficulty and the extent that a change will have a favorable impact on the organization.[9] The CRAP detector seeks out processes that will provide breakthrough performance when they are eliminated.

Executives who are serious about having their companies become learning organizations should also incorporate the "workout" process used by General Electric. GE established the workout process as a vehicle for developing leaders and improving the company's performance. Workout sessions bring a group of managers together to identify and address a particular problem or situation. The executive who is responsible for that area is invited to attend the workout session, but the executive does not run the session. Instead, the executive is drilled on any possible dimension of the problem or situation by the younger managers. Workout sessions bring issues into the open so they can be addressed. They also provide valuable insights into GE's strategies, practices, and operations for the younger/newer managers. The insights play an integral role in developing future leaders for GE.[10]

GE also developed a "RAMMPP" process where reports, approvals, meetings, measures, policies, and practices are reviewed at all levels (self, department, group, company, and so forth) to determine ways to reduce bureaucracy and enhance performance. The corresponding group analyzes whether each item being reviewed can be eliminated, partially eliminated, delegated downward, done less often, done in a less complicated/time consuming manner, done with fewer people involved, or done using more productive technology.[11]

Creating a Learning Organization Involves Acquiring, Developing, and Using Knowledge

Context Integration, which was acquired by eForce, demonstrated how a company can turn knowledge into a competitive weapon. Context Integration was a Web solutions company that was committed to gathering and sharing information with all of its people. Context Integration developed a knowledge management system called IAN (Intellectual Assets Network). IAN stored best practices, tracked new ideas, fielded questions, and operated as a kind of group mind. Every day, IAN distributed articles and tips to employees who might find them relevant. When a problem arose, the network tracked down the best qualified people to solve it. Before being acquired, Bruce Strong, VP of strategic services noted, "We have positioned ourselves on the frothing part of the knowledge wave. . . .

If we're not sharing ideas with one another, with our clients, and with our partners, we're in deep trouble."[12]

Learning organizations do not spend all their time developing new knowledge. They recognize there is no reason to reinvent the wheel if the knowledge they need already exists. Learning organizations develop knowledge networks so they can access critical information. Context Integration's IAN served as an idea-recycling center. Teams at Context Integration began every new project by searching IAN for past work that was similar to what they were doing, looking for ideas and practices that they could borrow. The goal was to use anything—models, architecture, source code—that would help them avoid duplicating another team's work.[13]

Less experienced employees usually do not have a wealth of contacts in their professional network within and outside the firm. This means they will not be able to access information as quickly as veteran employees who are well networked.

Thomas Edison indicated that success is the product of 10 percent inspiration and 90 percent perspiration. Bob Young, cofounder of Red Hat, redefined the formula for success. He stated it is the product of "1 percent inspiration and 99 percent theft."[14] While Bob Young may not have been advocating actual theft, he did recognize that the solutions to some business problems may already exist.

Xerox Business Services created Camp Lur'ning so its employees get a chance to share their ideas and learn from others, including XBS's customers. XBS employees are encouraged to find ways to better serve their customers by asking probing questions, gathering evidence, formulating a theory, testing it, modifying it with the help of others, and crafting a solution.[15]

Learning organizations try to minimize the role that habits may play when making decisions. The U.S. Army's Opposing Force (OPFOR) brigade's job is to help prepare soldiers for combat. It stresses the need to do a perceptive analysis before decisions are made as well as after they are implemented. The army recognizes that how you make decisions needs to incorporate continuous improvement. It has developed an extensive debriefing program called "After Action Reviews" (AAR). The

Army recognized that all too often when a group completed a project, it was either disbanded or went on to the next project. In both cases, no time was provided to deliberately reflect on and document what was learned from the experience as well as what could be done better if the group or some other group faces a similar situation in the future.[16]

The U.S. Army's Opposing Force makes learning an integral part of every activity by analyzing what was learned and how it could be improved in the future. Too many people rely on their memories about what they experienced before—which may not be complete or accurate—when they are called on to do something again. AAR provides lessons learned similar to Context Integration's IAN to help people do whatever they are expected to do better. It also provides valuable insights for people who are doing something for the first time, based on the experience of others who have done it before them. The army also believes in conducting "Before Action Reviews" (BAR), pre-briefings before undertaking activities. The pre-briefings make a deliberate effort to learn what has been learned before in AAR processes so the unit is more knowledgeable and has a better chance for success.[17]

Learning from your mistakes is one of the most important parts of learning. People who hide their mistakes increase the likelihood that other people may make the same mistakes. Learning organizations make a deliberate effort to create an environment where mistakes are identified, discussed, and addressed in a way that they are viewed as "learning opportunities." Brogan and Partners—an advertising agency—actually has a "mistake of the month" award which honors people who confess their blunders to the rest of the staff. CEO Maurice Brogan noted, "Sharing a mistake is just as valuable as sharing a best practice."[18] The same principle applies to "near misses." While they may not be considered mistakes, they need to be identified and dealt with in a similar fashion so they are handled better in the future.

Developing New Mental Models and Paradigms to Meet New Challenges

Creating your company's future involves making decisions today that will ultimately affect its future. Today's decisions will influence tomorrow's decisions, because today's decisions have a bearing on the company's markets, products, services, and processes in the years ahead.

Companies that are successful today may find it difficult to prepare for tomorrow. The "paradox of success" causes many companies to cling to their current way of doing business. This paradox is reflected in the "You can't argue with success" mentality that plagues many companies today. Celebration of successes can backfire because it makes it more difficult for people to challenge the way things are being done. Success may cause executives to be blind to new realities. It may also cause them to be deaf to the challenges made by people within the company and to the complaints or suggestions made by customers and other stakeholders outside the company.

The better the company is at something, the more successful it has been, and the greater the market share it enjoys, the greater the likelihood that it will fail to see a major shift in the market. Success tends to put executives in a "mental comfort zone." Few executives seek breakthroughs when they are in their comfort zones. In times of rapid change, it will not take long for their companies to be dethroned by maverick companies that fail to pay homage to them or their way of doing business.

What causes so many executives to miss the emergence of critical new realities? Every person has "mental models" that serve as the basis for how they see the world. One's mental models can either help a person deal with the changing world or they can be an anchor that keeps them from journeying effectively into the future.

Alvin Toffler coined the term "future shock" to capture the anxiety that occurs when the future invades the present. When people are surprised, they tend to operate from a reactive stance. It is difficult and unusual for a company to thrive under "red alert" conditions. Companies that are out of touch will not be able to align and synchronize their strategies and operations with new realities. History provides numerous examples of people and companies that were blindsided by new realities. Here are a few of the more noteworthy examples:

They couldn't hit an elephant at this dist. . . .[19]

—General John B. Sedgwick's last words in the Battle of Spotsylvania, 1864

Heavier than air flying machines are impossible.[20]

—Lord Kelvin, British mathematician, physicist, and president of the British Royal Society, 1895

Who the hell wants to hear actors talk?[21]

—Harry M. Warner, Warner Brothers Pictures, 1927

We don't like their sound. Groups with guitars are on the way out.[22]

—Decca Recording Company executive, turning down the Beatles in 1962

There is no reason for any individual to have a computer in their home.[23]

—Ken Olson, President of Digital Equipment Corp., 1977

Each of these statements reflects the negative impact mental models can have on one's perceptions, decisions, and behavior. In some cases, the people were still able to adjust and survive. General Sedgwick's mental model, however, cost him his life. Mental models filter information and screen people's perceptions of the world around them. People tend to see things that are consistent with their mental models. Mental models are like boxes. Their walls keep people from going outside the box—or thinking the unthinkable. Their boundaries keep them from seeing changes the future may bring. Mental models also affect their ability to see certain things that may be in clear sight, in some cases right in front of them.

IBM and Microsoft provide examples of the role mental models can play in the developing corporate strategies. Each of these examples emphasizes the need for companies to bring together people with a variety of backgrounds and to create an environment where people are encouraged to challenge the way things are done. IBM seemed to be fixated for years on making mainframe and personal computers. IBM's top brass did not recognize the valuable role "offering business solutions"—especially via the Internet—could play in IBM's future. It is said that Bill Gates also failed to recognize the early signs of the role the Internet could play in business strategy and operations. Supposedly, members of his management team had to gang up on him to get him to incorporate the Internet into Microsoft's strategy.

Beware of Corporate Maginot Lines

People who are infatuated with the past do not have the ability to prepare for a different future. Executives need to recognize that mental models that may have served them well may be totally inappropriate when conditions change. The Maginot Line provides a good example of how a mental model can make sense at one time and be totally obsolete at a later date. The French built a fortified line of defense following World War I to protect their country from a German invasion. The Maginot Line was massive, expensive, and visually impressive, but it was rendered useless in 1940 by the Axis forces in the early stage of

World War II. The French were so focused on a frontal assault along their border with Germany that they did not expect the Germans to invade France through Belgium, nor did they expect Axis planes to drop paratroopers to the west of the wall in strategic locations.

It is not unusual for people at lower levels of an organization or who operate at an organization's fringes to have mental models that are quite different from the models being used by people at the top. Major General Billy Mitchell, considered the father of the U.S. Air Force, provided an excellent example of what can happen when different mental models collide in an organization. He was known for his innovativeness and willingness to challenge the status quo during World War I. However, those in command of U.S. military forces did not share his ideas about the role air power would play in future wars. During his court martial in 1925, Mitchell boldly predicted that planes launched from aircraft carriers would attack the U.S.! It is ironic that later Frank Knox, Secretary of the U.S. Navy, claimed, "No matter what happens, the U.S. Navy is not going to be caught napping" *three days* before the Japanese attack on Pearl Harbor on December 7, 1941.

Executives whose mental models are more in sync than others have the potential to achieve breakthroughs. If your firm has the ability to circumvent your industry's mental Maginot Lines to see the new realities and to develop new approaches, then it may be able to be an ever-evolving enterprise.

To Reduce Surprises, Lengthen and Broaden Your Mental Radar and Sonar

Surprise occurs when reality is not what we expected it to be. People and companies are surprised because they have the tendency to be blind, deaf, rigid, and "legacy brained." Executives who want to reduce the likelihood of being surprised need to:

- Knock down the walls of their mental boxes so they can see new realities.
- Extend their mental radar so they can catch a glimpse of what may be on the horizon.
- Activate their mental sonar so they can sense what may be lurking just below the surface.
- Open their ears so they can hear voices that have not been heard.
- Develop new perspectives and broaden their education so they can think new thoughts.

- Stimulate their minds so they will have the dexterity needed to try new things.
- Exercise their bodies so they will have the energy needed to leave their comfort zone.
- Let go of their memories of the past and infatuation with the present so they can welcome a different tomorrow.

Mental models filter our vision and blind us to what may be going on around us. Mental models block signals of what the future may hold. Companies suffer when their executives do not see the signals, will not acknowledge the signals, or are unwilling to deal constructively with the signals. While most executives exclaim, "How could we have known?" a closer look reveals in most cases that the new realities were visible at the time. Executives are often surprised, not because the new realities cannot be seen; they are surprised because: (1) they are not looking for the signals, (2) they do not know how to read the signals even if they see them, (3) they fail to incorporate the signals into their decision processes when they see them, and/or (4) they do not act on them when they have the opportunity to do something about the new realities.

Prescription: No More Legacy Mindsets and a Stiff Dose of Reality

Executives of established companies can benefit from the irreverence to the status quo and candor demonstrated by most entrepreneurs. Executives need to create an environment where every person can challenge every idea, every decision, and every plan. Every business plan and almost every decision is based on mental models about what the future holds. Every mental model includes assumptions about what competitors, customers, employees, distributors, suppliers, legislatures, the economy, and the public will or might do. If mental models are the product of past experiences and present perceptions, then they are far from being infallible.

Executives need to make sure that plans and decisions are fair game to reality checks. Assumptions and perceptions need to be identified and tested on an ongoing basis. The more rapid and radical the change, the more frequently the reality checks should be conducted. To be effective, mental models must be based on a realistic set of assumptions. They must also be explicit so they can be monitored. Early warning alarms need to go off when performance indicators show signs that the plan may not be providing the results sought, so the models can be modified or new ones developed that are in tune with the new realities.

It is amazing how long some companies can be in trouble before their executives wake up and change their mental models. Some companies are able to see the new realities in time to develop new models and change the way they do business. In other companies, new executives need to be brought in to help develop a new model for doing business.

The company will not be able to see and deal with reality unless it has a culture that encourages people to challenge its prevailing mental models. Executives need to make sure internal and external messengers are not shot. People must feel their candor will not place them in jeopardy. Employees at all levels of the company must feel that their views are solicited, welcomed, valued, and rewarded. Customers, suppliers, and distributors must also feel their feedback and suggestions are welcomed and not treated as criticisms.

It would be interesting to take a trip back in time to see the reaction of the officers and soldiers who were trying to attack Troy when someone suggested, "We should build a large wooden horse on wheels, fill it with our soldiers, and leave it outside the gate at night so the enemy will bring it into the city . . . and when they are asleep we will be able to attack!"

Preparing Yourself and Your Company for a Different Future

Most executives feel more comfortable dealing with profit and loss components than discussing mental models and business paradigms. Yet, companies will be able to generate profits and build wealth only to the extent their executives use mental models and business paradigms that are in tune with market realities. The following observations and recommendations may help executives: (1) ensure their mental models are in sync with the ever-evolving marketplace, (2) sense change earlier, and (3) make sure their companies are in sync with new realities:

Observations about People and Learning

- People who say it cannot be done will be trampled by those who make the impossible possible.
- Those who hesitate lose to those who seize the moment.
- If you cannot anticipate trends, then position your firm to at least participate in trends.

- Market niche/segment "waves of opportunity" are forming more quickly, cresting earlier, and closing out more rapidly.
- Change usually hits us when and where we least expect it.
- Bad things can and will happen, and they will happen twice as soon as you expect.
- Your observations, insights, and ideas will probably not be embraced by others . . . especially those who have the most to lose by change.
- If it is your idea, then it will take twice as long for others to accept and implement it than if it was their idea.
- Just because an idea is not the same as what is being done does not mean that it is a bad idea.
- Remember Alvin Toffler, "The future has a habit of invading the present."
- "Maybe" will probably become "certainly."
- There will come a time when the impossible will be possible.
- Go from whether or not . . . to when?
- It is rarely an issue of whether or not something will occur. It will occur, so get ready. Deal with it. Make change your ally rather than your adversary.
- Predictable threats and errors are preventable threats and errors if you position your firm properly.
- Conventional wisdom may be an oxymoron.

Recommendations for Enhancing Learning

- Recognize your mental models are the product of a lifetime of experiences and education. You will gain new insights and develop new mental models only if you perceive the world in a different manner. To gain new insights you will need to have new experiences.
- Get out of your comfort zone—now!
- Feel uncomfortable when you feel comfortable!
- Remember Murphy's Law, "If something can go wrong, it will—and at the most inopportune time."
- Have out-of-mind, out-of-body, out-of-specialty, out-of-company, out-of-industry, out-of-the-present types of experiences—and have them often!
- To think outside the box, bring people in from outside the firm.
- Escape the "conventional thinking" mental box.
- Get on your tiptoes to extend your mental horizon.
- Spend at least two hours a week contemplating two to five years out.
- Periodically do a 360 degree rotation so you see the whole world around you and reduce the likelihood that someone is sneaking up on you or that you will be blindsided.

- Have at least one meeting per month with people who have different vantage points to discuss the future of business.
- Prevent "group think." Have people play the Devil's advocate or what Andrew Grove while at Intel, called, "Helpful Cassandras" so people do not act like lemmings who just "go with the flow."
- Do not shoot the messenger of bad news.
- Make sure bad news travels even more quickly than good news.
- Keep your cool when things get tough; it enables people to share their thoughts.
- Read what the people at the fringe are writing and do not be so quick to discount radical ideas or trends.
- Get to the fringe; interact with people who are different from you—the weirder, the better.
- Interact with people from different walks of life . . . the more different, the better.
- Take newcomers in your company to lunch, and listen to what they have to say.
- Go to conferences that deal with remotely related trends and technology.
- Identify at least three things from three very different industries that may have applications to your business.
- Assume nothing.
- Challenge every assumption.
- Do not rely on anecdotal information; separate facts from assumptions.
- Realize that someday could be tomorrow.
- Never say "never."
- Expect the obvious, but prepare for the unexpected.
- Hope for the best, but prepare for the worst.
- Constantly run "What if . . . ?" scenarios.
- Think the unthinkable.
- Run "worst case" scenarios, and then run scenarios that are twice as bad.
- Have spirited discussions, robust dialogues, deep probing, and so forth about real and significant issues.
- Recognize that dumb questions may produce smart answers.
- Have people leave their egos and corresponding turf at the door.
- Disagree over ideas, not personalities.
- Analyze "near miss" situations where your firm barely succeeded. Treat a near miss as an "almost failed situation." Pilots consider near misses to be "near hits or near collisions."
- Sense current realities and possible future realities.
- Hire people who are able to learn fast, who are curious, and who can admit when they are wrong.

- Create a system where people can anonymously ask questions, identify areas of nonconformity with organizational values and processes, and make suggestions.
- Create an environment where people do not hesitate to ask for help.
- Find out what you do not know and learn it.
- Surround yourself with people who are smarter than you in the things that matter.
- Create an environment where people have the freedom to experiment.
- Capture what people know *before* they leave the firm.
- Make your organization transparent to its members. Practice open-book management to foster organizational awareness.
- Beware of consultants. They have a tendency to provide off-the-shelf solutions that are not tailored to your unique situation or enterprise.
- Determine what strategy could help your company become the first mover or a fast follower.
- Look at your firm through your competitors' eyes. Identify where you are vulnerable and fix the areas before your competitors attack them.
- Do not get too caught up in what your competitors are doing right now. Anticipate what they might be doing in the next two years.
- Identify what could be the "forward pass" in your industry that makes the conventional running game look about as graceful as elephants trying to mate.
- Make sure you have an external orientation.
- Ask, "What is it, that if it was changed, would change everything?"
- Ask, ask, ask, and then listen, listen, listen to your customers, competitors, employees, and suppliers.
- Consider every complaint to be a learning opportunity.
- Look at the firm from an outsider's (customer, supplier, competitor, legislator, and so forth) perspective.
- Constantly ask, "Where are the emerging opportunities? How can we create and capitalize on them?"
- When you prepare your "To-do" list, also make a "Not-to-do List."
- Demonstrate leadership by having the courage to kill bureaucracy, sacred cows, silo mentality, and all the other practices that impede learning, change, and improvement.
- Create a sense of urgency to do what needs to be done NOW.
- Have the guts to do "the right thing" rather than what is expedient.
- Before you consider "your" idea to be new, do a Google search to see if it already exists.
- There are usually multiple ways to solve a problem or to address a situation. Seek additional, alternative approaches.
- Find a better way, every day.

- Beware of the types of mistakes or errors that Bill Gore calls "below the waterline." Bill Gore notes that mistakes that are above the waterline can be handled; the ones below the waterline can be devastating.
- Learn, learn, and learn. Step back and learn from every situation. A line in the film, *The Natural* noted, "I believe we have two lives ... the life we learn with and the life we live with after that." Live the second life.

Decisiveness Is Essential: Going from Thought to Action

This chapter started off by stressing the need for learning to be followed by value-added action. Knowing is not enough. Acting on what you have learned may make the difference between success and failure. The best learning organizations avoid paralysis by analysis. The best learning organizations know there is a time to think, a time to analyze, a time to decide, and a time to act. Richard Johnson—who started HotJobs—noted that success is often contingent on being able "to quickly go from thought to action."

The best learning organizations do not fall prey to the "ready, aim ... aim ... aim ... " syndrome. They know there comes a time to move on, when twenty questions can become one hundred questions, but the world will not allow you to keep studying the situation. The Marine Corps has the "70 percent solution rule." According to the 70 percent rule, "If you have 70 percent of the information, have done 70 percent of the analysis, and feel 70 percent confident, then move." The best learning organizations know that perfection takes twice as much time as excellence. They also know some things do not have to be done in an excellent manner—they just have to be done.

Do Not Expect Challenging the Status Quo to Be an Easy Journey

You need to recognize four important points when you make a commitment to creating your company's future. First, there will always be surprises, but you can reduce the likelihood of being blindsided by extending your mental radar, doing a 360 degree sweep, and checking the reality of your mental models. Second, there will be problems and setbacks; know the difference between problems that come with trying to make progress and the problems that come with clinging to the past or present. Third, even the savviest executives will make mistakes. That is part of learning. The attitude, "If I don't try anything new, then I won't make any mistakes" will speed the company's slide into mediocrity. The greatest mistake a company can make is to not experiment with new products, new services, and new processes. Fourth, you will have to challenge prevailing wisdom and break the rules to position your company for a better tomorrow. John Gardner noted, "I would lay it down as a basic principle of human organizations that the individuals who hold the reins of power in any enterprise cannot trust themselves to be adequately self-critical. For those in power the danger of self-deception is very great, the danger of failing to see the problems or refusing to see them is ever-present."[24]

Concluding Comments: Opportunities to Improve Learning Are Not Hard to Find

The variety of learning impairments indicates that they can be found in almost every facet of the firm. Some learning impairments are easier to address than others. Yet there is no panacea, and there are no quick fixes. Your firm's managers and employees must play a central role in reducing and eliminating your organization's learning impairments. In some cases, it is their attitudes, mindsets, habits, and behavior that impair learning. Some people will welcome the opportunity to adopt the concepts and approaches associated with being a learning organization. Some people will need encouragement and time to embrace the learning processes. Some people will be openly resistant to management's efforts to become a learning organization. Some will be more covert in their efforts to keep things the way they are.

Louis Armstrong, Jr., the great trumpet player, observed, "Some people don't know and you just can't tell them." Management must be prepared to eject the people who are not willing to get on the learning bus and to make the changes that need to be made. In any event, you will need to be persistent and set the right example in your efforts to transform your firm into a learning organization and ultimately an ever-evolving enterprise.

Your effort to become a learning organization will need to involve short- and long-term planning. You will need to identify areas where you can get early victories by showing that the ideas associated with being a learning organization can make a difference. You will also need to plant some seeds now that will foster learning and more substantive change in the years ahead. Your first step, however, is to identify and reduce the forces that are preventing your organization from learning. Take the Learning Organization Quiz in Table 8.1 to learn the extent to which your firm has the qualities of a learning organization.

The illiterate of the 21st Century will not be those who cannot read or write, but those who cannot learn, unlearn, and relearn.

—Alvin Toffler, author of *Future Shock*

TABLE 8.1.   Learning Organization Quiz

How does your firm rate on the following dimensions?
*Scoring Level 1 = not at all, 2 = slightly true,
3 = somewhat true, 4 = mostly true, 5 = completely true

		Level*
1.	Top executives set the example for championing learning.	1-2-3-4-5
2.	Top executives are in tune with the rest of the firm and its external environment.	1-2-3-4-5
3.	Managers at all levels are open-minded. Management at all levels actively solicits employee ideas.	1-2-3-4-5
4.	Management empowers employees to try new approaches.	1-2-3-4-5
5.	Your firm has a system in place for acquiring and sharing information to enhance performance.	1-2-3-4-5
6.	Management uses mental models that are in sync with current and emerging business realities.	1-2-3-4-5
7.	Management is not preoccupied with short-term results and seeking quick fixes.	1-2-3-4-5
8.	Management supports ongoing training and employee development.	1-2-3-4-5
9.	Management embraces state-of-the-art technology.	1-2-3-4-5
10.	Management is truly committed to reducing bureaucracy, rigidity, politics, and other activities that impede learning and change.	1-2-3-4-5
11.	Your firm embraces employee diversity as well as the cross-pollination of ideas.	1-2-3-4-5
12.	The merit of prevailing business practices is challenged on a regular basis.	1-2-3-4-5
13.	Your firm demonstrates future-oriented, anticipatory learning.	1-2-3-4-5
14.	Your firm demonstrates genuine customer-centricity.	1-2-3-4-5

(continued)

TABLE 8.1.   (Continued)

How does your firm rate on the following dimensions? *Scoring Level 1 = not at all, 2 = slightly true, 3 = somewhat true, 4 = mostly true, 5 = completely true	Level*
15. Management thinks things through looking for potential opportunities and pitfalls when making decisions.	1-2-3-4-5
16. Management at all levels makes a deliberate effort to do before and after-action reviews that enhance learning and future performance.	1-2-3-4-5
Total points	

Scoring Key

72–80	Congratulations, your firm demonstrates most of the qualities of a learning organization.
64–71	Your organization has many strengths, but still has areas that need to be improved.
56–63	Your organization has some strengths, but there is a lot of room for improvement.
48–55	Your organization either has some significant learning impairments or is weak in most areas. Tweaking your firm's learning environment will not be enough to make a real difference.
16–47	Your organization may be beyond hope. It will take a radical change in management, corporate culture, systems, and processes to have any chance of being competitive in the future.

Notes

Some of the material in this chapter originally appeared in the article, "Is Your Organization Learning-Impaired?" by the author and David J. Glew in *Industrial Management*, March/April, 2008. Reprinted with the permission of the Institute of Industrial Engineers, 3577 Parkway Lane, Suite 200, Norcross, GA 30092, www.iienet.org. Copyright 2008 by the Institute of Industrial Engineers.

1. Peter Senge, *The Fifth Discipline* (New York: Currency Doubleday, 1990), 3.

2. Kurt Lewin, "Frontiers in Group Dynamics: Concepts, Method, and Reality in Social Science," *Human Relations*, no. 1 (1947): 5–41.

3. Jeff Papows, *In Enterprise.com* (Reading, Massachusetts: Perseus Books, 1998), 105.

4. John Gardner, *No Easy Victories* (New York: Harper Colophon, 1968), 42.

5. By the author and David Glew, who is also a professor at the University of North Carolina Wilmington.

6. Diane Brady, "Can GE Still Manage?" *Bloomberg Business Week*, April 25, (2010): 30.

7. Noel M. Tichy and Stratford Sherman, *Control Your Destiny or Someone Else Will* (New York: HarperBusiness, 1993), 165.

8. Ibid., 159.

9. Ibid., 433, 434.

10. Ibid., 244.

11. Dave Ulrich, Steve Kerr, and Ron Ashkenas, *GE Work-Out* (New York: McGraw-Hill, 2002), 32, 33.

12. Chuck Salter, "ideas.com," *Fast Company*, no. 27 (1999): 294.

13. Ibid., 302.

14. Presentation to the Coastal Entrepreneurial Council, April 18, 2000.

15. Michael Morgan, "My Five Days at Camp Lur'ning," *Fast Company*, no. 5 (1996): 49.

16. Marilyn Darling, Charles Parry, and Joseph Moore, "Learning in the Thick of It," *Harvard Business Review* 27, no 2 (2005).

17. Ibid., 86.

18. Jennifer Gill, "The Mistake of the Month Award," *Inc. Magazine*, 27, no. 2 (2005): 34.

19. Christopher Cerf and Victor Navasky, *The Experts Speak* (New York: Pantheon Books, 1984), 135.

20. Ibid., 236.

21. Ibid., 172.

22. Ibid., 182.

23. Ibid., 209.

24. Gardner, ibid., 42.

Chapter 9

Creating a Corporate Culture That Fosters Innovation

America is in a product war, and the management of innovation is a strategic weapon. . . . Our ability to get better at the innovative process—to drive products from idea to market faster and with fewer mistakes—is the key to winning the war.[1]

—Robert Cooper

The marketplace is changing too rapidly for companies that are not very innovative. Firms that are not able to be better than their competitors at providing value to their target markets will go bankrupt. Innovation is essential if your firm is to gain and sustain competitive advantages. Being innovative not only involves developing compelling products and services, it also involves developing processes that give your firm an edge through speed, lower costs, enhanced quality, attracting talent, and so forth.

A study by Eureka Ranch found that firms that foster innovation grow at over five times the rate of other firms.[2] Your company's culture can play a critical role in fostering innovation. Yet most executives have difficulty articulating the nature of corporate culture and its effects on performance. The relatively intangible nature of corporate culture makes it rather elusive when executives develop the company's strategy and design the company's organizational processes.

Every company has a distinct culture just as every person has a unique personality that predisposes him or her to think and behave in certain ways. A company's culture is the result of numerous factors and forces. It affects the type of people the company hires as well as how it motivates and rewards them. It determines the type of ideas the company will embrace as well as the extent to which people are encouraged to experiment, explore, innovate, and take risks.

Corporate culture reflects what the company values. The ever-accelerating rate of change and de-layered nature of today's companies force people to make judgment calls every day. It is during these "moments of truth" that the company's culture affects whether the company will move forward or fall by the wayside. The company's culture in these moments serves as a compass for making decisions. When one's boss is not available for guidance or the company's policy manual does not provide the answer for how a situation should be handled, then the culture of a company often indicates what should be done.

Corporate culture can be characterized in three dimensions. First, the culture may be strong or weak. Strong cultures have a dramatic effect on employees. Southwest Airlines, Google, and 3M are known for having a culture that has a pervasive impact on every person at every level. Other companies have cultures that are so weak that they seem to lack any core values or common thread to direct ongoing decisions and behavior.

Second, the culture may or may not be in sync with the company's strategy. A company's strategy can be implemented only if the company's culture reflects the attitudes, values, and skills needed to make it happen. If the strategy calls for the development of innovative products, then the company will need a culture that welcomes exploration and experimentation. If the prevailing culture abhors risk-taking and punishes mistakes, then the company's strategy will not get the traction it needs to gain a competitive edge.

Third, the culture may or may not be very adaptive. Some cultures are so rigid that their companies are unable to change with changing times. Cultures that have failed to embrace the power of information technology, women in the executive ranks, a global perspective, and collaborative endeavors are out of sync with current realities. Most executives believe their companies should have strong cultures. Yet companies that have strong but inflexible or inappropriate cultures will have difficulty staying in the game.

Some Thoughts about Innovation

When all think alike, then no one is thinking.

—Walter Lippman

It's easy to come up with new ideas; the hard part is letting go of what worked for you two years ago, but will soon be out of date.

—Roger von Oech

Discovery consists of seeing what everybody has seen and thinking what nobody has thought.

—Albert von Szent-Gyorgy

To raise new questions, new possibilities, to regard old problems from a new angle, requires creative imagination. . . .

—Albert Einstein

Once we rid ourselves of traditional thinking we can get on with creating the future.

—James Bertrand

The essential part of creativity is not being afraid to fail.

—Edwin H. Land

The achievement of excellence can only occur if the organization promotes a culture of creative dissatisfaction.

—Lawrence Miller

The uncreative mind can spot wrong answers, but it takes a very creative mind to spot wrong questions.

—Anthony Jay

Every act of creation is first of all an act of destruction.

—Picasso

Some men look at things the way they are and ask why? I dream of things that are not and ask why not?

—Robert Kennedy

Mindless habitual behavior is the enemy of innovation.

—Rosabeth Moss Kanter

The people who get on in this world are the people who get up and look for what they want, and if they can't find them, make them.

—George Bernard Shaw

Never before in history has innovation offered promise of so much to so many in so short a period of time.

—Bill Gates

Nothing is so embarrassing as watching someone do something that you said could not be done.

—Steve Jobs

Culture Is about People, "Alignment," and Commitment

Your company's culture has a lot to do with whether your people are committed to creating your company's future, whether your company languishes in the present, or whether it clings to the past. All products, services, processes, patents, and profits come from people. Your company's future is directly related to: (1) the extent your people's interests are aligned with the company's goals, (2) the quality of ideas that are developed today, and (3) the extent they are executed well.

Executives need to recognize that it is a lot easier to change the company's strategy than it is to change its culture. While the strategy may call for a major shift in the company's product portfolio, in most cases the products will be developed by people within the company. If people are not committed to the company or if they do not relish the opportunity to create products that did not exist before, the company's strategy will be nothing more than words and numbers on a sheet of paper.

The company will have a higher probability of having a high level of commitment from its people if it makes a deliberate effort to attract people whose values and goals are aligned with the company's values and objectives. This does not mean the company should identify the ideal employee and try to clone a whole workforce from that profile. The concept of "goodness of fit" is tied to the need for alignment. Certain employees will thrive in certain corporate cultures. The company will succeed to the extent it attracts people who are aligned and rewards them for their contribution to the company's goals.

Innovation Comes from Diversity, Not Conformity

Executives often overemphasize the merit of the "goodness of fit" concept. The goodness of fit concept indicates that people should be hired who are similar so they can "fit in." Yet goodness of fit may be detrimental to a firm if it is taken too far. Innovation springs from diversity. If you are hiring like-minded people or assigning them to a team, then you are just adding another body. Innovative firms bring in people with very different backgrounds and perspectives. If your company hires the same type of person, then it will lack the rich diversity that is the seed for innovative ideas.

> Reality Check: Alignment is not the same as goodness of fit. Alignment means that people share the company's values. Goodness of fit implies similar thinking and behavior.

If your firm is to out-innovate its competitors, then it will need to have a cadre of people at all levels who can think outside the "conventional box." Breakthrough ideas rarely come from people with similar perspectives. While it may be easier (and human nature) to prefer to hire and work with people who are similar to you, you should make every effort to bring together people with different perspectives, experiences, and skills. Some of the most innovative companies have used cross-functional teams to develop breakthrough products, services, and processes. If companies are to truly capitalize on the talents of their people, then their executives should make every effort to create cross-functional companies.

Innovative companies are like salads. They value diversity and have created an environment where different perspectives are encouraged, a variety of people thrive, and new ideas are rewarded. Some of the most innovative companies take pride in their unconventional hiring practices. They hire people from the "fringe" or from unrelated fields and industries. People who are not from within your firm are more likely to ask probing questions, to challenge assumptions, and to suggest new ways to do things and new things to do. Younger people may also add value because they: (1) have less mental "unfreezing" to do because they do not have as many habits or legacy-based mental models that are based on why or how things have been done in the past, (2) are not the people whose ideas will have to be discontinued to make way for the new approaches, and (3) tend to be less risk-averse.

Some of the most innovative companies take pride in their unconventional hiring practices. Seth Godin noted, "The next time you review resumes, try ignoring all of the 'perfectly qualified' applicants. In fact, disqualify everyone who is clearly competent to do the job at hand. Do what Southwest Airlines does: Don't hire people with experience at another airline unless you're sure that they can unlearn what they've learned at the other airline. . . . Instead look for folks who are quick enough to master a task and restless enough to try something new. . . . "[3]

Some people are very creative. Other people are great at providing a sense of reality. One of the keys to enhancing innovation is to make sure the creative people are in creative situations and that the "reality check-ers" are brought in when it is time to make sure the idea really solves the problem or provides the benefit the targeted customer is seeking. Crea-tivity often arises in an open, freewheeling and nonevaluative environ-ment. Tom Kelley of IDEO—the award winning design firm—noted that the innovative process works best when you separate the children (creative people) from the adults (pragmatists).[4] The pragmatists play a key role in the innovative processes by making sure the innovative ideas can be turned into profitable products and services. While creative ideas may come from "aha" moments, they still need to be subjected to constructive scrutiny to determine whether they have potential to be profitable. This "mindfulness" is healthy because it keeps the creative types from getting drunk on the creative Kool-Aid. Some firms have "buddy systems" where they pair creative types with more seasoned executives. The creative types are free to suggest ideas to the executives who provide "wisdom" about issues that still need to be considered. The "wise" buddies help the innovative process by providing a balanced and supportive perspective.

Leaders Must Create an Environment That Fosters Innovation

Leaders can enhance innovation in many ways. They can provide "air cover" for the troops by keeping an open mind and providing resources. While they may not be in a position to champion individual innovative efforts, they can champion innovation throughout the company. They can knock down barriers, create opportunities for people at all levels of the company to have an open dialogue with top management, struc-ture the organization's processes so ideas can be shared easily, and cheer the troops on at strategic moments.

Leaders need to ensure that ideas are not subjected to legacy mind-sets. They also need to make sure ideas are not subjected to ridicule, territorialism, parochialism, or bureaucratic barriers. A list of "idea killers" that inhibit people in most organizations is widely circulated, even though the original author is not known.[5] The idea killers include: (1) "They'll never buy it!" (2) "Are we ready for this?" (3)"What will they say upstairs?" (4) "You can't argue with success," and (5) "Let's be realistic." The greatest idea killer may be, "The last guy who came up with that idea isn't here anymore!"

Other attitudes including "That's not my job" and "I am not creative" also keep people from developing innovative products, services, and processes. Firms with these and other managerial/mental disabilities are relegated to a perpetual firefighting existence.

Creating an environment that fosters innovation and creativity involves more than minimizing or eliminating a few idea killers; it also involves creating an atmosphere full of "idea enhancers." Ideas should be solicited on a regular basis and rewarded handsomely. Every effort must be made to promote: (1) looking at things from new perspectives, (2) ongoing experimentation, and (3) transforming mistakes into learning experiences. Executives should heed the value statement that runs throughout 3M, "Thou shall not kill a new product idea."

To Be an Innovative Organization Your Firm Will Need to Be a Learning Organization

Chapter eight noted that a company cannot be at the leading edge if it merely tries to keep up with other companies. For the company to excel, it must be a learning organization. It must also be innovative in its products, services, and processes. Creating the company's future requires more than just keeping pace with the changes that are happening outside the company. The ever-accelerating rate of change places a premium on the company's ability to evolve in a revolutionary manner. Companies that learn quicker and innovate better than their competitors are more likely to be out in front. Companies that are slow to learn and merely imitate innovative companies will either be relegated to a very precarious existence or become extinct.

Your company will not at the leading edge unless it masters strategic and adaptive learning. Strategic learning involves developing innovative ways to identify and capitalize on the opportunities that may be on the horizon. It also involves positioning the company to avoid potential threats. Strategic learning uses innovation to create the firm's future by identifying the markets the firm should be in, the types of customers it should target, the types of products and services it should offer, and how it will gain and maintain a competitive edge.

Adaptive learning helps the company keep pace with changing external conditions on an ongoing basis. It is directed to continuously improving the company's operations and modifying the firm's products and services. It also involves correcting deviations from planned performance.

Chuck Salter noted, "Winning companies don't just outhustle or outmuscle the competition. They out-think. Business today is about brains, not brawn. It's about how many ideas you generate, not how many factories you own. . . . Every so often, a company will invent a breakthrough business model that reinvents the rules of competition in an industry."[6] He also noted there is a day-to-day side to competing on ideas. While breakthrough ideas may make headlines and enable the company to leapfrog competition, your firm's success is also contingent on its ability to learn and innovate on a continuous basis.

Innovative Corporate Cultures Are Multifaceted

Innovative firms make a deliberate effort to increase the odds for success by making sure various factors that foster innovation are in place. Their mission statements stress innovation. Their vision statements include stretch goals. Their strategies embrace innovation to create and maintain customers. Their management systems and organizational structures enhance innovation. Their leaders champion innovation by providing encouragement, rewards, and financial support.

Companies that are truly innovative also recognize that innovation is not an end in itself. It is an important means to an end; it must be targeted to create value for the firm's targeted customers and profit for the firm. Chapter six profiled the difference between the "R&D push" strategy and "demand pull" strategy. Both strategies have merit. The R&D strategy works if the people in R&D can come up with products that people will buy. It is the *Field of Dreams*, "If you build it, they will come" strategy. 3M uses an R&D push strategy in some of its new product development efforts. It develops innovative products and then looks for customers who will benefit from their products. 3M has been successful because it has been able to develop a pipeline full of innovative products which appeal to current and future customers.

The R&D push innovation strategy is not as market-centric as the demand pull strategy. The demand pull strategy is based on the premise that firms should be "customer problem-solvers." Companies using this strategy seek every opportunity to interact with people and companies to learn where their needs are not being met well or at all. This strategy begins by listening to the marketplace. It looks for "customers in search of products." It recognizes that "gaps" with existing and potential customers can be a source of ideas that may be transformed into revolutionary products, services, and processes.

Most innovative companies use a hybrid strategy that incorporates the best of both strategies. They are committed to developing breakthrough products that change the marketplace and competitive landscape. They are also committed to solving their current customers' problems so they and their customers are more profitable.

> Reality Check: Being customer-centric can be a "Catch 22." This book has already noted that firms should avoid focusing only on their current customers. They also need to focus on their noncustomers whom they would like to convert into customers. They also need to concern themselves with future customers.

> Reality Check: Customer-centric people observe customers rather than just ask them what they want. By taking an "anthropological" approach to market research, they learn how people actually behave, even if they are not saying it.

> Reality Check: There may be times when your firm may have to make the leap and "lead" current and potential customers by introducing products and services that are beyond the list of minor modifications—to provide products and services beyond what they even considered or considered to be feasible.

There Are Numerous Shades of Gray for Innovation

Innovation is not an "either/or" proposition. There are various levels of innovation. Innovation can be revolutionary, or it can be evolutionary.

There is breakthrough innovation when people exclaim, "Wow, I didn't know that was even possible!" Breakthrough innovation can change the competitive landscape . . . and in some cases create new business models. It can be evolutionary by involving a series of significant changes. It can even be in the form of continuous improvements which may involve ongoing efforts to enhance the way things are done. When Tom Smith was CEO of Food Lion he was asked how his firm had done so well. He responded, "We're one percent better on 1,000 different things."

Reality Check: Avoid overengineering products with features that do not provide real value. There is a difference between offering features and providing benefits. Make sure you know the difference. Clayton Christenson, author of *The Innovator's Dilemma*, stresses the need for firms to not get caught up in offering all the whistles and bells. He stresses the value of disruptive innovation by being "minimal," which involves offering only the basics to attract nonconsumers.

Reality Check: Tom Peters cautions about being preoccupied with continuous improvement. He noted that if a firm is "100%" into continuous improvement, then it is "zero percent" into innovation.

Reality Check: "Managing Our Way to Economic Decline" written by Robert H. Hayes and William J. Abernathy in 1980 was one of the most widely read articles in the history of the *Harvard Business Review*. The authors expressed their concern about the tendency for firms to limit their risks and investments in innovation. They cited a senior executive who noted, "It's much more difficult to come up with a synthetic meat product than a lemon-lime cake mix. But you work on the lemon-lime cake mix because you know exactly what that return is going to be. A synthetic steak is going to take a lot longer, require a much bigger investment, and the risk of failure will be greater."[7] It is a shame that in the decades since the article came out, that that attitude may actually be even more prevalent today.

Innovation comes from having the right types of people in the right situations in the right environment, or culture. Top executives need to create a culture that provides: (1) the "air cover" needed to support innovative efforts, (2) critical resources even in tough times, and

(3) opportunities for fast failures that foster fast learning. They also need to provide an environment that (1) breaks bureaucratic barriers, (2) reduces risk aversion, and (3) welcomes constructive criticism.

Innovation comes from a mindset that reflects various dimensions. When Thomas Watson was the head of IBM, he encouraged his people to "Think." Years later, the people at upstart Apple Computer were encouraged to "Think Different." Innovation is reflected in many ways. It often starts with a questioning mind. It is reflected in a curiosity and inquisitiveness that asks, "Why, why, why, and why not?" You cannot have innovative answers unless you ask perceptive questions. The questioning mind is reflected in contempt for the status quo and challenging conventional wisdom. It is reflected in the belief that there is always a better way to do things and better things to do. Someone once noted that to be a truly innovative person in an established firm, you need to ask the type of questions and make the type of suggestions that could get you fired.

Innovative people have the courage of their convictions. The prelude to *Star Trek*, "To boldly go where no one has gone before," captures the essence of an innovative corporate culture. It encourages people to develop products, services, processes, and even business models that have not existed before. Howard Schultz had the courage of his convictions when he transformed Starbucks into one of the world's most recognized brands. He elevated the coffee experience to a whole new level. He also had the courage to offer products and services beyond most people's expectations.

A considerable part of our quality of life and the strength of our market economy has been the product of people who had the courage to challenge existing paradigms and the innovativeness to develop new ones. They were the ones who boldly challenged the status quo by asking: "Why do people have to leave their home or office to do banking, to buy stock, to buy a book, to get an education, or to buy plane tickets?" They were the ones who challenged the need for computers to be stationary, the need for planes to have propellers, and the need for most products to be made of wood or metal. Once they realized there must be a better way, they developed products that changed the way people work and live. They were the ones who developed voice recognition software, the mouse, laptops, personal digital assistants, the microwave oven, e-books, e-mail, and the rest of the never-ending list of products that make things possible that people did not think were possible before they were invented.

People who challenged prevailing paradigms created their future in spite of the choruses of doubters who were heard saying:

"But that's not the way it's done."
"But who would want to do it that way?"
"There's no way . . ."
"You've got to be kidding."
"No one in her right mind would . . . "
"What fool came up with that idea?"

It is interesting to note that a number of these products were considered frivolous by most people when they were first introduced. For example, purchasing specialists and accountants wondered why people would need a Xerox photocopier when carbon paper had done just fine.

The next generation of managers, purchasing specialists, and accountants wondered why people would want Post-it notes when a piece of paper with a strip of tape could do the job. Microwave ovens were also subjected to considerable skepticism. Skeptics wondered why anyone would spend hundreds of dollars to cook a hot dog, bake a potato, or pop popcorn in a few seconds. Skeptics challenged why anyone really needed to "zap" a cup of coffee. Skeptics also played the health issue card to challenge whether the food was really "cooked." Skeptics raised the microwave "leakage" issue as well.

Skeptics also challenged how any serious computer company could expect adults to use a "childish" mouse. It is ironic that products that were ridiculed, like cell phones, are now considered by many people to be necessities. Frequent users are often heard asking their elders, "How could you live without them?" It is amazing how attitudes and behavior for millions of people can change in such a short period of time.

Reality Check: Jim Collins cautioned firms to make sure "it's good enough" does not take root in your firm's culture. Your firm starts its slide into mediocrity the moment that good is good enough.

Reality Check: Beware of the tendency to be arrogant when you are successful. Arrogance often leads to complacency, which then leads to mediocrity, which then makes your firm irrelevant.

How Can Companies Foster Innovation?

Companies need to recognize how their structures, systems and hiring practices are interrelated. If you want an innovative culture, you need an organization that is market-centric. It also needs to attract and support people with a wide variety of ideas.

Top management must create a strategy that focuses on innovation. Tom Peters noted that if you really want innovation, then you should set "10X performance goals." If you set the goal for the product to be 10 times faster or one-tenth its current cost, then your people will have to be truly innovative. While the goal may seem unrealistic, his point is that if your innovation goals are modest (such as 10% better), then your people may try to tweak the product or service rather than approach it from a truly innovative perspective.

3M has been very innovative over the years because it has a goal that a certain percent of its sales must come from products that it did not offer at the time the goal was set. A goal for innovation may be that 30 percent of sales in four years must come from products that the firm does not offer today. Yet setting goals for corporate innovation is not enough. The company must establish a performance review system that expects innovation and rewards it.

The innovative process involves introducing or trying something new. The willingness to try is directly related to the freedom to fail. The greater the risk and punishment for failure, the less people will be willing to suggest new ways to do things and to try new things. Jim Collins stresses the difference between failure and "fallure." Fallure occurs when you try something and it does not work out. Failure is to not try at all. Executives need to encourage innovative efforts and to learn from the ones that may not succeed. Some firms even celebrate efforts that may not have met expectations to show that experimentation is valued

3M is known for asking the following three questions before it invests in new products. They are: "Can we make it?" "Will they buy it?" and "Can we make traditional 3M margin with it?" 3M's due diligence forces prospective new product managers to identify who will buy the product (at what price), who will be the competitors, how will they compete, when will they enter the market, and numerous other questions.

Reality Check: Executives who are preoccupied with what is immediately within their reach are prone to develop corporate strategies that merely "fine tune" present products and practices. The tendency for executives to direct their attention almost exclusively to existing tangible factors and the here and now is called "Management by Braille." Their perceptual fields are composed primarily of existing markets, existing customers, existing technology, existing competitors, existing capabilities, existing strengths, and existing weaknesses. Management by Braille limits one's depth perception. Their preoccupation with what can be quantified and measured keeps them from considering less tangible factors and scanning the horizon for faint signals of what may be ahead. This keeps them from seeing emerging trends and their corresponding opportunities.

Reality Check: Most managers, including those who make it to the top, rarely break out of their industry's boundaries to experience the dynamics of a world undergoing an incredible transformation or learn the perceptions and visions of executives in other fields and markets. Innovation often comes from having an out-of-body experience. Today, executives would be wise to have out-of-company and out-of-industry experiences often.

Reality Check: There are times when you should not try to reinvent the wheel. The "not-invented-here" syndrome has done a complete about-face in that it is now valued rather than discouraged by many firms. More firms are outsourcing, open sourcing, and crowdsourcing innovation.

The Art and Science of Innovation

There are things you can do to foster innovation, but the innovative process is not like plumbing or electricity where you can plan it and be certain of the outcome. Innovation is not for perfectionists or control freaks; it can be chaotic at times. Innovation cannot be forced. You may occasionally be able to come up with an innovative breakthrough, but you cannot count on it. Innovation takes time, and certain conditions must exist for it to occur. Having lead time gives you the opportunity to do a true situational analysis, to think things through, to tap knowledge networks, to develop new product ideas, to test them on prospective consumers, to make modifications from their feedback, to get the bugs out of the production and distribution processes, and to plan for the launch.

Creativity and innovation are more likely to occur if you create an environment that allows people's minds to be free from distractions and other factors that can impede freedom of thought, intuitive leaps, and the cross-pollination of ideas. Certain problem solving techniques—including brainstorming—increase the odds for innovation by providing processes for systematically approaching a situation. Brainstorming increases the odds by having numerous guidelines including: (1) generating as many ideas as possible in the time allotted, (2) initially prohibiting idea evaluation and criticism, and (3) including people with various perspectives, so people can build on each other's ideas. These simple guidelines often provide breakthroughs that might not have been possible under different conditions and/or by people acting alone.

Most creative techniques place a premium on giving the brain time for mental "incubation." The subconscious mind can be the source of innovative ideas. If it is given time to address the situation, it can run free—uninhibited by conventional thinking and by the "mental walls" that channel thinking down prescribed or conventional paths. The subconscious mind has the incredible ability to jump walls and to combine ideas that appear unrelated to the conscious mind. Its imagination is unbounded. In some ways, it is like the dreams that we have when we wake up wondering how in the world so many things that may not have been directly related to each other were combined in the dream. Yet, our "Where did that come from?" dreams illustrate how imaginative our subconscious mind can be and how it may be able to be a source of innovation.

There is a story about a graduate student who came late to class, looking disheveled. When the professor probed why the student was late and looked like a mess, the student responded that he had been working without a break on the three problems that were assigned in the preceding class and that he had only solved one of the problems. The student was so frustrated with his inability to do all the problems that he thought he must not have what it takes to earn his doctorate. The professor realized that the student had come late to the preceding class and had missed the discussion between the professor and the other students. That discussion centered around identifying three mathematical problems that have yet to be solved by anyone on the planet. The exhausted student thought that the three problems on the blackboard were the homework assignment. He went home that day and solved one of them! This shows what can happen when the impossible is not considered impossible. Corporate cultures that free people to come up with innovative solutions and to make possible what consumers did not consider possible may be in a position to own the marketplace.

> Reality Check: When you are in a hurry, you may just satisfice and take the first acceptable idea that comes along. Satisficing may be OK in low importance issues, but not in medium to high importance issues that can wow customers and truly separate your firm from the pack.

> Reality Check: Your firm cannot be the most innovative firm in your industry at everything. Pick the things that will make the biggest long-term difference from a return on investment, risk-return perspective.

> Reality Check: Avram Miller observed, "There is no certainty that the market will embrace your innovation . . . so get it in the hands of a group of consumers to find out how they feel, make changes quickly, and get it back in the marketplace."

Fostering Creativity and Innovation

John Gardner noted, "There's never been a shortage of ideas. The problem is getting a hearing for them."[8] Your job is to create an environment that actively solicits and rewards ideas. Ideas should be solicited on an ongoing basis. Every effort must be made to promote: (1) looking at things from new perspectives, (2) the free flow of ideas, (3) ongoing experimentation, and (4) transforming mistakes into learning experiences.

Creativity and innovation should not be left to chance, luck, or divine intervention. If you want to take your firm to the next level and beyond, then you will need to keep your firm from being a bureaucratic quagmire, where questions that challenge the status quo die or are punished, or where innovative ideas die from neglect. Even though innovation cannot be managed with the same precision as a production line, it can be fostered when: (1) objectives are set for it, (2) people are trained for it, (3) funds are invested in it, and (4) performance is reviewed in terms of it, and (5) rewards are provided for it.

Management's assumptions about people's abilities to be innovative can be a self-fulfilling prophecy. Creativity and innovation tend to be a product of the company's culture. If executives believe people have innovative ability, then they will put processes in place that encourage, enhance, and reward innovation. If they believe most people cannot be innovative, then they will design organizational processes that end up constraining creativity.

Efforts to enhance innovation can range all the way from being an integral part of your firm's strategic plan down to the layout of the firm's facilities. People at all levels of the firm should be empowered to size up situations and to come up with innovative ideas that will give the company an edge. 3M also encourages its people to "bootleg" resources from their existing budget to use in pursuing innovation that is not officially part of the plan. It also encourages "skunkworks" where people from various areas work together to foster innovation. In some instances. 3M may provide the developer of an idea with the opportunity to oversee the development of a division that will commercialize the idea. Yet innovation often comes from little things as well. For example, Chan Suh, CEO of Agency.com, installed chalkboards on the office doors of his New York-based ad agency so people can jot down on-the-spot brainstorming and ideas.[9]

Tips and Approaches That Foster Innovation

- Provide enough latitude for people to explore possibilities.
- Establish a separate fund for innovation that is available for special initiatives.
- Minimize bureaucracy so people do not have to jump many hurdles.
- Make sure ideas can flourish, be heard, and be acted on. Jack Welch, when he was the CEO of GE, noted that revolutions begin with ideas.
- Form cross-functional teams where synergistic results come from cross-pollinating brains.
- Develop an innovation index that monitors the overall number of new ideas or the number of ideas per employee for products, services, and/or processes.
- Ensure ideas are encouraged and rewarded rather than subjected to ridicule, territorialism, parochialism, or bureaucratic barriers.

- Hire and develop people who have considerable mental dexterity to see things from new perspectives, to ask probing questions, and to think new thoughts.
- Provide avenues for people at all levels and positions to learn how to be more creative, because creativity and innovation can be learned.
- Provide opportunities for people at all levels to learn more about changes in the marketplace.
- Use "stage-gate" processes to reduce the risks and capital investment associated with new product idea "concepts" by getting quick feedback from potential customers. Have screens at each stage of development (from idea to launch) that kill potential products that do not meet predetermined expectations.
- Use rapid and iterative prototyping to get your products into the hands of potential customers. Learn from them, modify your products, and put them back in their hands for further improvement; then launch them without getting caught in analysis paralysis.
- Identify today's and tomorrow's "lead users." Get to know them and their challenges. They may be the source of ideas. Help them solve their problems. They may also be your first beta site, your first customer for a new product, and possibly a source of funding if you are looking into doing a joint venture.
- Pay particular attention to your noncustomers. Find out what they want that your firm is not offering.
- Investigate what is keeping people from being consumers. Find out what your firm will need to offer for them to enter the marketplace and become consumers.
- Pay attention to changes taking place in what your customers' customers want. They will determine what your customers will need.
- Encourage your people—not just salespeople—to interact with customers and potential customers (and analyze your competitors' offerings); then provide avenues that make it easy for them to share their observations and ideas with you.
- Consider "crowdsourcing" where people outside the firm have the opportunity to provide innovative ideas and/or provide suggestions about your products, ideas, marketing programs, and so forth.
- Create an environment where people can be "champions" for new products, services, and processes.
- Recognize that coming up with good ideas usually involves first coming up with a large number of ideas. Separate idea generation (brainstorming) from idea evaluation.
- Recognize there is nothing wrong with a "selective imitation" strategy (if you do not violate intellectual property issues) where you incorporate

the best ideas from numerous competitors' products into the development of your new product.

- Make sure that innovative ideas are acted on and do not die from neglect and inaction by putting them off to "someday." Ideas that have merit should have action plans with key milestones so they are acted on. Make sure there is a direct and immediate link "from idea to action."
- Avoid being a perfectionist. Most ideas are diamonds in the rough. Your job is to help them grow into marketable products and services and/or operational processes that will enhance performance.
- Make sure managers do not have a "That's not your job; it's R&D's job to come up with innovative products and services" attitude. Everyone—regardless of position—has the ability to come up with innovative ideas if he or she is provided with an environment that truly welcomes their ideas.

The power of incentives to encourage people to develop ways to improve performance should not be underestimated. Numerous firms have created incentive plans to encourage people throughout the firm to develop ways to enhance performance. Some plans provide recognition for people who come up with good ideas. When an employee with a computer chip firm was asked what gets him out of bed in the morning, he responded, "I want to see my ideas at work." Many plans combine recognition with financial incentives. While recognition has its benefits, money can be a very effective way to get people to find new ways to do things and new things to do. Profit sharing and gain sharing systems that reward people at the individual, group, divisional, and company-wide levels can have a profound impact on the desire for people to learn, to be creative, and to experiment.

Leading by Example: The Leader's Role in Fostering Innovation

True leaders cast a shadow in everything they do. Every word, every decision, every action you do has an effect on what people think and do throughout your firm. If you want your people to be innovative, then you need to set the right example and do everything you can to create an environment that fosters innovation.

The Following Tips Highlight What You Can Do to Foster Innovation:

- Empower people at lower levels of the company to size up situations and to come up with innovative approaches.

- Stay the course and avoid jackrabbiting from one idea to the next without giving each idea the time and attention it deserves.
- Be actively engaged in conversations and discussions about ideas.
- Treat failed experiments and innocent mistakes as learning opportunities. Henry Ford noted, "Failure is only the opportunity to begin again more intelligently."
- Do not wait until it is convenient or you are in a crisis to be innovative.
- Make innovation in your firms' products, services, and processes part of every agenda.
- Provide "air cover" in terms of financial and emotional support as well as resources for the people in your firm who are in a position to champion innovative ideas.
- Do not fall victim to the "Don't rock the boat" mentality. Your role is to foster the innovative spirit, not inhibit it.
- Constantly ask, "What can we do that will change the way the game is played so that we can make our competition irrelevant?"

Reality Check: There is a tendency for executives to reduce the funding for innovation when things get tough and the budget gets tight. Make sure you and your staff maintain the commitment to innovation. Cutting your firm's innovation budget is like a farmer eating his seed corn. When that happens there will be no corn to harvest in the future. Innovation is an investment; it is the way to create your firm's future. People will look to you in times of crisis to see if your commitment to innovation caves under the pressure.

Concluding Comments: Ideas Can Be the Source of Competitive Advantage.

It used to be "Lead, follow, or get out of the way." Today, following is not a viable strategy. If you do not have compelling competitive advantages, then you are dead. For the company to excel, it must be an innovative organization. It must be innovative in its products, services, and processes. Truly innovative firms demonstrate anticipatory innovation. They anticipate what the market will want so they have the lead time needed to develop innovative solutions to be in sync with ever-evolving consumer needs, wants, and desires. Innovative firms also have processes in place for discontinuing what they are doing so they can invest in the future.

Innovation can put the firm in a position to be a first mover and trend setter rather than a trend follower. The possibilities for innovation are limited only by one's imagination. That is why the firm's culture is so important. If all your people are plugged in and your firm is relentless in its pursuit of innovation, then great things are possible.

Creating your company's future requires more than just keeping pace with the changes that are happening outside the company. The ever-accelerating rate of change places a premium on the company's ability to evolve in a revolutionary manner. Companies that learn more quickly and innovate better than other companies are more likely to be out in front. Companies that are slow to learn and merely imitate innovative companies will become irrelevant.

If you create an environment that encourages and rewards innovation, then people in your company will direct their resourcefulness to efforts that will benefit the company. If you create an environment that does not tap their resourcefulness, then they may direct their creative talents to activities that do not enhance the company's performance. In some cases, employees who find their creative talents constrained jump ship and share their talents with a competitor. In other cases, they may even create their own companies to compete against your company. When it comes to creative talent, you either use it or lose it! Take the Innovation Culture Quiz in Table 9.1 to learn the extent to which your firm is positioned to foster innovation.

A new idea is delicate. It can be killed by a sneer or yawn: it can be stabbed to death by a joke or by a worried frown on the right person's brow.

—Charles Brower, former President of Batten,
Barton, Durstine & Osborne advertising agency

TABLE 9.1.   The Innovation Culture Quiz

How does your firm rate on the following dimensions? *Rating Level: 1 = not at all, 2 = slightly true, 3 = somewhat true, 4 = mostly true, 5 = completely true	Level*
1. Your firm has stretch goals that can only be accomplished by high levels of innovation.	1-2-3-4-5
2. The firm's leaders champion innovation.	1-2-3-4-5
3. The firm has systems and processes that foster innovation.	1-2-3-4-5
4. The firm has a diversity of people who provide numerous perspectives.	1-2-3-4-5

TABLE 9.1.   (Continued)

How does your firm rate on the following dimensions? *Rating Level: 1 = not at all, 2 = slightly true, 3 = somewhat true, 4 = mostly true, 5 = completely true	Level*
5. The firm provides rewards for innovative ideas.	1-2-3-4-5
6. Management encourages experimentation and does not punish ideas that fail to meet expectations.	1-2-3-4-5
7. Management solicits innovative ideas from people in and outside the firm, including crowdsourcing.	1-2-3-4-5
8. Management provides sufficient lead time so ideas have a chance to incubate.	1-2-3-4-5
9. The firm uses the stage gate process to screen ideas for their relative merit so ideas with limited merit do not get continued funding.	1-2-3-4-5
10. Management allows people to work on projects that are not part of their regular responsibilities.	1-2-3-4-5
11. The firm is consistently in sync with changing market conditions	1-2-3-4-5
12. The firm's culture and innovative processes are in sync with the firm's strategy.	1-2-3-4-5
13. There is a deliberate effort to phase out products, services, and processes that have limited future potential.	1-2-3-4-5
14. Management distinguishes when it is time to generate ideas and when it is time to reality test the ideas. It has the right type of people in each of the different roles.	1-2-3-4-5
15. People at all levels are encouraged to challenge current practices and conventional wisdom.	1-2-3-4-5
16. Management makes a deliberate and continuous effort to reduce bureaucracy and eliminate idea killers.	1-2-3-4-5
17. People in the new product development process make a deliberate effort to avoid overengineering products. They avoid adding features that are not considered benefits by the targeted consumers.	1-2-3-4-5
18. The firm is truly in sync with its customers' current and future needs.	1-2-3-4-5
19. The firm is monitoring its customers' customers to make sure it is in sync with their current and emerging needs.	1-2-3-4-5

(continued)

TABLE 9.1.   (Continued)

How does your firm rate on the following dimensions? *Rating Level: 1 = not at all, 2 = slightly true, 3 = somewhat true, 4 = mostly true, 5 = completely true	Level*
20. The firm does rapid prototyping so it gets its ideas into the hands of prospective consumers quickly and benefits from their feedback.	1-2-3-4-5
Total points	

Scoring Key

90–100	Congratulations, your firm has the qualities of a corporate culture that fosters innovation.
80–89	Your organization has many strengths, but still has room for improvement.
70–79	Your organization has some strengths, but there is a lot of room for improvement.
60–69	Your organization either has some significant impairments or is weak in most areas. Tweaking your firm's culture and processes will not be enough to make a real difference.
20–59	Your organization may be beyond hope. It will take a radical change in management, strategy, corporate culture, systems, and processes to have any chance of being innovative in the future.

Notes

1. Robert G. Cooper, 'Stage-Gate Systems' A Tool for Managing New Products," *Business Horizons* 33, no. 3 (1990): 44.

2. Maynard Brusman, "Nurturing New Ideas," Bnet Web site, http://bnet.com, May, 11, 2007.

3. Seth Godin, "In the Face of Change, the Competent Are Helpless," *Fast Company*, no. 31 (2000): 234.

4. "The Deep Dive—One Company's Secret Weapon for Innovation" video (Hamilton, NJ: Films for Humanities, 1999).

5. The author would like to know who is the original author for this list.

6. Chuck Salter, "Ideas.com," *Fast Company*, no. 31 (1999): 294.

7. The executive's comments originally appeared in *Business Week*, no. 2419 (1976): 57.

8. John Gardner, *No Easy Victories* (New York: Harper Colophon, 1968), 41.

9. Ellen Neuborne, "The Shape of Things to Come," *Business Week*, no. 3639 (1999): 64.

Chapter 10

Developing a Competitive Edge through Smart Execution

Thinking well is wise; planning well, wiser; doing well wisest and best of all.

—Persian Proverb

Nothing good happens if you cannot transform plans into reality. Yet Murphy's Law, "If anything can go wrong, it will, and at the most inopportune time" seems to plague most organizations today. The corollary to Murphy's Law, "Nothing is as easy as it looks" captures the challenges managers are facing in a world of spinning plates and ever-increasing complexity. Firms that approach execution and implementation from a proactive and systematic perspective will separate themselves from the pack.

In an ideal world, a firm would have exceptional ideas, exceptional strategies, and exceptional execution. A multitude of books and articles have been written about developing breakthrough ideas and crafting formidable competitive strategies. But firms will go nowhere if they are not able to execute their plans and tactics. Cypress Semiconductor, under the leadership of T. J. Rogers, has demonstrated a total commitment to identifying performance objectives and monitoring whether they are being accomplished. Rogers stated, "Most companies don't fail for lack of talent or vision. They fail for lack of execution—the mundane blocking and tackling that the great companies consistently do well and strive to do better."[1]

Executives who foster exceptional execution will give their firms a competitive advantage. This chapter focuses on the challenges of execution and implementation that will help a firm become an exceptional enterprise. It places particular attention on the managerial and behavioral dimensions of execution.

While the business world may still be infatuated with executives who capture the media's attention for being bold and bigger than life, today's environment beckons for a very rare breed of executive. It beckons for executives who have a solid grasp of today's realities as well as emerging realities and who can make the right things happen, the right way, at the right time, and within budget. Investors, consumers, and employees at all levels are calling out for executives and managers who are willing to make commitments and who can create environments where the commitments are fulfilled.

Some Thoughts about Execution and Implementation

Ideas are easy, it is the execution that is difficult.

—Jeff Bezos, founder of Amazon

Unless you can translate big thoughts into concrete steps for action, they're pointless. Without execution, the breakthrough thinking breaks down, learning adds no value, people don't meet stretch goals, and the revolution stops dead in its tracks.[2]

—Larry Bossidy and Ram Charan, authors of *Execution*

Every time you set foot on the track, you have to assume that something unexpected will happen.

—Sarah Fisher, Indy Driver

Execution and Implementation: What Is the Difference?

The terms "execution" and "implementation" are often used interchangeably with little distinction made between the two. However, there is a distinction between them that is worth making. Both are crucial to success. Execution is about performance. It focuses on "*whether*" certain goals were accomplished. Implementation, on the other hand, focuses on "*how*" the goals will be accomplished. Implementation refers to the activities required to *transform* an organization's vision, strategy, initiative, or project into reality.

In most cases, effective execution occurs when what was set out to be accomplished is accomplished. Execution means that organizational tasks and responsibilities are carried out effectively and in accordance with organizational goals, strategies and tactics. It may be reflected in getting a new assembly operation up and running by, or before, the target date. It may be reflected in delivering an order that meets the quality, quantity, time, and cost targets. It may even be as small as responding to a customer inquiry in a timely fashion. It can apply to the organization as a whole, a business unit, a department, a project, and even an individual.

New Realities: More of the Same Will Not Cut It

The "expectations bar" has been raised in the last few years and it is expected to continue being raised in the years ahead. The days of for-giveness are over. Customers expect results and will not accept excuses. They show no mercy to firms that cannot meet their quality, quantity, time, convenience, and cost expectations. Customers want it their way, and they want it now. They want their products to be of higher and more consistent quality, priced lower, and more convenient to access and use. Customers no longer expect their suppliers to fulfill their commitments; they demand it. Customers live in a world of alternatives. Customers will seek out other sources of supply if they cannot count on their current suppliers. In some cases, they will become their own suppliers. Your customers may even become your competitors.

The time has come for firms to get their acts together or to prepare for their demise. New realities require new approaches to execution and implementation. The following realities must be incorporated into how firms approach execution and implementation:

Today's Realities

- **It is not about coping any more**. Just getting by will not cut it. Barely meeting deadlines will not cut it. Relying on overnight delivery to make up for operational mistakes will not cut it.
- **Things are becoming more complicated**. The world is changing on all fronts; nothing is simple anymore. When was the last time things seemed simple, when things were stable, and when things could be predicted?
- **The good old days are over**. Manufacturers used to be able to enjoy long standardized production runs. The new world looks more like a job shop than an assembly line. Customization and new projects are no longer the exception; they are the rule.

- **Being first-to-market does not assure success.** Being at the leading edge and being fast have considerable appeal, but being the first to the "customer satisfaction" finish line is what really counts. There was a time when you might be able to get away with a "Launch it now, and we'll fix the problems later." strategy. Now, if you do not get it right the first time, you may not be around to fix it later.
- **We live in a networked world.** The strategy of outsourcing everything but the areas where you have core competencies sounds good in theory, but being dependent on other firms also creates considerable vulnerability. Each supplier and/or corporate ally is like a link in a chain. Firms that adopt just-in-time practices and use single sources of supply need to choose their partners very carefully. Supplier dependability is far more important than shave a few cents of expenses on the income statement.
- **We live in a world of spinning plates.** We live in a "today" mentality where immediacy and a preoccupation with today's bottom line are preventing many firms from building a solid foundation for a better tomorrow. This is particularly true for publicly traded firms.
- **We live in a world of specialists with silo mentalities.** Specialists' functional orientation and perspective keep them from seeing the big picture and having an "integrated systems perspective." They do not see the whole-parts-whole nature of business that is essential for effective execution.
- **We live in a world where people are cautious to a fault.** People are so afraid of making a mistake that they do things "by the book." Unfortunately, today's book does not look like yesterday's book. And tomorrow's book will not look like today's book. Today's book will need to be thrown out sooner rather than later in favor of new approaches that foster resourcefulness and innovation. Moreover, innovation does not have to come at the expense of effective execution. It just means that thinking things through must play an integral role when the firm is being innovative.

Execution and Implementation Problems: In the Eye of the Beholder

It is ironic how everyone seems to complain about execution problems, but no one seems to take responsibility for them. Top management exclaims: "Can't anyone get it right down there?" They are like the basketball coach who tried to dodge accountability by saying, "I can't shoot the foul shots for my players during the game!" Mid-level managers who are supposed to serve as linking pins that connect the dots between strategy and tactics by developing action plans, budgets and timelines exclaim, "Who in the world came up with these ideas?" and "Doesn't anyone up there have any sense of reality?" Front-line managers accuse top management and middle managers of being like seagulls "who fly in from a distance, make a lot of noise, drop a lot of 'stuff' on them, and then fly away."

Failure at the Top: Many Executives Hamstring the Firm's Ability to Execute

If you are looking for the root cause for execution problems, then you have to start your search at the top of the enterprise. Management's job is to create an environment that is conducive to performance. If performance is not there, the problem is not with the people on the front lines; it is with top management's failure to create an environment that fosters exceptional execution.

Reality Check: The Rule of Finger states, "When you point the finger of blame, take a look at your hand—you will find three fingers are pointing back at you!" A reality check often reveals that those at the top just do not grasp the role they need to play and the dynamics of exceptional execution. Napoleon Bonaparte once noted, "Soldiers win battles and generals get the credit." Unfortunately, when things go wrong today executives dodge accountability and employees get the ax.

How Executives Undermine Effective Execution and Implementation

If one's attitudes are the basis for one's approach to managing, then it is clear that executives and managers who have the following attitudes about execution will jeopardize their enterprise's ability to execute in an exceptional manner.

Situation 1: Some executives just do not want to take the time to deal with execution issues. They consider their role to be the firm's visionary and to come up with the next new thing.

Solution 1: Executives also need to champion execution. Everything they do needs to send the message that execution is an integral part of every person's job. Harvey S. Firestone noted, "Success is the sum of detail. It might perhaps be pleasing to imagine oneself beyond detail and engaged only in great things, but as I have often observed, if one only attends to great things and lets the little things pass, the great things become little; that is, the business shrinks."

Situation 2: Some executives believe it is the ideas that really matter and that good ideas almost implement themselves.

Solution 2: Executives cannot afford to take implementation for granted. Exceptional performance is not possible without exceptional execution. Exceptional execution may provide the enterprise with a significant competitive advantage.

Situation 3: Some executives consider themselves to be "above" having to deal with implementation issues. They stand at the summit and tell their troops, "Just make it happen!"

Solution 3: General George Patton observed, "You will never know what is going on unless you hear the whistle of the bullets."

Situation 4: This situation has some similarities to situation #3. Some executives are so afraid of being accused of micromanaging that they overcompensate by distancing themselves from discussions about execution issues, from monitoring ongoing performance, and from intervening when it necessary.

Solution 4: T.J. Rogers of Cypress Semiconductor noted that in his industry, management needs to create a "no surprises" environment because there is little room for error. Cypress Semiconductor's comprehensive system sets and monitors more than 6,000 performance factors on an ongoing basis.[3]

Situation 5: Too many executives have learned to play it safe by setting goals that are merely increments of the last period's goals. Incremental goals merely encourage people to tweak what they have already done.

Solution 5: If you want people to find innovative ways to do things, then set objectives that cannot be accomplished by tweaking how things have been done in the past. Stretch goals encourage people to find or develop innovative ways to get things done. While reengineering may have received some bad press as a way to cut payroll, its real value is that it forces people to start with a clean sheet of paper.

Situation 6: Some executives do not see the essential connection between setting set stretch goals like being "the best in our industry" and the level of commitment needed by the troops to make them happen. As *deciders*, executives fail to recognize how critical it is for the grass roots *doers* to be committed. They assume those who are doing the blocking and tackling in the trenches will be committed because they are loyal to the enterprise.

Solution 6: Commitment does not come from loyalty; it comes from having your ideas solicited and your contributions valued.

Situation 7: Some executives are so fixated on making sure things are done the right way that they do not step back and ask if they are doing the right things. They spend all their time reviewing metrics and fail to ask themselves if they are even using the right metrics.

Solution 7: Managers must guard against being so preoccupied with measuring moment-to-moment progress as they are cutting their way through the forest that they fail to check to make sure they are in the *right* forest. They should look at their firms and ask, "If we were to start the firm from scratch today, what should we be doing and how should we be doing those things?"

Situation 8: Some executives have adopted the, "Don't sweat the small stuff" attitude toward execution issues. They fail to grasp how little glitches can have dramatic consequences. They never read the proverb Ben Franklin included in Poor Richard's Almanac in 1758, "For the want of a nail, the shoe was lost; for the want of a shoe the horse was lost; and for the want of a horse the rider was lost, being overtaken and slain by the enemy, all for the want of care about a horseshoe nail."

Solution 8: When Ray Kroc was running McDonald's, he treated the process for making French fries as if it were a religion. He knew that their quality could not be subject to variability. Executives need to send the message that everything the firm does is a "moment of truth." Every decision and every action, regardless of how small it may seem at the time, either enhances the firm's performance or jeopardizes its very existence.

Situation 9: Some executives have adopted the attitude, "Well, 'stuff' happens!" They consider mistakes to be the norm, not the exception. Mistakes are expected and accepted. They are so accustomed to missing deadlines by a day or two, having to do rework as a matter of routine, scheduling overtime, and having crises every day, that they really do not consider these situations to be moments of truth that determine their firm's future.

Solution 9: People at all levels must be held accountable for getting the job done right the first time, every time. Most firms' performance review processes and criteria do not measure the various facets of execution and/or their incentive plans reward factors not directly related to execution effectiveness. If you want exceptional execution, then you need to create a "zero tolerance for lame excuses" environment.

Situation 10: Some executives do not understand the challenges associated with execution. They are like freshly minted MBAs who believe everything can be distilled into a glitzy PowerPoint presentation and Excel spreadsheet. They have not been in the trenches, and they just do not grasp the messiness and multitude of issues involved in executing plans.

Solution 10: Tom Peters noted, "Unpredictability cannot be removed, or even substantially reduced, by excessive planning." Instead of spending all the time on putting their ideas in slick presentations, freshly minted MBAs should spend some time in the trenches getting a first-hand feel for where the rubber meets the road and developing scar tissue from true "learning opportunities."

Situation 11: Some executives emphasize the importance of execution but fail to provide sufficient resources and the air cover needed for the troops to do their jobs well.

Solution 11: Executives need to make sure that funding for state-of-the-art information systems, training, and continuous improvement processes are not the casualties of austerity drives. They must be able to show that they are necessities, not luxuries, and that these efforts have a direct effect on the firm's top line by creating and maintaining customers, as well as its bottom line by enhancing operating efficiency.

Situation 12: Some executives do not have the courage to support execution efforts when things get tough. They fail to take a stand on tough execution issues. Instead of defending the need to get things right, they waffle, rationalize, deny reality, or step aside. Instead of leading, they let the forces of expediency steamroll the processes that foster effective execution and the people who are committed to getting it right.

Solution 12: Adlai Stevenson, former governor of Illinois and presidential candidate, once stated, "On the plains of hesitation lie the blackened bones of countless millions who at the dawn of victory lay down to rest, and in resting died." Executives and managers at all levels must be unwavering in their commitment to make the right things happen the right way.

Situation 13: Some executives get so wrapped up in detailed planning that they fail to recognize that the purpose of planning is not to develop plans—it is to implement plans that make good things happen.

Solution 13: Planning needs to be flexible, and it needs to be adaptive. It should point the firm in the right direction, but it should not become a straight jacket for its developers or its implementers. Explorers Lewis and Clark knew they could not plan for everything in advance and that they would need to have resources in reserve so they could adjust to various realities. They started their expedition with over 1,000 pounds of trinkets to trade with the Indians.

Situation 14: Too many executives are reactive. Instead of preventing fires, they operate via a "red alert" fire-fighting, problem-solving mode.

Solution 14: Executives need to adopt anticipatory management techniques profiled earlier in the book that foster problem identification and problem prevention. Mental horizons need to be extended, "what if?" scenarios need to be run, variances need to be identified early, and contingency plans need to be ready to be implemented to ensure effective execution. Success in the years ahead will involve more than coming up with the answers to the key questions. Success will take more than knowing which questions need to be answered. If the firm wants to be exceptional, then it will need to develop the answers before anyone else—competitors or customers—even know the questions.

Situation 15: While some executives are prone to overanalyzing and over-planning, other executives are the exact opposite. They operate with a "We'll cross that bridge when we get to it" mentality.

Solution 15: While this approach may sound appropriate in some situations, executives need to know which situations are *those* situations. There is a big difference between waiting to see what should be done and procrastination.

Situation 16: Some executives are not willing to create the type of environment where the firm learns from its mistakes. Instead of seizing the moment, leaving no stone unturned, investigating why things went wrong, and fixing the problem, they spend their time rationalizing, denying, pointing the finger of blame elsewhere, and protecting sacred cows.

Solution 16: Executives need to ensure the enterprise is a learning organization. People need to be encouraged, reviewed, and rewarded for challenging assumptions, asking tough questions, probing for the root causes of problems, breaking down bureaucratic barriers, killing sacred cows, engaging in robust dialogues, and pursuing new ideas. Goals, action plans, and incentives also need to be established for fixing things, improving things, and for innovation.

Some Thoughts about Planning

An ounce of application is worth a ton of abstraction.

—Booker's Law

In the final analysis, planning cannot be meaningful without management foresight, management support, management decision, and management follow-through.

—P.J. Lovewell, as Director of Research, Stanford University

It's a bad plan that admits no modification.

—Publilius Syrus, Roman Writer, 42 B.C.

Execution and Implementation Need to Be Approached in a Holistic Manner

Executives who are committed to creating an environment that fosters exceptional execution need to recognize that it is not just about identifying and taking care of the details. Execution and implementation are as multi-faceted as a diamond. Execution and implementation are far more strategic and comprehensive than "making sure the i's are dotted and the t's crossed."

Executives need to approach execution and implementation from a systems perspective that incorporates the four critical dimensions: people, culture, strategy, as well as systems and structure. These dimensions cannot be considered independent of each other. Each must contribute to the other. Inconsistencies among dimensions will undermine the enterprise's ability to execute in an exceptional manner. The Exceptional

FIGURE 10.1.   Exceptional Execution Model

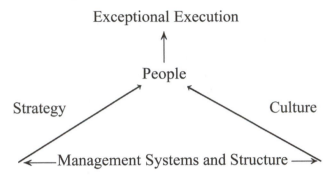

Execution Model profiled in Figure 10.1 reflects the interrelatedness of the four dimensions.

- **People:** The firm must have the right people with the right skills and the right attitudes. They must also be in the right positions to utilize their skills and abilities. Firms should seek people with diverse perspectives and with varied experiences. They are more likely to see potential problems and to come up with innovative approaches for making the right things happen. The diversity should include people who are freethinkers, people who are comfortable playing the devil's advocate role, specialists who bring valuable skills to the situation, generalists who can see the big picture, and people who, like project managers, can choreograph resources, talent, and ideas into highly productive efforts.
- **Culture:** A commitment to exceptional execution must be part of the very fabric of the enterprise. It must be one of the firm's key values. The firm's culture must breathe execution to the point that execution is embraced by each person in each job. The culture must have little tolerance for execution errors, especially those that are repeated. The culture represents a delicate balance between fanaticism for getting things right and a continuous quest for finding better ways to get things done. The culture must have a continuous experimentation mentality. People are encouraged to find better ways to execute, but when it comes to fulfilling commitments to internal and external customers—execution perfection is expected.
- **Strategy:** Execution and implementation must be an integral part of the firm's strategy. The firm's strategy must point the firm in the right direction, yet it must enable the firm to adapt to market realities. Management must translate the firm's vision into tangible action plans. The strategy should incorporate the dynamics and challenges involved in implementation from the very beginning. Particular attention should be directed to soliciting input from the people who will be implementing the strategy.

- **Management Systems and Structure:** The firm's management systems must support effective implementation and execution. Information systems should function more like intelligence systems that let people know what is going on in an anticipatory manner. The firm's recruiting, selection, and training efforts must be designed to foster exceptional performance. The firm's performance review system must hold people accountable for executing plans. The firm's incentive system must reward those who demonstrate exceptional execution. The firm's structure must also enable people to communicate and interact freely so they are not encumbered by bureaucratic processes, functional silos, and/or a multitude of organizational layers. Frank Blake as CEO of Home Depot developed an interesting way of finding out whether decisions made at headquarters were being implemented in Home Depot's stores. When his son Frank was the manager of one of Home Depot's stores in Wilmington, North Carolina, he would call him to see if he was aware of the change and if it was being implemented. The Blakes referred to this reality check as "The Wilmington Connection."

Identifying and Capitalizing on Exceptional Implementers: Profile of "Go-To" People

Corporate success in the years ahead will be contingent on the extent to which firms are able to develop competitive advantages. While a great deal of attention has been directed to the need to develop breakthrough strategies as well as innovative products and services, it is clear that they will succeed only to the extent they are implemented well. Yet little attention has been directed to understanding the managers who turn business strategies into actual results.

Learning more about what makes people exceptional implementers is of considerable practical importance for firms, for executives who are looking for the right person to implement various initiatives, and for people who want to be exceptional implementers. Firms will profit from increasing the number and quality of exceptional implementers they hire and develop. The ability to take an idea from the 30,000 foot level and to make it a reality will provide their organizations with a significant competitive advantage.

This section provides insights into personal characteristics and critical skills firms should seek in their hiring practices. It also highlights implementation skills that may be enhanced in their training programs and their efforts to place people in situations where they can develop their implementation skills. This section is based on an investigation of people who are exceptional implementers.[4] It provides insights from interviews with senior executives from various industries. It also highlights the personal characteristics and critical skills exhibited by "go-to" people who have an uncanny ability to consistently bring various initiatives in on time and within the budget.

Scattered throughout most successful businesses are a handful of "go-to" people that executives rely on to make things happen. When a project or new initiative is crucially important, these "go-to" people are called upon to oversee the management of that effort. They are the people who transform ideas into reality.

Some Thoughts on the Role People Play in Execution and Implementation

Problems can be reduced by allowing employees to help plan changes rather than directing them to execute a plan made by others.

—Eugene Raudsepp, former President, Creative Research, Inc., MTS Digest, April/June, 1987

Good people can fix a lot of flaws in poor planning, but it's never the other way around.

—Roland Schmitt, former Senior V.P. General Electric

Common Characteristics and Skills of Exceptional Implementers

No two exceptional implementers are exactly alike, but most of them share certain attributes. The attributes can be broken into two basic categories: personal characteristics and critical skills. Taken collectively, the most common of these attributes describe what might be considered the truly exceptional implementer.

Key Personal Characteristics

The following personal characteristics play a key role in an exceptional implementer's performance:

- **Tenacious:** They have an internal desire to press forward, avoid delay, and engage the task.
- **Challenge seeking:** They go beyond simply having a desire to act; they just move ahead. They seek opportunities to improve performance and take the firm to the next level.

- **Self-directed:** Their tenacity and propensity to seek challenges are primary factors when executives select people to oversee specific tasks.
- **Able to draw on a rich and diverse experience base:** They have varied functional expertise and the ability to work across functions effectively.
- **Versatile and adaptive:** They welcome and embrace change. They have the ability to turn on a dime.
- **Willing to take risks:** They are usually assigned nonroutine challenges, so being a little bit of a maverick helps them take risks.

Critical Implementation Skills

The following behavioral skills are employed by exceptional implementers to complete their tasks successfully:

- **Management and organizational skills:** They are always looking ahead and try to preempt situations. They are also able to put the pieces together in a way that is understandable and manageable.
- **Facilitation skills:** They are often asked to take on major projects where their ability to engage and capitalize on others' talents are essential to success. Exceptional implementers often rely on finesse in getting the people whom they do not have authority over involved and committed to the endeavor.
- **Multifaceted communication skills:** They prefer "face-to-face" communications, letting people know they are a part of the team, and giving them a sense of ownership in the overall project. They find out what kind of problems are being encountered before the problems blow up. They also have the ability to act as an interpreter among different areas of the organization.
- **Problem-solving skills:** Their ability to handle very ambiguous situations and to *frame* problems is often called "mindfulness." They are able to see the whole-parts-whole as well as the cause and effect nature of situations. They are able to focus on the things that matter most. They can also develop creative and unique solutions.

The Devil Is in the Details: Guidelines for Enhancing "Tactical Implementation"

Tactical implementation is the details, the nuts and bolts, and the rolled-up shirtsleeves of an organization. It involves the real-time decisions and day-to-day activities that are required by those on the front line. For example, front-line managers are primarily responsible for implementing the firm's strategy. They are responsible for the design, development, and execution of tactical initiatives that enable the firm to meet quality and quantity expectations as well as to be on time and within the budget. "The devil is in the details" perfectly describes some of the challenges people face who are responsible for implementing action plans and who are on the corporate firing line. This section encourages those at the top to be savvier to the challenges faced by first-line managers and employees who will determine whether their visions will become a reality. Their strategies will give their firms a competitive edge only if they are skillfully implemented.[5]

Some Thoughts about the Importance of Paying Attention to the Details

Vision is important, because you have to have a path where the company is going to go. But visions that you don't execute on are called hallucinations. The implementation—the execution—is the difficult part. And that's in the details.

—John Roth, former CEO of Nortel

An executive cannot gradually dismiss details. Business is made up of details and the chief executive that dismisses them is quite likely to dismiss his business.

—Harvey S. Firestone

It's my role as leader to create leaders who pay attention to details at every level of the organization.

—David Novak, CEO of Tricon Global Restaurants

It isn't so much that I have to manage the details, I have to ensure the details are managed.

—John Roth, former CEO of Nortel

The only way you get a sense of the big picture is through a keen understanding of details. How things play out in the retail store is more important than what a document at headquarters says is happening. So I go shop at the stores like a customer. When I tour the stores I ask questions like where can I find printer cartridge #6534? Hopefully the sales rep points me to the two-for-one counter. That's nirvana.

—Thomas Stemberg, former CEO of Staples

Reality Check: The following quote, however, indicates the "Catch-22" nature of paying so much attention to details that you fail to see the big picture and the role that innovation can play in enhancing organizational success. Francois Duc de La Rochefoucauld, a French Moralist, noted in the seventeenth century, *"Those who apply themselves too closely to little things often become incapable of great things."*

> Reality Check: Being on time and under budget are only valuable if the resulting tactics are appropriate and accurate representations of the strategic plans. Here again is the need to make sure you are in the right forest.

Principles of Tactical Implementation

There is nothing sexy or glamorous about implementation—especially tactical implementation. Implementers are like offensive linemen in football. They are the unsung heroes if things go as planned, and they are often the only ones singled out when something goes wrong. Too often, senior managers who are responsible for formulating strategy lose sight of challenges faced by those responsible for implementing their strategies. Seven key principles of tactical implementation profiled in this section make the "doing things right" nature of implementation far more challenging than figuring out "the right things to do" that is associated with strategy formulation.

Plans should incorporate various reality checks that take into account implementation issues. Executives also need to recognize that the implementers will have to engage in even more detailed implementation planning that involve a cascade of "additional" decisions that include raising and then answering many of the "who, what, when, where, how, how much" questions that are left out of most strategies and initiatives. The implementers are the ones who are expected to develop detailed agendas, to do lists, schedules, budgets, and the like for specific tasks that are part of the initiative.

> Reality Check: It is almost inevitable that as detailed action planning takes place, additional strategic issues will emerge that will have to be addressed well after the strategic plans have been approved. Make sure the people involved in implementing a plan recognize in advance that the plan may need to be ever-evolving.

The following principles describe important characteristics of implementation that frequently make implementation devilishly difficult. The chapter concludes by proposing nine recommendations to help managers cope better with the challenges of implementation.

Principle 1: What May Seem to Be Simple Can Be Deceptively Complex

Sometimes tactical initiatives are so simple in concept that it seems that they could almost implement themselves. Managers must recognize that simplicity or intuitiveness of the strategic concept has very little to do with the challenge of implementation. The challenge of effective implementation begins not at the start of implementation but rather during the upfront decision making process that can be critically important for successful implementation. Reliance on the "We'll cross the implementation bridge when we get to it" philosophy may place the firm in a precarious position.

Principle 2: Buy-in Is Crucial

Decisions, plans, and strategies by nature involve change. Management needs to recognize few people welcome change, especially when it is initiated by others. Employee resistance can range from subtle foot-dragging all the way to covert sabotage. One of the most critical implementation tasks involves building the mental commitment (or buy-in) to the initiative on the part of those groups and individuals who are asked to carry out key implementation tasks.

Top management may garner a higher level of buy-in if it considers the people on the firing line as internal customers or even internal consultants. Managers seeking to increase employee buy-in should make a deliberate effort to bring employees on the firing line into the loop. If top management stresses the value and importance of the endeavor and genuinely asks employees to provide suggestions and recommendations to enhance and improve the endeavor, it will be increasing the commitment to making it a success. Management may also be able to increase the level of commitment by front-line personnel if the personnel have a link to the firm's customers.

Senior management buy-in is also essential. Senior managers often falter in their support of the program when the needs for training, funding and other resources become more explicit. Management's reluctance to provide "air cover" and commit resources highlights the need for getting senior managers to formally sign off on the commitment of the corresponding resources. Senior management's visibility by people at all levels in the organization for an endeavor can also affect the perceived importance of the project and hence the buy-in of those participants required to implement them.

Principle 3: Metrics Play a Key Role in Implementation

Management must also set clear and measurable metrics for assessing the performance for the endeavor as well as for the individuals carrying out implementation activities. Buy-in problems are frequently based on misunderstandings about the responsibilities and obligations of the endeavor's participants. Metrics help clarify tactical goals as well as the expected deliverables of the project or program.

Principle 4: Mindfulness Plays a Key Role in Implementation

Effective implementers have a sense for the situation holistically. They also have mental alertness to potential problems. Mindfulness is a valuable attribute, but it is often perceived by some people in organizations as being cynical, negative, not being a team player, or downright nuts. Just as organizations need open-minded, freewheeling people who can think outside the box in brainstorming and new product development sessions, organizations also need people who are able to find flaws and who are willing to provide a timely sense of reality.

Reality Check: People who challenge assumptions and the status quo need to be protected from those who do not like to be challenged. A Turkish proverb noted, "Those who tell the truth should have one foot in the stirrup."

Principle 5: Implementation Success Involves Anticipating and Avoiding Surprises

Those involved in planning should recognize the two rules of implementation: Rule 1 is "Stuff" happens. Rule 2 is "When things seem to be going smoothly, remember Rule 1." Effective implementation often boils down to the ability to anticipate and hence avoid potential problems that can occur on a project. Although problems during implementation are a fact of life, highly effective implementers are successful in part because they are more diligent in identifying and assessing potential risks. They look for causal linkages between project elements and potential negative outcomes.

The increasing incidence of discontinuities in today's marketplace makes it impossible for even the savviest people to anticipate all possible ways that events may unfold. Those organizing for implementation should be able to reduce the frequency and severity of implementation surprises by: (1) utilizing more experienced managers, (2) engaging in a more fine-grained level of planning and (3) actively considering risks and developing contingency plans.

Research has shown that more experienced individuals are better able to anticipate unusual or uncommon occurrences. Managers who have varied experiences tend to take into account more unusual events. Experience plays a key role in the development of perceptiveness and intuition. Perceptiveness involves the ability to see things others may not see. Intuition involves coming up with the answer without really knowing how you got it. These skills are particularly valuable when time is of the essence and/or there is limited information.

Risk analysis is a general form of anticipatory management that was profiled earlier in the book. It involves running "What if" scenarios to identify factors that could impact the endeavor. Risk analysis helps the people involved: (1) identify potential problems, (2) assess the probability that these events will occur, and (3) make changes in the plan where needed.

When undesired events occur and there is little time to review the situation and craft a whole new game plan, having developed fairly explicit contingency plans in the original planning process will provide a company with a "quick response" capability, giving it an edge over firms that are more reactive. Contingency plans need to be developed if: (1) the consequences of error are too severe, (2) the probability of error is too high, (3) the consequences of reacting slowly are too high, and/or (4) a combination of two or more of these factors occur.

Principle 6: Implementation Needs to Adapt to Emerging Issues

Effective implementers are extremely vigilant for the potential emergence of problems. They are prepared to respond to the unexpected events *sooner and with fewer resources*. The uncertainty and unpredictability of what lies ahead means that they will have to: (1) size up the uniqueness of the situation, (2) scan the surroundings for clues that modifications need to be made during implementation, (3) determine what actions need to be taken, and (4) make adjustments when it becomes apparent that the original plan will not be successful. Early warning systems enable earlier detection and quicker response to problems before they can escalate into major problems.

Reality Check: Front-line managers rarely have the luxury of focusing on one project at a time. They operate in a world of "spinning plates." At any time, first-line managers might be working on several projects, attending to their daily responsibilities, and handling the latest crisis their manager dropped in their lap. More and more time is spent running back and forth from one wobbling plate to the next to keep them from crashing. In a zero-sum world, the time devoted to problem solving keeps them from having the time to do problem seeking. This is unfortunate because the more time that can be invested in identifying potential fires, the less time and resources that will be needed to put them out.

Principle 7: Improvisation Is Often a Necessity

Murphy's Law places a premium on having the ability to improvise. The experience of Jim Lovell, Jack Swigert and Fred Haise on Apollo 13 provides a dramatic example of how improvisation can play a critical role when Murphy's Law enters the scene. They were more than 200,000 miles from earth when their No. 2 oxygen tank blew up, causing tank No. 1 to fail also. The command module's normal supply of electricity, light, and water was lost. What followed was an epic struggle against the hostile environment of space by the skilled and highly trained astronauts working in close coordination with the ground-based team at Mission Control. Through improvisation sparked by tenacity and ingenuity, the astronauts and ground crew overcame seemingly insurmountable odds to bring the Apollo 13 astronauts safely back to Earth. They confirmed the belief that necessity is truly the mother of invention.

While the kind of problems that occur during the implementation of tactical initiatives in the corporate arena may not match the drama of the Apollo 13 mission, they do require many of the same skills. Front-line managers must be prepared to improvise appropriate and unique responses in the face of critical, unanticipated problems. Highly effective implementers are alert to the potential for opportunities to improvise improvements in the plans or standard routines.

Managerial Interventions/Recommendations

Many people consider the ideas presented in this chapter to be common sense. If implementation is simply a matter of common sense, then why do firms struggle so mightily to implement various initiatives? The following section highlights some "uncommon" sense about improving implementation effectiveness.

- **Implementation is a skill that needs to be honed.** Getting to the top today takes more than an MBA from a prestigious business school; you have to demonstrate that you can make things happen, which requires excellence in implementation. While implementation may not be glamorous, earning the label of "someone who gets things done by paying attention to the details" can be more valuable than having a freshly minted, brand name MBA. First-time managers are frequently thrown into the fire and have to learn on the job. Firms must provide the appropriate types of training programs that will provide insights into planning and implementing projects. They must also make an effort to provide people with a variety of experiences that will help them be more mindful and effective.
- **Like a good wine, "Don't empower your people before their time."** Without considerable information and knowledge, empowerment for those on the firing line could lead to chaos. Implementers can be like deer frozen in a car's headlights if they do not have adequate preparation.
- **Top management must provide direction, not directions.** Top management must provide the implementers with a sense for what the final result should be. Yet top management cannot foresee how situations can change from one moment to the next, nor does it have extensive experience with all the potential challenges people on the firing line may encounter. Richard Ellenberger, former CEO of Broadwing (formerly Cincinnati Bell) commented, "I give my senior management team as much room as a Loran positioning system, which is used by ships and aircraft. With a Loran you know where you are within the confines of a grid, and a beep goes off when you reach the outer edges of the box. Within the grid our executives get a lot of autonomy."[6] People on the firing line must be free to analyze the unique situation, to figure out what needs to be done, to develop the details, and to improvise when necessary. Anyone who has remodeled a house knows that plans will have to be modified as soon as the first board is removed!

- **Use the right tools for the job.** Tactical initiatives usually have all the characteristics of projects—they are unique, complex, and require a great deal of coordination and planning. Useful project management tools and techniques have been developed for planning and managing projects. However, managers on the firing line who are required to implement tactical initiatives often fail to take advantage of these tools. Too few implementation managers use project management software or tools such as PERT charts and/or "What if?" simulations.

- **Choose your partners carefully.** Firms are embracing the core competency strategy that states, "Only do what you do best; partner with firms where you aren't the best." When it comes to implementing tactical initiatives, many firms turn to outside partners to plan and execute the program details. The "outsource nearly everything" concept has merits, but it can also place a firm in jeopardy. Depending on others may increase the firm's vulnerability. Managers should practice due diligence, make sure each partner places a premium on your relationship, and always have contingency plans.

- **Have an intolerance for execution errors.** Implementation effectiveness can be significantly affected by the organizational culture. Some organizations appear to be highly effective at implementation, while others continually struggle to implement their strategies and tactics. The common thread between organizations that are great at implementation is they have an intolerance for execution errors. This intolerance for implementation errors pervades the organizational culture and leads to an increased level of diligence and attention to detail during implementation planning and execution.

Reality Check: Do not confuse intolerance for errors with intolerance for experimentation and its corresponding mistakes. Intolerance for errors applies to errors that could have been foreseen and for making the same mistake twice. If you want innovation, then you need to have a culture that recognizes that mistakes are part of learning.

- **Make simplicity a virtue.** Implementers live by the axiom, KISS—Keep it Simple Stupid. Initiatives that are kept simple and straightforward will save time and produce far fewer mistakes during implementation. The challenge for implementers is to determine correctly whether initiatives are legitimately straightforward or are seemingly simple but deceptively complex.

Concluding Comments: Perceptive and Agile Implementation Will Give Your Firm an Edge

Execution would be a lot easier if times were stable and actions could be repeated over and over. The true test of implementation in the years ahead will be whether people will be able to execute well the first time. Competing in the marketplace will be like exploring new terrain. Ever-evolving enterprises are like the early explorers. They do not have precise maps to guide them. Like explorers, they need people who can size up the unique situation, develop a plan of action, monitor success, and make quick changes.

Planning and implementation in the years ahead will need to incorporate the concepts and techniques associated with rapid prototyping. Planning will need to be done more quickly and be far more flexible. Implementation efforts will also need to do a better job answering the who, what, when, where, how, and how much questions—and to do it quickly. The ability to continuously monitor the things that can make a difference and to adjust and improvise will be even more important. Being quicker than anyone else will make the difference between thriving and dying. Take the Effective Execution Quiz in Table 10.1 to learn the extent to which your firm is doing the things that enhance performance.

If you are embarking around the world, don't forget the toilet paper. Once, we had to wait for an incoming fax.

—Richard Branson

TABLE 10.1.   The Effective Execution Quiz

How does your firm rate on the following execution dimensions? *Scoring Level: 1 = not at all, 2 = slightly true, 3 = partly true, 4 = mostly true, 5 = completely true	Level*
People	
1. Do your firm's chief executive and executive team really understand the challenges of execution?	1-2-3-4-5
2. Does your firm recruit people who have different backgrounds and perspectives to foster robust and diverse discussions, insights, and the cross-pollination of ideas?	1-2-3-4-5
3. Does your firm cross-train people so they have a broader perspective and numerous capabilities, and so your firm is not vulnerable when there is staff turnover?	1-2-3-4-5
4. Does your company attract, encourage, protect, and reward people who foster a reality-orientation by challenging assumptions and asking tough questions?	1-2-3-4-5

TABLE 10.1. (Continued)

How does your firm rate on the following execution dimensions? *Scoring Level: 1 = not at all, 2 = slightly true, 3 = partly true, 4 = mostly true, 5 = completely true	Level*
People	
5. Do the people who are responsible for implementation have a project management mentality that fosters a whole-parts-whole framework?	1-2-3-4-5
6. Do the people involved with implementation have the mental dexterity and courage to improvise when the situation warrants changing the game plan and finding innovative ways to get to get the job done?	1-2-3-4-5
Strategy	
7. Does your firm's strategy include specific time-based milestones for transforming its mission and vision into reality?	1-2-3-4-5
8. Does your firm's strategy identify the managers who will be held accountable for performance?	1-2-3-4-5
9. Does your firm operate with a "concurrent" strategy/ execution mentality?	1-2-3-4-5
10. Does your firm embrace anticipatory management where it runs "What if?" scenarios and the development of contingency plans?	1-2-3-4-5
11. Does your firm keep resources in reserve so it can change its actions quickly?	1-2-3-4-5
12. Does your firm have the people who will be implementing action plans participate or at least have their ideas solicited when the strategies and actions plans are being developed?	1-2-3-4-5
Systems and Structure	
13. Does your firm have a management information system that has built-in early warning systems that enable quick awareness of emerging or potential variances and quick response to them?	1-2-3-4-5
14. Does your firm deliberately and continuously seek out best practices in execution in as well as outside your industry?	1-2-3-4-5
15. Does your firm continuously seek ways to simplify operations including using reengineering efforts?	1-2-3-4-5
16. Does your firm have a knowledge management system that makes it possible to learn from others in and outside the firm, to hit the ground running, and to have a higher likelihood of success?	1-2-3-4-5

(continued)

TABLE 10.1. (Continued)

How does your firm rate on the following execution dimensions? *Scoring Level: 1 = not at all, 2 = slightly true, 3 = partly true, 4 = mostly true, 5 = completely true	Level*
People	
17. Does your firm's performance review system hold people accountable for results?	1-2-3-4-5
18. Does your firm's incentive system tie rewards to performance?	1-2-3-4-5
19. Does your firm provide a lot of latitude for people who are implementing action plans to make substantive changes without having to secure management approval?	1-2-3-4-5
Culture	
20. Does your firm make a deliberate effort to seek new ways of doing things rather than doing them as they have been done?	1-2-3-4-5
21. Does your firm encourage experimentation with ways to enhance execution?	1-2-3-4-5
22. Does your firm have a culture that abhors bureaucracy and fosters the free flow of information from any person to any person?	1-2-3-4-5
23. Does your firm encourage people to speak up when they think things do not seem right?	1-2-3-4-5
24. Does your firm celebrate execution success and successful teams?	1-2-3-4-5
25. Does your firm acknowledge people who have smooth operations via problem prevention as much as it recognizes people who solve problems?	1-2-3-4-5
Total score	

Scoring Key

113–125	Congratulations, your firm demonstrates the qualities needed for exceptional execution and implementation.
100–112	Your organization has many of the factors that contribute to effective implementation, but still has areas that need to be improved.
78–99	Your organization has some strengths, but there is a lot of room for improvement.
65–77	Your organization either has some significant shortcomings or is weak in most areas. Changing just a few areas will not be enough to make a real difference.
25–65	Your organization may be beyond hope. It will take a radical change in management to improve the strategy, corporate culture, systems, and processes to have any chance of being competitive in the future.

Notes

Some of the material in this chapter originally appeared in the articles, "Traversing the Execution Minefield" by the author and Thomas W. Porter in *Industrial Management*, September/October, 2003 and "Exceptional Implementers" by the author, Thomas W. Porter, and David J. Glew in *Industrial Management*, September/October, 2007. Reprinted with the permission of the Institute of Industrial Engineers, 3577 Parkway Lane, Suite 200, Norcross, GA 30092, www.iienet.org. Copyright 2009 by the Institute of Industrial Engineers.

Some of the material in this chapter originally appeared in *Business Horizons*. Reprinted with permission from *Business Horizons*, vol. 46, no. 1, by Thomas W. Porter and Stephen C. Harper, "Tactical Implementation: The Devil is in the Details," (Copyright 2003): 53–60, with permission from Elsevier.

1. T. J. Rogers, "No Excuses Management," *Harvard Business Review* 68, no. 4 (1990): 84.

2. Larry Bossidy and Ram Charan, *Execution* (New York: Crown, 2002), 19.

3. Rogers, ibid., 87.

4. The interviews were part of the article, "Exceptional Implementers" by Thomas Porter, Stephen C. Harper, and David Glew, *Industrial Management*, September/October (2007): 15–20.

5. Thomas W. Porter and Stephen C. Harper, "Tactical Implementation: The Devil Is in the Details," *Business Horizons*, 46, no. 1 (2003): 53–60.

6. Jonathan Fahey, Silvia Sansoni, Nathan Vardi, and Josephine Lee, "Master of Minutiae?" *Forbes* 168, no. 1 (2001): 32.

Epilogue

The phrase "Change or die" is used often in the corporate arena, but it is not correct. A firm can change in many ways and still die. For your firm to succeed in the years ahead, it must initiate the right changes, at the right time, with the right speed, and be implemented well; that is what *evolving* is all about. Yet evolving is not just about surviving; it is about thriving. Surviving involves coping. Thriving involves sensing and seizing the opportunities that will emerge in the years ahead. To thrive in the future, the firm must create its future.

Creating your firm's future involves recognizing:

- What worked well yesterday will be less effective today, ineffective tomorrow, and may be obsolete the day after tomorrow.
- Change should never be just for the sake of change. Changes must focus on improving performance.
- Changes that are not in sync with prevailing realities will fail. Firms that are out of touch get out of sync, and then go out of business.
- You have to be in the right forest (markets) at the right time. If you are not in the right forest, then everything you do will be an exercise in futility and your firm will be irrelevant.
- Change is no longer an exceptional occurrence. Change is the rule. Change can be evolutionary or it can be revolutionary, depending on how executives approach the future.
- Improving the company's current situation will not be enough. Executives need to direct more of their attention to creating their company's future.
- With ever-accelerating change, evolution will need to be anticipatory and fast.
- Breakthrough leadership will be required. Traditional management techniques like continuous improvement that have served their companies well will not be enough for their companies to break away from the pack.
- Breakthrough leadership should not be the chief executive officer's exclusive domain. To excel, companies need to have breakthrough leaders at all

levels and in every unit. Every person has the potential to make a difference, and every person should play an integral role in moving the company forward and creating its future.

In short, you must recognize that the strategy that got you to where you are today—regardless of how successful it may currently be—will not get you where you want to go.

You cannot have an ever-evolving enterprise without ever-evolving leaders who seize the moment and seize the future. Winston Churchill noted, "To every man there comes in his lifetime that special moment when he is figuratively tapped on the shoulder and offered that chance to do a very special thing, unique to him and fitted to his talent; what a tragedy if that moment finds him unprepared or unqualified for the work that could have been his finest hour."

Churchill's comment also applies to organizations. This book has stressed the need for organizations to be ever-evolving enterprises. It will be a shame if your firm is not prepared to seize the opportunities that lie ahead. If you miss the opportunity to create your firm's future, then you will have jeopardized your firm's future.

Ever-evolving leaders need to have the energy to take things in stride and be cool under fire. Things will not always go smoothly. Murphy's Law will still occur even with the best-laid plans. It is at those times that you will have to adapt and adjust. There will always be challenges. Creating your company's future takes courage to do what no other firm has done. Teddy Roosevelt noted,

> It is not the critic who counts: not the man who points out how the strong man stumbles or where the doer of deeds could have done better. The credit belongs to the man who is actually in the arena, whose face is marred by dust and sweat and blood, who strives valiantly, who errs and comes up short again and again, because there is no effort without error or shortcoming, but who knows the great enthusiasms, the great devotions, who spends himself for a worthy cause; who, at the best, knows, in the end, the triumph of high achievement, and who, at the worst, if he fails, at least he fails while daring greatly, so that his place shall never be with those cold and timid souls who knew neither victory nor defeat.

Ever-evolving enterprises approaches change with a "portfolio" approach. They recognize some change efforts must focus on the short or near term. Some change efforts should focus on the middle term.

Some change efforts should be invested in the long term. They recognize some change efforts must be directed to continuous improvement. Some change efforts may be evolutionary while some change efforts must be revolutionary. They recognize there is a time to start with a blank sheet of paper by reengineering, there is a time to reengineer your business strategy, and there is a time to look for a whole new forest. They recognize there will be times when detailed planning may work, and there will be times to improvise. They recognize there is a time to leverage your core competencies and time to develop new ones. They recognize there are times to be bold and to seek breakthroughs and times to resist the temptation to be seduced by short-lived opportunities. They recognize there are times to be the first mover, and there are times when it is smarter to be a fast follower. They recognize that even though organic growth may be the best way to grow, there will be times when acquiring another firm may represent an opportunity to access great people, great technology, and great markets more quickly than doing it organically.

Ever-evolving enterprises recognize numerous other factors. They need to have a rich pipeline of new product and service offerings. They recognize that to move ahead you have to be able to let go. They recognize that you have to learn and to unlearn. They recognize that you do not become the best by adopting best practices of other firms; you become the best by developing best practices that other firms will emulate. They recognize that when you focus on beating your competition, you take your eyes off delighting your customers.

When all is said and done, if you want to your firm to be an ever-evolving enterprise and to create its future, then you must recognize you must set the example by being an ever-evolving leader.

Every moment you are not evolving is a step toward extinction!

Index

About the Author

STEPHEN C. HARPER, Ph.D., is the Progress Energy/Betty Cameron Distinguished Professor of Entrepreneurship at The University of North Carolina Wilmington. Steve is the author of six books on leadership and entrepreneurship including: *Extraordinary Entrepreneurship: The Professional's Guide to Starting an Exceptional Enterprise* (2004), *The McGraw-Hill Guide to Starting Your Own Business* (2003), *The Forward-Focused Organization* (2001), *The McGraw-Hill Guide to Managing Growth in Your Emerging Business* (1995), and *Management: Who Ever Said It Would Be Easy?* (editor and coauthor, 1983). He is also the author of dozens of articles that have appeared in national and international magazines.

Steve is the recipient of numerous awards including: The University of North Carolina Board of Governors' Award for Teaching Excellence, The University of North Carolina Wilmington's Distinguished Teaching Professorship Award, The Board of Trustees' Teaching Excellence Award, and the Chancellor's Teaching Excellence Award. He served on the faculty at Arizona State University where he earned his Ph.D., and as a Visiting Professor in Duke University's executive MBA program.

Steve was President of Harper and Associates Inc.—a business consulting firm—from 1976 through 2009. He has also been the cofounder and President of numerous economic development organizations including: The Coastal Entrepreneurial Council, In-Ventures Inc., and DARE Inc. He has also served on the board of directors for numerous organizations.

Steve has conducted hundreds of seminars on strategic thinking, breakthrough leadership, corporate entrepreneurship, and the management of change for corporations, not-for-profit enterprises, and government agencies at the national, state, and municipal levels in the United States and Canada. He has also made presentations to more than one hundred professional associations and has been a speaker for Inc. Resources.